MW01596817

ABOUT THE PUBLISHER

The New York Institute of Finance ...

... more than just books.

NYIF offers practical, applied education and training in a wide range of financial topics:

* *Classroom training:* evenings, mornings, noon-hour
* *Seminars:* one- and two-day professional and introductory programs
* *Customized training:* need-specific, on your site or ours, in New York City, throughout the United States, anywhere in the world
* *Independent study:* self-paced learning—basic, intermediate, advanced
* *Exam preparation:* NASD licensing (including Series 7), CFA prep, state life and health insurance licensing

Subjects of books and training programs include the following:

* *Account Executive Training*
* *Brokerage Operations*
* *Futures Trading*
* *International Corporate Finance*
* *Options as a Strategic Investment*
* *Securities Transfer*
* *Technical Analysis*

*When Wall Street professionals think **training**, they think **NYIF**.*

Please write or call for our catalog:

 **New York Institute of Finance**
70 Pine Street
New York, NY 10270–0003
212 / 344–2900

Simon & Schuster, Inc.   A Gulf + Western Company
"Where Wall Street Goes to School" ™

Currency and Interest Rate Hedging

A User's Guide to Options, Futures, Swaps, and Forward Contracts

Torben Juul Andersen

New York Institute of Finance
Prentice-Hall

Library of Congress Cataloging in Publication Data

Andersen, Torben Juul.
  Currency and interest rate hedging.

  Includes index
  1. Forward exchange. 2. Hedging (Finance).
  3. Financial futures. 4. Interest rate futures.
  5. Option (Contract) I. Title.
  HG3853.A53   1987   332.64'5   87–7758
  ISBN 0–13–195645–0

©1987 by NYIF CORP.
A Division of Simon & Schuster, Inc.
70 Pine Street, New York, NY   10270-0003

All rights reserved.
No part of this book may be reproduced
in any part or by any means
without permission in writing from the author.

This publication is designed to provide accurate and authoritative information in regard to the subject matter covered. It is sold with the understanding that the publisher is not engaged in rendering legal, accounting, or other professional service. If legal advice or other expert assistance is required, the services of a competent professional person should be sought.

—From a Declaration of Principles jointly adopted by a Committee of the American Bar Association and a committee of Publishers and Associations

Printed in the United States of America
10 9 8 7 6 5 4 3 2 1

New York Institute of Finance
(NYIF Corp.)
70 Pine St.
New York, New York   10270-0003

Contents

Part III
Options, 105

Chapter 6
The Options Contract, 107

Chapter 7
Types of Contract, 103

Chapter 8
Profitability Patterns, 147

Chapter 9
Hedging with Option Contracts, 158

Preface

Being a witness to the dynamic evolution of the market for international financial services which has taken place over the last few years, I felt a lack of a single source which could give a complete overview of the new market developments and an explanation of their mechanics. Several books have been written which provide very detailed discussions on special aspects of the new financial markets, but only a few provide a full and comparable overview of all the new market developments. In lack of such a single descriptive source I decided that I had to make it myself.

The main focus of the book is the presentation and discussion of new hedging techniques with a brief introduction to the new investment banker jargon which requires familiarity when approaching the financial markets. The book takes a pragmatic rather than a normative view. The aim has not been to write a complicated book on international finance, but rather to present the situation as simple as it is and to illustrate the potential applications of the new hedging instruments. However, despite the attempted straight-forwardness of the book it should bring the reader to an informative level which makes her or him well equipped for a qualified discussion on the topic and which should allow the professional financial manager to better assess the hedging opportunities existing in today's markets. It is my hope that potential readers feel the same way also after reading the book.

Working in an international environment has provided valuable insights and has furnished my interest in the development on the international financial markets. The financial futures and options exchanges of the London International Financial Futures Exchange, the Chicago Mercantile Exchange, the Chicago Board of Trade, the New York Futures Exchange, the Philadelphia Stock Exchange, the Montreal Exchange and the European Options Exchange very openly provided information on the contracts offered and the principles of trading these on the respective exchanges. The *Wall Street Journal*, the *Financial Times*, the *Montreal Gazette* and the *New York Times* kindly permitted reprinting of their daily quotations.

I am in debt to Stephen Stone and Barbara Rockefeller of Citibank, N.A. New York and to Alfred Dangoor of Citifutures Limited for commenting on essential parts of the book as well as to William E. Easley III for providing insights into the new market approach of the Montreal Exchange. I also wish to thank Mr. Edwin Ford of Citicorp Investment Bank for bringing some insights into the current uses of currency and interest rate swaps. However, any discrepancies or miscalculations overlooked are my sole responsibility.

I thank my wife, Mette, for not only bearing with me in spending free evenings and week-ends writing this book, but she also on top of providing the moral support transformed my handwritten scriblings into a readable typewritten format.

Finally I wish to express my appreciation to Mr. Fred Dahl and his associates at the New York Institute of Finance for supporting the completion of this book.

Torben Juul Andersen
Libreville

PART I

The Argument for Hedging

Chapter **1**

International Trade and Payments

The major part of the cross-border payment flows emanates from, or is a consequence of, international trade transactions. The payments relate directly to compensation for export and import of goods and services, or they relate to international capital transactions caused by surpluses or deficits on the current balance of payments. To the extent that there is imbalance between the incoming and outgoing payments on trade transactions in a country, private institutions or the central government will either deposit (invest) or borrow funds on the international financial markets. Hence a significant part of international cash flows relates to debt service and interest compensation from international borrowers and investors. The interest payments are registered on the country's current balance of payment, whereas repayment of principal is included in the capital balance section of the balance of payment account.

THE INTERNATIONAL FINANCIAL SYSTEM

Since World War II, many attempts have been made to further unrestricted international trade, to the economic benefit of the countries involved. Negotiations in the late 1940s among the major Western countries led to the General Agreement on Tariffs and Trade (GATT), in which the countries agreed to eliminate tariff barriers on imported goods. The agreement has since been revised a few times, and today continues to play an important role in international political discussions. Under the auspices of the United Nations, attempts have been made to standardize international trade practice and international trade law in order to reduce the inherent risks of intercountry trade transactions. The liberalization of international trade has had a visible effect on economic growth in the Western world during the 1950s and 1960s.

The *Bretton-Woods Agreement* of 1944 also reflected the vision of rebuilding the world economic system by promoting international trade. For this to succeed, an unrestricted international payment system was required. This was accomplished by creating a "clearing center" where countries with a current balance of payment deficit could get temporary credit until stabilizing economic policy measures had reversed unfavorable balance of payments trends. The credit would be provided by the countries with registered balance of payment surpluses. This clearing center was instituted through the establishment of the *International Monetary Fund (IMF)*. At the same time the World Bank was established for the purpose of extending longer-term credits in support of socioeconomic projects in countries in need of funds for their economic development.

Each participating country deposited a certain quota in gold (25%) and the domestic currency (75%) with the IMF, the quota being determined by the relative sizes of the countries' GNPs and international trade volume. The clearing system was arranged so that a country at any time could draw an amount equivalent to the current gold holding of the country's quota. The gold holding is equal in size to the initial gold deposit, plus the amount of gold that other countries had paid in, in exchange for the country's domestic currency. To obtain further drawings on the IMF quota, the countries had to negotiate directly with the IMF, which then set its conditions for further credits, with due regard for the economic situation of the countries in question.

In the IMF system each country determined a fixed foreign exchange rate (value) against gold. The U.S. dollar was fully convertible into gold at a fixed price of US$ 35 per ounce. Hence the U.S. dollar became the international reserve currency which the central banks on request could convert into gold. Each member country was obliged to maintain a foreign exchange rate with a maximum deviation of plus or minus 1% from the fixed foreign exchange rate. Due to the limited supply of gold, *special drawing rights (SDRs)* were created in 1970, with the view of creating sufficient international liquidity to further the increase in trade flows. The value of the SDR was determined by a weighted average of sixteen international currencies.

Already in 1968 the gold convertibility of the U.S. dollar was abolished, and in 1971 the *Smithsonian Agreement* widened the maximum allowable variation from the fixed foreign exchange rate to plus or minus 2¼%. Until the final collapse of the insituted international financial system in 1973, the system went through a whole array of crises. The final consequence was a return to freely floating foreign exchange rates.

The increased volatility among the European currencies was found unacceptable by the member countries of the European Economic Community (EEC). So, in 1972 the member countries, plus a few other European countries, agreed to keep swings of their respective currencies within half the allowable band as determined by the *Smithsonian Agreement.* This made up the so-called *snake,* which moved inside the Smithsonian foreign exchange rate boundaries, the *tunnel.* Following the collapse of the international fixed rate policy in 1973, France decided to leave the European fixed rate agreement.

Following several years of political discussions, the EEC member countries, excluding only the United Kingdom, established the *European Monetary System (EMS)* in 1979. In this system each currency can move within a band of plus or minus 2¼% from a fixed foreign exchange rate set against each of the EEC currencies.

The implementation of this fixed rate monetary system was supported by swap arrangements among the countries' central banks, whereby each country could obtain short-term credits in the other European currencies to support the stability of the foreign exchange rate development. The EMS was formalized further by the creation of a *European Currency Unit (ECU)*, the value of which is determined by a weighted average of the EEC currencies. For European visionaries the ECU constitutes the future common currency of a European Monetary Union which consequently would become an alternative international reserve currency. However, the EMS has not been unconditionally successful. Since its inauguration in 1979, ten adjustments of the fixed rate parities have taken place, the last one in January 1987.

It is outside the scope of this book to discuss the normative aspects of fixed versus floating rate foreign exchange rate systems. Suffice it to say that, based on past economic history, sovereign governments can use foreign exchange rate policies to manage their external balance problems, and they will utilize this economic policy tool whenever it is found opportune to do so.

BALANCE OF PAYMENT DEVELOPMENTS AND INTERNATIONAL CREDIT INTERMEDIATION

In the wake of the increase in the international oil prices in the early 1970s, the energy-importing economies—in developed as well as in developing countries—increasingly registered balance of payments deficits. The balance of payments surpluses of the oil-producing countries were transferred to the countries with balance of payments deficits primarily through the intermediation of the international banks. The balance of payments deficits registered on the European continent and in Japan in the early 1980s triggered a general tightening of fiscal and monetary policies, whereas the United States during the same period appeared to go through an unwarranted fiscal expansion. This has reversed the balance of payments pattern over the prior years bringing the United States into a position of a major deficit country. The balance of payments development shows a cyclical pattern reflecting the effects of a generally uncoordinated economic policy among the major industrialized countries.

Table 1-1. *Current Balance of Payment Development.*

(US$ Millions)	1980	1981	1982	1983	1984	1985
Belgium	– 4,940	– 4,190	– 2,400	– 540	–45	606
Denmark	– 2,380	– 1,720	– 2,310	– 1,220	–1,815	–2,685
France	– 4,170	– 4,740	–12,070	– 4,430	–754	–165
Germany	–15,740	– 5,500	3,380	,115	6,990	13,201
Italy	– 9,680	– 8,115	– 5,480	760	–2,953	–
Japan	–10,750	4,770	6,850	20,800	35,003	49,169
Netherlands	– 2,940	2,770	3,560	3,660	5,081	5,428
Norway	1,100	2,170	640	2,060	2,984	2,982
Sweden	– 4,540	– 2,780	– 3,510	– 940	359	–1,100
United Kingdom	8,090	14,050	8,545	3,860	2,087	4,878
United States	3,723	4,471	–11,211	–41,563	–107,358	–117,676
Total	–42,227	1,186	–14,006	–13,438	–60,421	–45,362

Source: Monthly Review of Statistics, May 1986, Denmark's Central Bureau of Statistics.

There are no immediate signs that this behavioristic pattern will change in the near future. In the early 1980s the energy-importing developed countries as a whole registered a significant balance of payments deficit which slowly has been diminished as a consequence of stricter energy policies and continued development of alternative energy sources. The dramatic drop in the price of crude oil during 1986 should continue to improve the balance of payments positions of the industrialized countries over the latter years of the 1980s, at the expense of the oil-exporting countries.

The unevenness in external balance developments will continue to put high demands on the credit intermediation of the international capital markets. Despite more restrictive economic policy measures in Western Europe, we have also witnessed a tendency toward further liberalization of foreign exchange regulations, which will further the internationalization of credit intermediation in general. Any institution in need of funds will consider the domestic as well as the international supply of credit, as well as investors will evaluate global investment alternatives. The volume of funds raised on the international capital markets continues to be significant. The role of direct bank intermediation in cross-border credits, however, has diminished, and new ways of intermediating cross-border capital flows are currently being developed.

Table 1-2. *Funds Raised by some Developed Countries on the International Markets.*

(US$ Millions)	1982	1983	1984	1985
Australia	–	5,826.1	8,814.4	14,407.3
Belgium	2,380.9	1,324.9	2,702.1	3,269.1
Denmark	2,643.8	4,679.6	5,596.0	3,589.4
France	15,159.9	11,303.3	12,103.8	18,772.6
Germany	1,401.0	2,998.3	2,063.4	3,452.1
Italy	6,874.1	4,720.6	8,855.9	11,008.2
Japan	8,335.2	15,089.1	17,346.1	21,268.8
Netherlands	1,134.2	1,255.3	1,399.4	2,298.7
New Zealand	5,196.0	928.9	3,492.0	2,707.3
Norway	2,276.1	1,550.3	2,685.2	3,905.1
Portugal	1,951.8	1,130.4	1,752.2	2,381.9
Spain	3,021.6	4,452.9	5,830.4	3,912.9
Sweden	4,512.7	6,867.5	13,109.7	9,889.9
United Kingdom	3,490.5	3,416.3	9,524.6	25,454.2
United States	25,315.8	20,687.0	59,983.1	68,893.5
Total	83,693.6	86,230.5	155,258.3	195,211.0

Source: Financial Statistics (Monthly), February 2, 1986, OECD Financial Statistics, Part 1.

Table 1-3. *Funds Raised on the International Markets (Breakdown by Type of Instrument).*

(US$ Millions)	1982	1983	1984	1985
International Bonds	50,329	50,098	81,717	135,431
Foreign Bonds	25,199	27,050	27,801	31,025
Special Placements	–	–	2,000	1,300
International Bank Loans	90,750	60,209	53,219	53,461
Foreign Bank Loans	7,428	6,965	8,761	6,647
Other International Facilities	5,386	13,505	55,276	56,856
Total	179,092	157,827	228,774	284,720

Source: Financial Statistics (Monthly), February 2, 1986, OECD Financial Statistics, Part 1.

Development in
Interest Rates and Foreign Exchange Rates

The interest rates on foreign currencies quoted on the Eurocurrency markets are determined by the domestic interest rate movements, and they relate to the interest rates of other foreign currencies through the interest rate parity factor.

Arbitrage between the domestic money market and the equivalent Eurocurrency market will cause the interest rate level of the two markets to follow each other, given that no regulatory restrictions prevent arbitrage transactions to take place. The domestic interest rate is determined by the economy's current demand for credit and the monetary authorities' regulation of credit availability. The latter is managed in response to the development of the balance of payment, the unemployment rate, the inflation rate, and other economic policy measures.

The interest rate of a given currency will be influenced by the interest rate development of other currencies and the financial markets' expectations on the future foreign exchange rates of the currencies. Due to the prevalence of a forward foreign exchange market, international interest rate arbitrage transactions can easily be closed. Hence a currency's interest rate will be determined vis-a-vis the interest rate of other foreign currencies in accordance with the expected future foreign exchange rates as determined by the quotes on the forward foreign exchange market. The return to floating foreign exchange rates during the 1970s and the disintegrated economic policies of the Western economies thus have had a destabilizing effect on the interest rate development of the major international currencies.

The development of the foreign exchange rates over the past years has been characterized by the continuing strengthening of the U.S. dollar against the other international currencies. From early 1983 to early 1985, the U.S. dollar showed a strengthening of 35–40% against the major European currencies. However, this fairly steady long-term trend in the exchange rate development covers overly volatile day-to-day and erratic intra-day movements on the foreign exchange markets.

The value of the U.S. dollar peaked in March 1985, and the former strength of the dollar as an international currency had a drastic turning point following the meeting between the finance ministers and central bankers of the five leading industrial countries on September 22, 1985. The movement against the dollar was brought about by strong intervention, led by the Bank of Japan and the U.S. Federal Reserve and supported by the Central Banks of Germany, England, and France. Even during this period of intervention, however, the day-to-day volatility in the foreign exchange market remained.

Table 1-4. *Some Interest Rates on the International Markets.*

The Eurocurrency Market Three-Month Deposit
(pct. p.a.)

Month	1984								1985								
	M	J	J	A	S	O	N	D	J	F	M	A	M	J	J	A	S
U.S. Dollars*	11.60	11.73	12.05	11.87	11.71	10.81	9.56	8.96	8.45	9.11	9.39	8.75	8.18	7.66	7.95	8.08	8.21
Pounds Sterling	9.42	—	11.66	11.03	10.84	10.66	9.98	9.83	11.48	13.77	13.63	12.76	12.66	12.45	12.07	11.47	11.56
Swiss Francs*	3.88	—	4.75	4.87	5.02	5.28	5.03	4.96	5.09	5.73	5.79	5.38	5.15	5.22	5.11	4.66	4.60
German Marks	5.95	—	5.82	5.60	5.59	5.83	5.76	5.64	576	6.12	6.17	5.88	5.62	5.54	5.14	4.62	4.54
Dutch Guilders	6.14	—	6.44	6.36	6.29	6.26	5.98	5.82	5.89	6.96	7.22	6.87	6.91	6.70	6.38	5.85	5.78
French Francs	12.78	—	12.08	11.60	11.36	11.57	11.13	10.81	1072	11.08	11.11	10.70	10.26	10.38	10.63	11.82	10.50

Source: Financial Statistics, (Monthly), December 12, 1985. OECD Financial Statistics, Part 1.

Figure 1-1. *Interest Rate Development (Three-month Eurocurrency Deposits).*

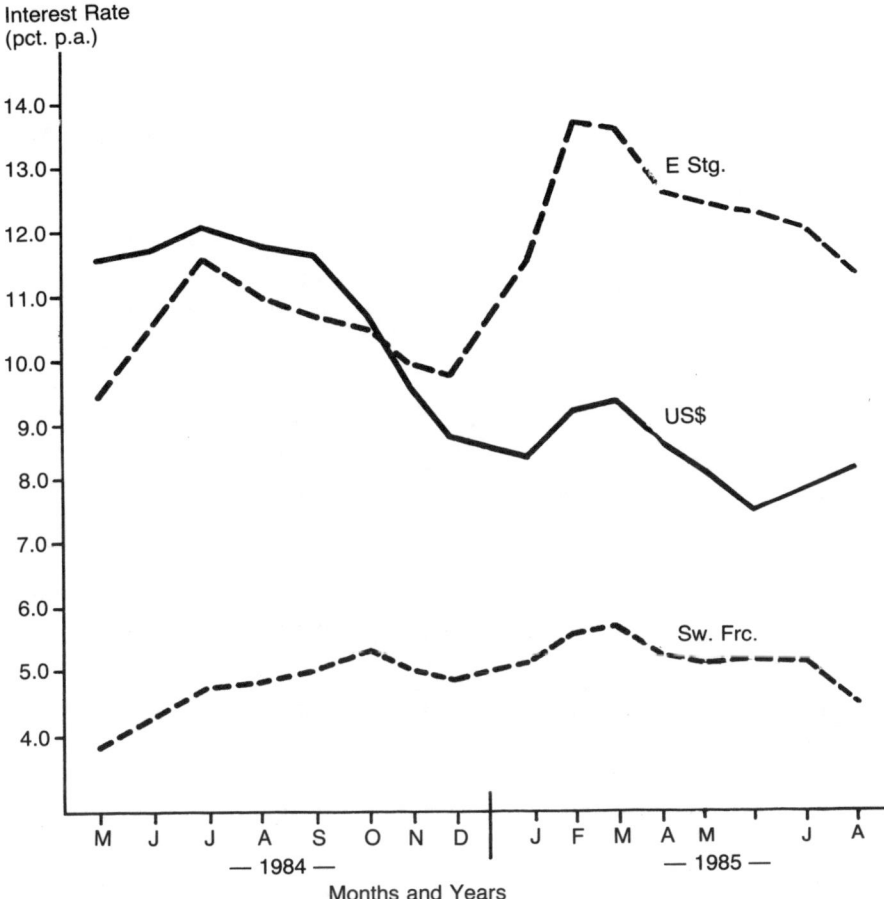

Under a floating rate regime and even in a managed floating rate environment, the determination of the foreign exchange rates is highly influenced by the expectations of the market participants leading to cyclical movements in the foreign exchange rates. The behavior of foreign exchange traders further unstabilize the short-term foreign exchange rate development periodically leading to substantial rate volatility.

Table 1-5. *Some Foreign Exchange Rates on the International Markets (Monthly Averages).*

Month (Year)	German Marks	Pounds Sterling*	French Francs	Swiss Francs
(1983)				
March	2.4069	0.6697	6.9872	2.0590
April	2.4370	0.6491	7.3051	2.0538
May	2.4679	0.6347	7.4222	2.0592
June	2.5474	0.6451	7.6584	2.1103
July	2.5864	0.6541	7.7743	2.1154
August	2.6734	0.6660	8.0433	2.1622
September	2.6677	0.6670	8.0578	2.1629
October	2.6013	0.6676	7.9472	2.1094
November	2.6829	0.6768	8.1606	2.1692
December	2.7477	0.6971	8.3793	2.1952
(1984)				
January	2.8067	0.7091	8.5812	2.2337
February	2.7049	0.6952	8.3226	2.2068
March	2.5955	0.6862	7.9981	2.1470
April	2.6401	0.7024	8.1192	2.1859
May	2.7485	0.7198	8.4418	2.2662
June	2.7432	0.7269	8.4278	2.2848
July	2.8463	0.7572	8.7341	2.4053
August	2.8870	0.7616	8.8616	2.4182
September	3.0233	0.7944	9.2762	2.4980
October	3.0699	0.8200	9.4127	2.5245
November	2.9895	0.8048	9.1697	2.4628
December	3.1001	0.8409	9.4968	2.5569
(1985)				
January	3.1675	0.8854	9.6941	2.6553
February	3.2930	0.9119	10.0611	2.7958
March	3.3070	0.8930	10.1017	2.8094
April	3.1170	0.8138	9.4990	2.6177
May	3.0914	0.7857	9.4155	2.6105
June	3.0573	0.7724	9.3115	2.5635
July	2.7876	0.6998	8.4940	2.2800
August	2.7830	0.7142	8.4945	2.2830
September	2.6726	0.7103	8.1470	2.1855
October	2.6151	0.6930	7.9660	2.1434
November	2.5118	0.6734	7.6565	2.0809
December	2.4641	0.6962	7.5530	2.0764

Source: Cross rates calculated from *Monthly Review of Statistics*, May 1985, Denmark's Central Bureau of Statistics, and Paris fixing rates from Citibank, N.A. Paris.

Figure 1-2. *Foreign Exchange Rate Development (Monthly Averages).*

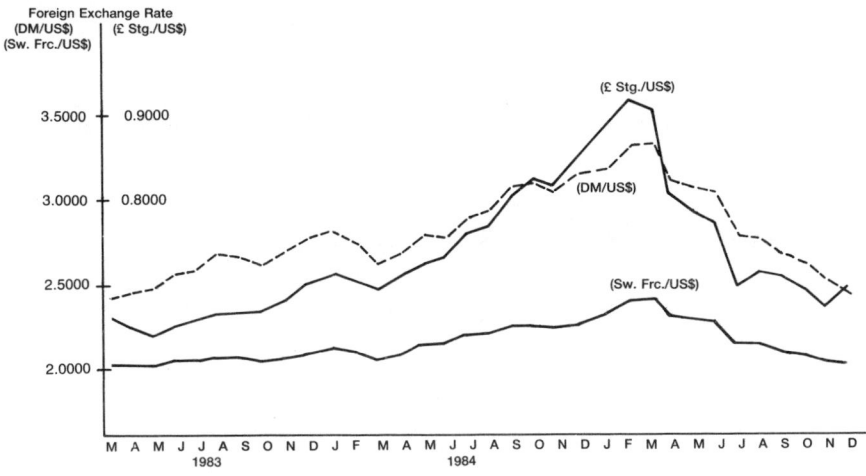

CONCLUSION

Substantial currency flows take place between the countries of the world economic system emanating from underlying trade and capital transactions. After World War II, the foreign exchange rates determining the currency exchange relating to these cross-border payments were managed within a fixed rate system under the auspices of the IMF. This system collapsed in the early 1970s leading to freely floating exchange rates, with certain European countries led by the EEC trying to establish a more stable foreign exchange rate zone on the European continent. As a consequence of this development, interest rates and foreign exchange rates have become increasingly volatile.

Financial Exposure

With the expansion of international financial relationships and the continued liberalization of cross-border cash flows, more and more institutions become exposed to international transactions. These take the form of future foreign currency cash receivables and payables caused by trade transactions and foreign currency denominated financial commitments. The increasing exposure requires enforced attention by the financial management of the institutions involved, and the management boards need to establish clear institutional policies stating the acceptable risk levels of the institution's international engagements.

In times of volatility in international interest rates and foreign exchange rates, an excessive financial exposure can have a very significant impact on an institution's financial performance and consequently requires management's constant attention.

An institution's financial exposure can be separated into two broad categories. *Interest rate exposure* arises when financial assets and liabilities have a mismatch in maturity or interest rate basis, or when floating rate financial commitments create uncertainty with regard to future cash flows. *Currency exposure* arises when foreign currency receivables and payables do not match each other in amount and timing because the future conversion value of the net flows into the domestic currency of accounting is unknown.

INTEREST RATE EXPOSURE

The concept of interest rate exposure is best described by means of a few examples.

Example: A company, after updating its liquidity budget in December, realizes that a liquidity gap of US$ 10,000,000 will appear throughout the twelve months commencing in June of the following accounting year, caused by planned engagement of a new project. Assume that the short-term dollar interest rate has moved between 8–12% p.a. over the past year. With a similar volatility in interest rates over the coming year, cash flow calculations on the project will show a variation of US$ 400,000 on interest expenses, which severely jeopardize the profitability of the project. Locking in the future rate would give the company a clearer picture of the project's profitability.

Example: A commercial bank extends floating rate U.S. dollar loans to its corporate client base. The bank itself issues a fixed coupon, dollar-denominated Eurobond to fund its dollar assets. However, the bank's assets carry floating rate interest whereas a part of the bank's liabilities carry a fixed interest rate. A drop in the dollar interest rate, in this combination of interest rate basis on the assets and liabilities, will bring the bank's future profitability in jeopardy.

Example: A leasing company provides long-term financial commitments to its client base with a locked-in return to the institution. The leasing company funds these activities through floating rate loans. In an increasing interest rate environment, the net profit will shrink and possibly even turn into a loss position.

The obvious solution to such interest-gapping positions is to match the interest rate basis of the assets and the liabilities. The following chapters deal with a wide variety of techniques whereby the interest rate basis of assets and liabilities can be

Figure 2-1. *Illustration of Types of Interest Rate Exposure.*

```
┌─────────────────────────────────────────────────────────────┐
│                    Interest Rate Exposure                     │
│   (1)        Assets                    Liabilities            │
│          ─────────────────────────────────────────────       │
│                                                               │
│            Fixed return            ┌──────────────┐           │
│                                    │ Floating rate │ % p.a. ? │
│                                    └──────────────┘           │
│                                                               │
│   (2)        Assets                    Liabilities            │
│          ─────────────────────────────────────────────       │
│  % p.a. ? ┌────────────────┐                                  │
│           │ Floating return │          Fixed rate            │
│           └────────────────┘                                  │
└─────────────────────────────────────────────────────────────┘
```

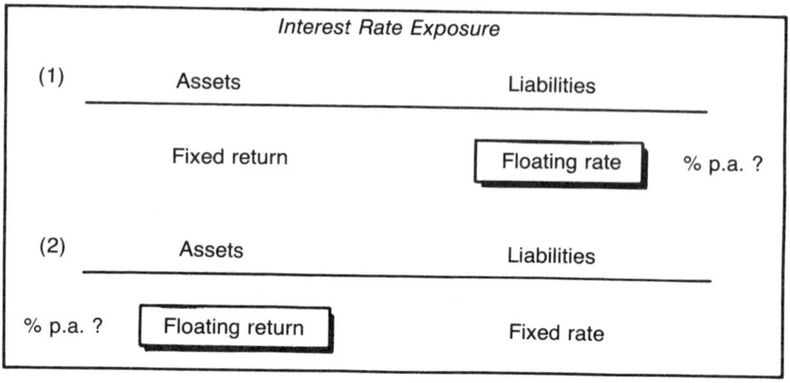

changed without conflicting with the underlying business practice of the institution.

CURRENCY EXPOSURE

Currency exposure can be best explained by an example.

Example: A German trading company makes a major part of its sales in U.S. dollars. The current need of working capital is funded through low interest Swiss franc loans. If the U.S. dollar depreciates against the Swiss franc, the company's overall profit will be squeezed. To the extent that the company can match cash inflows and outflows to the same foreign currency, the earnings squeeze will be eased. To the extent that the company has a net outflow of Swiss francs or a net inflow of U.S. dollars, the company runs a risk because the future foreign exchange rate, which translates the foreign currency flows into the domestic currency of accounting (Deutsche marks), is unknown. If the company has a net outflow of Swiss francs at repayment of the foreign-currency-denominated loans, a strengthening of the Swiss franc against the Deutsche mark would cause an increase in the company's interest expense measured in Deutsche mark. Conversely, if the company has a net inflow of U.S. dollars from exports, a weakening of the U.S. dollar

Figure 2-2. *Illustration of Currency Exposure.*

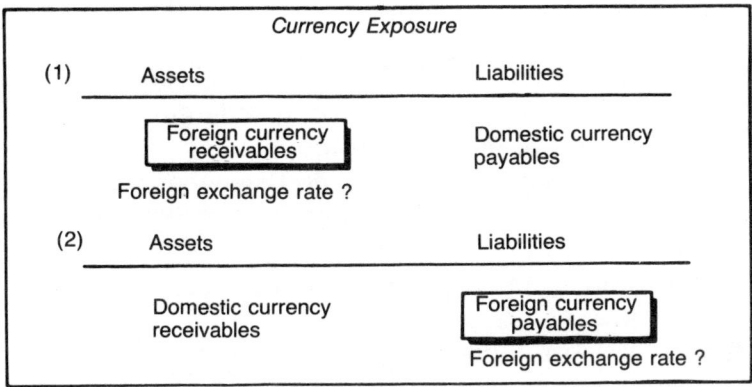

against the DM will cause a decrease in the company's DM earnings.

Textbooks discussing currency exposure often use a framework that distinguishes among three types of foreign exchange risks:[1]

1. Translation exposure.
2. Transaction exposure.
3. Economic exposure.

1. *Translation exposure* relates to the problem of converting foreign-currency-denominated assets and liabilities into the domestic currency of accounting with its implications for the profit and loss statement. Very often the discussion centers around the accounting issues regarding foreign subsidiaries in a multinational corporation vis-a-vis the U.S. or other national accounting rules.

2. *Transaction exposure* relates to the expected revenue and expenses over the coming accounting year and performs an analysis on the net income effect as registered on the profit and loss statement, from potential changes in the foreign exchange rates.

3. The *economic exposure* point of view on the effects of foreign exchange rate trends is longer term. Hence the discus-

sion centers on price competition in foreign markets, with its impact on export earnings, import costs, and the implications for coming years' profit and loss statements.

Ignoring the often technical discussion on conversion principles and accepted accounting rules in different countries, as well as the special problem regarding foreign subsidiaries, it can be argued that cash flows in the end are what really matters to any institution managed according to general business principles. Assets and liabilities, properly stated, should measure the present value of the expected future cash inflows and cash outflows of the institution. Therefore too much attention to translation exposure represents a short-term view to the exposure problem, which might have a negative impact on the institution's long-term cash flows.

The income statement of an institution based on the current accounting year usually doesn't match the actual cash flows of the institution over the accounting period, due to lags in the payment structure of the institution's commitments. Over a longer time span (say ten years), however, the net income registered on the institution's accounts will get very close to reflecting the net cash inflows of the institution. Hence the view that the main focus in a going concern should be on long-term cash flows remains valid, as the cash flows eventually will be fully reflected in the profitability measures of the institution.

In consequence any analysis of financial exposure must as a starting point involve a longer-term analysis of the institution's domestic as well as foreign-currency denominated cash flows. The analysis will indicate the maturities of both cash outflows and inflows, with a view to the interest rate basis of financial commitments. The simple cash flow statement in Figure 2-3 could be utilized with benefit.

With the cash flow statement that provides an overview of the institution's term exposure on interest rates and foreign exchange rates, a view is taken on the short-term volatility and long-term trends of the interest and foreign exchange rates in order to assess the mismatch risk of the foreign currency cash flows. If management's view is that all major currency and interest rate gaps should be closed because they otherwise bring the institution's profitability into jeopardy, a natural response

Figure 2-3. *Simplified Cash Flow Statement.*

Quarters	Cash Inflows		Cash Outflows		Liquidity Forecast Net Cash Inflows	
	Currency	Amount	Currency	Amount	Currency	Amount
1.	DM	130,000	DM	210,000	DM	–80,000
	US$	295,000	US$	105,000	US$	190,000
	Sw. Frc.	25,000	Sw. Frc.	75,000*	Sw. Frc.	–50,000
	£ Stg.	90,000*	£ Stg.	10,000	£ Stg.	80,000
	—	—	—	—	—	—
	—	—	—	—	—	—
2.	—	—	—	—	—	—
	—	—	—	—	—	—
	—	—	—	—	—	—
	—	—	—	—	—	—
3.	—	—	—	—	—	—
	—	—	—	—	—	—
4.	—	—	—	—	—	—
5.	—	—	—	—	—	—
6.	—	—	—	—	—	—
7.	—	—	—	—	—	—
.	—	—	—	—	—	—
.	—	—	—	—	—	—
.	—	—	—	—	—	—
.	—	—	—	—	—	—
.	—	—	—	—	—	—
.	—	—	—	—	—	—

*Financial commitments on floating rate basis, cash flow estimate based on present interest rates. *Note:* The cash flows denominated in foreign currencies could, for example, represent export receivables where amounts and due dates are predetermined, or it could represent principal and interest payments on financial commitments. In case a financial commitment is established on a floating rate basis, the future cash flow in the currency of accounting is uncertain not only because the foreign exchange rate is volatile, but also because the interest rate applied is likely to fluctuate.

In circumstances where the foreign currency cash flows represent predetermined receivables or payables the sole consideration would be the foreign exchange exposure. In the case of a foreign-currency-denominated financial commitment, one would have to consider both the currency and interest rate gapping aspects. The interest rate gapping in foreign currencies is an especially important consideration to many financial institutions.

would be to match the foreign exchange and interest rate basis of the cash inflows and cash outflows, or to lock in the future conversion of the net foreign currency cash inflows. The following chapters deal with a wide variety of techniques that convert the currency and/or the interest rate basis of cash flows and that lock in or guarantee the future foreign exchange rate as well as the future interest rate.

FORECASTING INTEREST RATES

The interest rate indicates the market-determined price on the availability of money which brings about an equilibrium between entities demanding funds and entities supplying funds. As such the interest rate is determined by supply and demand forces often illustrated by the *Marshallian cross* indicating volumes of funds in demand and supply as a function of the price. The term "interest rate level" is meant to be a general indicator of the interest rates on all the financial instruments available in the financial market which, through substitution effects, will have the same general movement in the interest rate.

The monetary authorities affect the interest rate level by monitoring and managing the reserve position of the commercial banks. This can, for example, take place through open market operations, through restrictions on credit expansion, by imposing reserve requirements on deposit growth, by quantitative regulations of the discount window, and so on. Hereby the supply of loanable funds in the banking system is regulated. If the credit availability is increased, the interest rate level will fall; and if the credit availability is tightened, the interest rate level will increase.

In the "Keynesian" models the interest rate is linked to the real economy through the interest rate sensitivity of investments and savings. For an open economy this has implications for the balance of payments development inasmuch as the discrepancy between the level of investments and the level of savings is equivalent to the balance of payments deficit. Hence if the balance of payment is in deficit, the monetary authorities will tighten the credit expansion, the interest rate level will increase,

Figure 2-4. *Interest Rate Level as Determined by Supply and Demand.*

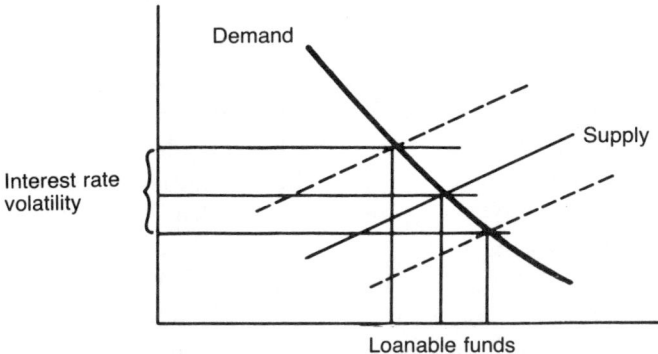

investment activities will fade, and the volume of savings will increase. Therefore the disposable income available for consumption will drop and the demand for imported goods will ease to the benefit of the balance of payments development. In the event of insufficient savings, the high demand for goods and services will induce an inflationary process.

The "monetarist" models take the view that an expansion in the availability of credit with a given production capacity in an economy will induce an inflationary process with time lags of one to two years. If inflation increases, savers and investors who give up consumption today to obtain consumption at a later point in time will require an extra interest rate compensation in order to secure the same "real" consumption at the future date. This will drive the interest rate level *upward*. The inflationary process will make domestically produced goods more expensive abroad with negative implications for the balance of payments development.

Hence the two economic schools appear to reach contradictory conclusions with regard to the monetary policy's impact on interest rate movements. In the one case a tightening of credit availability induces an increased interest rate level, and in the other case the same phenomenon is spurred by an expansion of the availability of credit. Without going into a detailed discussion of the evolution of the two major schools of thought, it can be concluded that when the economic profession is in disagreement about how the economic dynamics work, then what really matters is the market makers' perception of the economic realities. If the participants in a financial market believe in one set of economic dynamics vis-a-vis the interest rate, their collective expectations will make their belief come true.

Nevertheless, it becomes crucial to understand the position of the monetary authorities in order to understand their reaction to various developments in the real economy. To some public authorities the balance of payments development constitutes a major concern and to others the inflationary process is in focus. Very often forecasting the interest rate level is tantamount to foreseeing the reaction of monetary and fiscal authorities to a worsening of the balance of payments position or to an increase in the inflation rate. If the reaction pattern of the monetary authorities is well understood, the forecasting exercise boils down to the forecast of real economic events and the ability to foresee the political response and market reaction to such developments. However, this is an exercise that is *not* mastered by economic science, but rather that relies solely on the subjective judgment and experience of individuals.

Economic models can forecast the real economic consequences of different events under a given set of preconditions and therefore constitute a good tool for economic policy makers, as it answers their questions, "What happens if we introduce this or that policy measure?" To date, however, no forecasting model has been developed that can forecast the future interest rate satisfactorily. The exercise of forecasting interest rates at best is an uncertain task, and relying on interest rate forecasts in consequence is the same as making a bet on the future. So in many cases it is wise to hedge major interest rate gaps.

FORECASTING FOREIGN EXCHANGE RATES

The foreign exchange spot rate is determined by the current supply and demand situation of the two currencies in question. The supply and demand for a country's currency arise partly from trade-related cash flows into and out from the country.

Figure 2-5

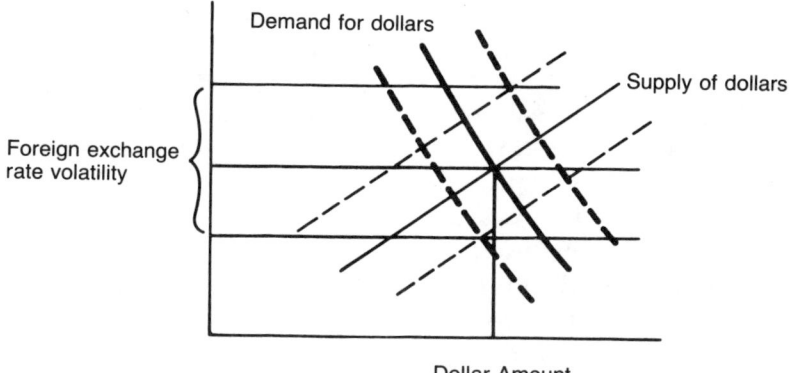

To pay for imports, foreign currency must be bought against the supply of the domestic currency: the higher the supply of the domestic currency, the lower the price on this currency. When an exporter receives payment from an importer in a foreign country the importer demands the exporters's currency against the supply of foreign currency. The higher the demand of the exporters's currency the higher will be the price for the exporter's domestic currency. Hence the higher the current balance of payment surplus of a country, the higher the likelihood is that the price of that country's currency will increase.

Yet, as proven by the foreign exchange rate development of the U.S. dollar in the mid-1980s, this rule of thumb is *not* satisfactory in explaining foreign exchange rate movements. This is because it ignores the other half of the balance of payments account, namely the capital account, which registers cash flows originating from international investments and foreign loan transactions. If foreign entities invest in a country, they will demand the currency of this country against the supply of foreign currency when effecting the investment. The increased demand from these investment transactions will force up the price of the country's currency.

The residual on the overall balance of payments account, including the current account and the capital account, is the country's international reserves. If there is a net cash inflow of foreign currency to the country its international reserve position will improve. Conversely, if a country has a net cash outflow of foreign currency, the country's international reserve position will weaken. Therefore some forecasters have used the international reserves of a country as an indicator of the general supply and demand position of that country's currency. However, even if the reserve position is volatile it might on average remain at a level that secures a stable foreign exchange rate development, and so it does not constitute a satisfactory indicator of foreign exchange rate movements.

A standard rule often used in foreign exchange rate analysis is the *purchasing power parity theory*. This theory basically says that, of two countries, the country with a higher inflation rate will have its currency depreciate against the other country's currency of a magnitude that is inversely related to the inflation rates of the two countries. This is because over time the country with the higher inflation rate will export more expensive goods and the country will receive cheaper imports from the lower inflation country. This will have a negative impact on the balance of payments development in the high inflation country which eventually will enforce a readjustment of the foreign exchange rate. This adjustment process, however, is slow. First of all, the adjustment process might take a long time to materialize; secondly, the international reserve position of any country makes up a buffer that can extend the duration of the foreign exchange rate adjustment. Hence this is not a satisfactory model for forecasting short-term foreign exchange rate movements. (As it turns out, the model holds fairly true in the long run, but who can forecast the inflation rates ten years ahead of time?)

Which indicators, then, *can* explain the short-term movements in foreign exchange rates? One is the comparison of relative interest rates between different foreign currencies. In countries with liberal foreign exchange rate regulations, the international investors will be attracted to the highest-yielding currency investments. What matters here is not the real interest rate, as indicated by the nominal interest rate minus the inflation rate, but rather the nominal interest rate itself. To foreign investors, the inflation rate of other countries does not matter because they will use the proceeds of the investment in their own country. So what matters is the relative size of different currency areas' nominal interest rates. All other things being equal, foreign investments will be attracted to the currency area of the highest nominal interest rate, which will strengthen the foreign exchange rate of that currency. This being the case, we come back to the problem of forecasting interest rates in order to determine future foreign exchange rates.

The expectation of a continued strengthening of a foreign currency will attract more foreign investors because they see a chance to increase the yield from the investment above the nominal interest rate of that currency area. This attraction vanishes quickly when the foreign exchange rate starts to weaken. This "rational" investor behavior causes the foreign exchange rates to follow cyclical trends, which are very hard to forecast. Another important element in the foreign currency investor behavior is the perceived security of the different alternative currency areas. The security element relates to political stability in the currency area in question and to potential political destabilization in the alternative currency areas.

The underlying factors that induce the behavioristic moves of foreign investors are very hard, if not impossible, to forecast, which appears to be proven by following up on professional foreign exchange rate forecasts of the mid-1980s. The economic technician would analyze the foreign exchange rate movements, for example, by performing a regression analysis involving all the explanatory variables:

$$S_t = a + bR + cM + dC + eI + fG + gS_{t-1}$$

S_t = Spot foreign exchange rate at time t.

R = Relative change in international reserves.

M = Relative change in money supply (M2).

C = Relative change in the consumer price index (CPI).

I = Relative three-month interest rates.

G = Relative yield on one-year government bonds.

S_{t-1} = Spot foreign exchange rate at time $t-1$.

$a...g$ = Regression coefficients.

Even if all the regression coefficients pass the significance test, we come back to the problem of forecasting the explanatory variables in order to end up with a forecast for the future foreign exchange rate. As already illustrated, this represents the true weakness of consequential models when used for forecasting purposes. In response, a variety of time series techniques has been developed. These models are pure statistical models that base their forecasting ability solely on a statistical analysis of the historical foreign exchange rates as represented in a sufficiently large time series. (See the Appendix in this chapter.)

A special technique, the so-called *technical analysis,* constitutes a group of the most simple time series analyses developed in the search for objective statistical forecasting methods. These models are usually based on the moving average concept applied on a time series of the historical daily foreign exchange rates. In essence, such a model compares the short-term movement in the foreign exchange rate with the longer-term movement in the foreign exchange rate. If the short-term movement differs significantly from the longer-term movement, the foreign exchange rate movement *might* have come to a turning point.

Example: The ten-day, five-day and two-day moving averages have been calculated on a time series of foreign exchange rates. We see that on the sixteenth day, the two-day moving average falls below the five-day moving average. This indicates the beginning of a downward trend in the foreign exchange rate. On the nineteenth day, the five-day moving average falls below the ten-day moving average, indicating with higher significance the downward trend in the foreign exchange rate. For a foreign currency investor, this would indicate that the currency in question should be sold. Conversely when the short-term moving averages exceed the longer-term moving averages from below, it indicates that the currency in question should be bought. (See Table 2-1 and Figure 2-6.)

The analysis is based on the observation that foreign exchange rates move in cycles where objective statistical measures can indicate the turning points of these cycles. The cyclical movements of the foreign exchange rates are very much a function of the market participants' behavior, which will be dis-

Table 2-1. *Technical Analysis.*

Day	(DM/US$)	Ten-day Moving Average	Five-day Moving Average	Two-day Moving Average	
1.	2.7500	–	–	–	
2.	2.7750	–	–	2.7625	
3.	2.8000	–	–	2.7825	
4.	2.8100	–	–	2.8050	
5.	2.8050	–	2.7880	2.8075	
6.	2.8220	–	2.8024	2.8135	
7.	2.8500	–	2.8174	2.8360	
8.	2.8600	–	2.8294	2.8550	
9.	2.8700	–	2.8414	2.8650	
10.	2.9000	2.8242	2.8604	2.8850	
11.	3.0000	2.8492	2.8960	2.9500	
12.	3.2500	2.8967	2.9760	3.1250	
13.	3.3000	2.9467	3.0640	3.2750	
14.	3.2500	2.9907	3.1400	3.2750	
15.	3.2000	3.0302	3.2000	3.2250	
16.	3.1500	3.0630	3.2300	3.1750	Sell
17.	3.0500	3.0830	3.1900	3.1000	signal 1
18.	2.9500	3.0920	3.1200	3.0000	
19.	2.9000	3.0950	3.0500	2.9250	Sell
20.	2.8500	3.0900	2.9800	2.8750	signal 2

Figure 2-6

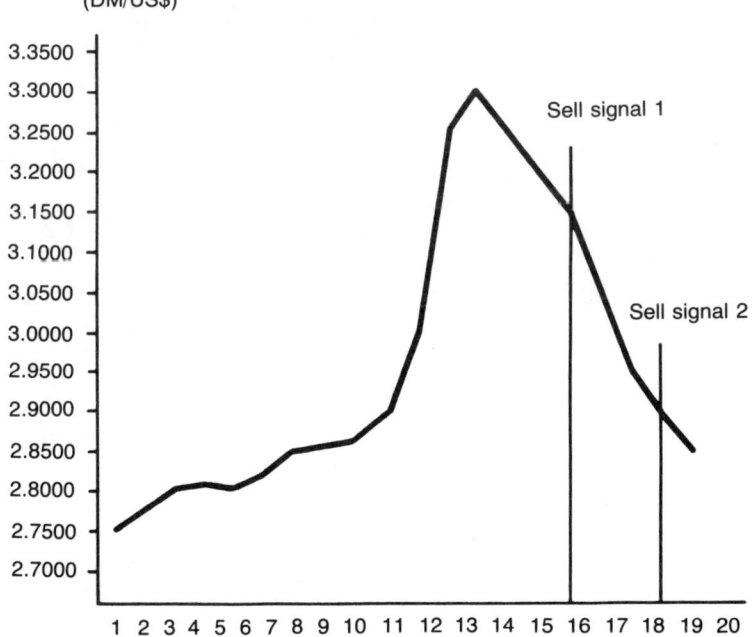

Foreign Exchange Rate
(DM/US$)

Sell signal 1

Sell signal 2

Day

carded when there is intervention in the foreign exchange markets. Hence this type of analysis has its limits, although the models have proven to be useful in managing short-term foreign currency positions, as well as leads and lags in foreign currency flows. The model, however, is reactive in nature and can serve only as an indicator for subjective evaluations on the future foreign exchange rate.

Therefore there are no reliable models to be used when forecasting foreign exchange rates and consequently it is often wise to hedge major foreign currency exposures so as to eliminate the risk of unfavorable foreign exchange rate movements.

CONCLUSION

The expansion in the volume of international commercial transactions and the liberalization of the foreign exchange regulations in many industrialized countries have made institutions engaging in international business more vulnerable to interest rate and foreign exchange exposures, a development that will require close attention by management.

There are differing attitudes to the question on whether or not to hedge financial exposure. Some feel that all foreign exchange and interest rate gaps should be closed to minimize the uncertainty of cash flows, while others feel that in the long run losses and gains will even out. The proper answer probably reflects the more balanced view that financial exposure should be managed. Given the volatility of the interest and foreign exchange rates, the apparent difficulties in forecasting their movements, and the increased impact from interest rate and currency gaps, it is often wiser to hedge major exposures.

High volatility in interest rates and foreign exchange rates can have a severe impact on an institution's cash flows if rate trends continue to run in an unfavorable direction. Hence it is crucial that management performs a thorough analysis of the institution's financial exposures in order to assess the potential risk of these positions. As forecasting interest rates and foreign exchange rates has proven virtually impossible, maintaining large open positions is to gamble on future rate movements.

In response to this, management should define its attitude to these types of risks and institute clear guidelines regarding the level of acceptable financial exposure.

APPENDIX: AUTOREGRESSIVE
INTEGRATED MOVING AVERAGE (ARIMA)

To this category of forecasting techniques belongs the *auto regressive integrated moving average* processes, the so-called ARIMA models, developed among others by Box and Jenkins during the early 1970s. A *moving average (MA) model* is a weighted average of a series of historical observations, which in its simplest form is described as follows:

$X_t = Z_t + bZ_{t-1}$

X_t = The moving average at time t.

Z_t = Observation at time t.

b = Coefficient (weight).

An *autoregressive (AR) model* is basically a regression equation where the explanatory variables are the historical observations themselves. In its simplest form, this model is expressed as follows:

$X_t = aX_{t-1} + Z_t$

X_t = The observed value at time t.

X_{t-1} = The observed value at time $t-1$.

a = Coefficient.

Z_t = The discrepancy between the forecasted value at time t and the actual value at time t.

These two models can now be combined to make an auto regressive moving average (ARMA) model, expressed simply as follows:

$X_t = aX_{t-1} + Z_t + bZ_{t-1}$

Often a nonstationary (that is, it follows a trend of some sort) time series can be made stationary by taking the difference between all observations and making the time series analysis on the differentiated values. This means that one has to integrate or sum up the differentiated model to get back to the nonstationary model. A simple differentiation of observations is as follows:

$$Y_t = (X_t - X_{t-1})$$

Hence the auto regressive integrated moving average (ARIMA) model, in its simple form, can be expressed as:

$$Y_t = aY_{t-1} + Z_t + bZ_{t-1}$$

$$(X_t - X_{t-1}) = a(X_{t-1} - X_{t-2}) + Z_t + bZ_{t-1}$$

$$X_t = (1+a)X_{t-1} - aX_{t-2} + Z_t + b2_{t+1}$$

This equation represents the simplest form of an ARIMA model containing an autoregressive process with one time lag, as well as a moving average process with one time lag and with the analysis based on the once differentiated observations.

These equations can be extended to include as many time lags as is found necessary to make a good model. The general model can therefore be represented as follows:

$$Y_t = a_1Y_{t-1} + a_2Y_{t-2} + \ldots + a_nY_{t-n} + Z_t + b_1Z_{t-1} + b_2Z_{t-2} + \ldots + b_nZ_{t-n}$$

$$Y_t = (X_t - X_{t-1})$$

$$n = \text{Number of time lags.}$$

A substantial amount of literature describes and discusses the analysis of time series in order to establish the optimal models, a task that soon easily becomes fairly technical.[2]

PART **II**

Financial Futures

The Futures Contract

Futures contracts have their roots in the markets for raw materials, such as agricultural products (corn, soybeans, wheat, sugar, cocoa) and metals (copper, tin, silver, gold, platinum), which also in the case of silver and gold serve as investment vehicles.

As opposed to making forward dealings in commodities, where the goods are physically exchanged at a future date at an agreed price, the idea of the futures contract is to create a standard instrument to be traded on an exchange floor.

An exchange-traded futures contract for a given commodity is interchangeable with other contracts on the same commodity, having common specifications for such terms as size of contract, commodity grade, delivery months, and so on (see Table 3-1). Standardized by the exchange on which it trades, the futures contract therefore is easily traded. A *futures contract* is therefore a legal commitment for the seller to make delivery and for the buyer to take delivery of a standardized quantity and quality of the underlying commodity at a specified time (the *expiration date*).

The value of a futures contract depends on the market price

Table 3-1. *Specifications of a Standard Contract: Gold.*

Commodity name	Gold
Exchange name	Commodity Exchange, New York (COMEX)
Size of contract	100 troy ounces
Delivery months	Current calendar month, the next two months, and Feb/Apr/June, Aug/Oct/Dec
First delivery date	First Friday of the delivery month; this is the first day on which delivery may be made.
First notice date	Two business days before the first delivery date; this is the first day on which a seller may issue notice of intention to deliver.
Expiration date	Second Friday before delivery of the futures contract; this is the last day on which an option may be exercised.
Minimum price fluctuation	$0.10 per ounce; this is the smallest change allowable in the price movement of a contract.

of the underlying commodity in the *spot,* or *cash,* market. To determine the value of a contract, multiply the spot market price by the size of the contract.

Example: If gold is quoted at $305 per ounce on COMEX, one contract of gold is worth $30,500 ($305 per ounce times 100). A minimum price movement of $0.10 in the price of gold is therefore equal to a $10 change in the price of the contract ($0.10 per ounce times 100 ounces in a contract).

Over the years, the underlying interests of futures contracts have changed and increased in number. For many years, contracts traded exclusively on agricultural commodities, such as corn, wheat, pork bellies, and soybeans, as well as on precious metals. In the early 1980s, futures contracts became available on oil and gasoline, debt instruments, and even stock indexes. Table 3-2 presents a small sampling of the many types of contract available today.

Table 3-2. *Representative Futures Contracts.*

Commodity Exchange Name	Delivery Months	Size of Contract	Minimum Price Fluctuation	Name
Wheat (hard red winter)	Mar/May/July/Sept/Dec	5,000 bushels	$0.0025 per bu. ($12.50)	Kansas City Board of Trade
Cattle, Live	Feb/Apr/Jun/Aug/Oct/Dec	20,000 pounds	$0.025 per lb. ($5)	Mid-American Commodities
U.S. Treasury Bonds	Mar/June Sept/Dec	$100,000 face value 8% coupon	1/32 point ($31.25)	Chicago Board of Trade
Standard & Poor's 500 Stock Index	Mar/June Sept/Dec	500 x S&P stock index value	5 points ($25)	Chicago Mercantile Exchange Index and Option Division
U.S. Dollar	Mar/June Sept/Dec	$100,000 U.S. dollars	$0.0001 ($10)	Toronto Futures Exchange
No. 2. Heating Oil (New York)	All months	42,000 gallons	$0.0001 per gal ($4.20)	New York Mercantile Exchange
Japanese Yen	Jan/Mar/Apr/Jun/July/Sep/Oct/Dec, and spot month	12,500,000 Japanese Yen	$0.000001	Singapore Inter-national Monetary Exchange

OPENING AND CLOSING TRANSACTIONS

A transaction in futures contracts must be identified as either "opening" or "closing" a position. The initial buying or selling of a futures contract results in an *open position* for the buyer or seller, respectively. The seller's position is open because it is considered *short*—the seller has sold a commodity that he or she does not own. The buyer's position is considered *long* because the contract is for a future purchase of the commodity. As a result, the buyer's position is also open.

A *closing* transaction is one that offsets a position. A commitment may be closed in two ways:

1. By an *offsetting* (liquidating) *transaction:* To close, or offset, a short position, a *seller* buys a comparable contract (a *closing purchase transaction*). A buyer closes a long position by selling a comparable contract (a *closing sale transaction*). All but a small percentage of positions are closed this way.
2. By *delivering* or *receiving* the commodity: A seller may also close a position by delivering the commodity, a buyer by receiving it.

ROLE OF THE EXCHANGES

A futures exchange provides the trading arena for standardized futures contracts. As in the case of stock exchanges, only members may trade on futures exchanges. Eligibility for membership depends on creditworthiness, past business history, character, and integrity.

ROLE OF THE CLEARING HOUSES

The clearing house is an exchange-affiliated agency that clears trades, guarantees performance, and handles fulfillment through delivery.

Clearing

For every trade, the buyer's and seller's firms submit the data on the trade to the clearing house. At the clearing house, data from the buying and selling firms are compared. If the data match, the trade is *cleared*. If not, the data are sent back to the firms for correction. Should the trade data still not match up, the trade is handled on an *out trade*—that is, as a special case.

Guaranteeing Performance

The clearing house thus acts as a third party to all trades. During the course of a trading day, Smith may sell a contract to Jones, Jones to Doe, and Doe to someone else. Once the trade is made, however, the contract no longer exists between the last buyer and seller. Rather, the clearing house becomes the contra to each transaction—a buyer to every seller and a seller to every buyer. Purchasers and sellers of the contracts create financial obligations not to one another but to the clearing corporation or to the exchange through its member firms.

Delivery

Although only a few percent of all futures contracts result in physical delivery, clearing corporations have to provide the mechanism for delivery of the underlying commodity when necessary.

QUOTATIONS

Figure 3-1 presents futures contract quotations, which are typically listed alphabetically by commodity, with the expiration dates grouped below each commodity. Corn, for example, is listed before soybeans, soybeans before wheat, and so on. Notice also that these commodities all fall under the heading of "Grains and Oilseeds." Other categories are "Livestock and Meat," "Metals and Petroleums," "Wood," and "Financial,"

Figure 3-1

FUTURES PRICES

Thursday, April 10, 1986.

Open Interest Reflects Previous Trading Day.

—GRAINS AND OILSEEDS—

	Open	High	Low	Settle	Change	Lifetime High	Low	Open Interest
CORN (CBT) 5,000 bu.; cents per bu.								
May	228½	229½	227	228	− ¼	291¼	222½	33,049
July	220¼	221¾	218½	219¼	− 1½	286	218½	30,339
Sept	204¼	205¼	202¾	203	− 1¾	270	202¾	8,086
Dec	200½	201¼	199	199¼	− 2	235½	199	37,218
Mar87	209½	210¼	207¾	207¾	− 2	242½	207¾	5,283
May	213½	213¾	212	212¼	− 1½	242	212	1,423
July	215	215	212¾	212¾	− 1¾	222	212¾	175
Est vol 49,000; vol Wed 46,044; open int 115,573, +4115.								
SOYBEANS (CBT) 5,000 bu.; cents per bu.								
May	525	529¼	521½	524¾	+ 1¾	657	489	23,833
July	521½	527¼	518½	522¾	+ 2¾	658	497	27,993
Aug	519½	526	517½	521¼	+ 2	609	498½	3,898
Sept	510½	514	508½	510	....	555½	496	3,265
Nov	509	511¾	504½	507¾	− 1	556½	498	19,093
Jan87	516¼	521	514	516¾	− ½	565	509	1,512
Mar	524½	529	522½	526	− ½	576	519½	1,367
May	531	533¼	527½	530½	− 1½	556	527½	142
Est vol 29,500; vol Wed 28,643; open int 81,115, +1,330.								
SOYBEAN MEAL (CBT) 100 tons; $ per ton								
May	154.40	156.00	153.50	154.90	+ 1.00	163.90	134.00	15,674
July	153.90	155.40	152.80	154.40	+ 1.00	167.00	134.00	13,588
Aug	153.20	154.80	152.30	154.10	+ 1.20	163.50	135.50	4,603
Sept	151.00	152.60	149.50	151.10	+ .60	159.30	137.50	3,306
Oct	148.10	149.00	146.50	148.50	+ .50	156.00	136.00	4,017
Dec	149.20	150.50	147.50	149.60	+ .40	157.00	136.00	6,910
Jan87	....	....	....	150.70	+ .50	157.50	136.00	820
Mar	....	....	....	151.00	....	159.00	149.00	275
Est vol 12,000; vol Wed 11,530; open int 49,193, −30.								
SOYBEAN OIL (CBT) 60,000 lbs.; cents per lb.								
May	17.50	17.64	17.41	17.43	+ .02	27.45	16.76	16,734
July	17.77	17.97	17.72	17.75	+ .04	25.25	17.02	16,469
Aug	17.85	18.05	17.80	17.88	+ .06	25.15	17.16	5,659
Sept	17.95	18.07	17.95	17.95	....	24.05	17.10	2,959
Oct	18.05	18.15	17.95	17.97	....	22.80	17.25	3,666
Dec	18.45	18.55	18.35	18.40	....	22.50	17.51	7,714
Jan87	18.60	18.65	18.50	18.50	− .05	22.35	17.70	1,127
Mar	19.00	19.05	18.85	18.90	....	20.25	18.20	398
Est vol 12,000; vol Wed 20,055; open int 54,762, +170.								
WHEAT (CBT) 5,000 bu.; cents per bu.								
May	295½	298	285	286¾	− 9¼	302	274	5,224
July	250½	251	246	246¼	− 4½	310	246	16,154
Sept	252	253	248½	249	− 3½	299	248½	6,627
Dec	260¾	260¾	256	256	− 4½	308¼	256	5,442
Mar87	261½	261¾	257	257	− 4¾	287	257	614
Est vol 11,000; vol Wed 8,921; open int 34,105, −269.								
WHEAT (KC) 5,000 bu.; cents per bu.								
May	280	281	272	272½	− 8½	301	263½	3,898
July	242	242¾	239½	239½	− 2½	298½	239½	8,425
Sept	245½	245¾	243½	243½	− 2	281½	243½	1,633
Dec	253½	253½	253	252½	− 2	283	253	799
Mar87	....	....	256	256	− 2	259¾	256	52
Est vol 2,962; vol Wed 3,115; open int 14,807, +143.								
WHEAT (MPLS) 5,000 bu.; cents per bu.								
May	338½	340	336¾	336¾	− 3¼	363	318¾	3,368
July	300½	301¾	299½	300	− 2½	247½	294	1,454
Sept	276	276	273¾	274	− 2½	350	273¾	1,221
Dec	282½	282½	281	281	− 2¼	302	281	335
Est vol 1,448; vol Wed 1,036; open int 6,378, −3.								
BARLEY (WPG) 20 metric tons; Can. $ per ton								
May	90.00	90.90	89.60	89.60	− 2.30	130.00	89.60	2,585
July	89.50	90.30	89.50	89.50	− 2.70	119.17	89.50	2,513
Oct	86.50	87.10	86.40	86.40	− 2.30	106.00	86.40	2,759
Dec	87.00	87.80	86.90	86.90	− 2.50	99.50	86.90	1,749
Est vol 2,420; vol Wed 566; open int 9,606, −68.								
FLAXSEED (WPG) 20 metric tons; Can. $ per ton								
May	281.80	281.80	279.70	279.70	− 2.10	352.50	279.60	2,739
July	289.20	289.20	287.30	287.50	− 1.70	326.20	287.30	1,426

	Open	High	Low	Settle	Change	Lifetime High	Low	Open Interest
Dec	38.95	39.15	38.80	38.81	− .35	59.25	38.45	9,459
Mar87	40.00	40.10	39.85	39.85	− .35	49.50	39.50	692
Est vol 3,000; vol Wed 4,119; open int 20,426, −297.								
ORANGE JUICE (CTN)—15,000 lbs.; cents per lb.								
May	94.55	95.00	94.20	94.50	− .95	162.50	82.60	1,706
July	94.40	94.80	93.70	93.70	− 1.00	157.50	83.50	1,823
Sept	93.70	93.90	92.60	92.60	− 1.40	127.25	82.00	1,020
Nov	93.60	93.60	92.50	92.50	− 1.35	125.00	82.50	467
Jan87	93.00	93.00	92.10	92.10	− 1.00	113.00	83.75	270
Mar	93.25	93.25	92.90	92.85	− .80	122.00	83.90	948
May	94.00	94.00	94.00	93.20	− 1.20	94.75	84.50	665
July	....	....	....	93.70	− 1.10	95.00	84.75	306
Est vol 650; vol Wed 743; open int 7,205, −122.								
SUGAR—WORLD (CSCE)—112,000 lbs.; cents per lb.								
May	9.45	9.45	8.85	8.91	− .46	9.58	3.58	31,072
July	9.45	9.45	8.65	8.74	− .61	9.50	3.79	27,053
Sept	9.39	9.42	8.83	8.83	− .50	9.42	4.05	357
Oct	9.38	9.40	8.80	8.80	− .50	9.40	4.02	42,446
Jan87	9.50	9.50	9.50	8.80	− .50	9.50	5.65	169
Mar	9.61	9.64	9.06	9.10	− .45	9.64	6.03	14,198
May	9.80	9.82	9.25	9.27	− .41	9.82	6.75	3,520
July	9.85	9.90	9.32	9.34	− .44	9.92	7.77	1,500
Est vol 28,688; vol Wed 23,784; open int 120,315, +314.								
SUGAR—DOMESTIC (CSCE)—112,000 lbs.; cents per lb.								
July	20.65	20.70	20.62	20.68	....	21.60	19.35	1,295
Sept	20.65	20.70	20.65	20.70	− .03	21.45	19.35	588
Nov	....	....	....	20.62	− .03	21.29	19.65	282
Est vol 100; vol Wed 183; open int 2,165, −113.								

—METALS & PETROLEUM—

	Open	High	Low	Settle	Change	Lifetime High	Low	Open Interest
COPPER (CMX)—25,000 lbs.; cents per lb.								
Apr	....	....	....	64.30	+ .40	65.25	63.00	0
May	64.00	64.75	64.00	64.55	+ .40	74.00	60.00	34,680
July	64.75	65.40	64.70	65.25	+ .40	72.55	60.35	26,994
Sept	65.35	65.85	65.35	65.80	+ .40	70.90	60.90	8,197
Dec	65.90	66.60	65.90	66.45	+ .40	70.30	61.60	6,976
Mar87	67.15	67.15	67.10	67.10	+ .40	70.00	62.55	1,558
May	....	....	....	67.45	+ .40	70.00	62.90	437
July	....	....	....	67.85	+ .40	69.95	63.25	197
Est vol 7,700; vol Wed 13,440; open int 79,141, +929.								
GOLD (CMX)—100 troy oz.; $ per troy oz.								
Apr	337.50	339.50	337.50	338.90	− .40	496.80	314.70	1,721
June	339.80	342.80	339.00	341.70	− .50	433.50	320.50	60,368
Aug	343.00	346.00	343.00	345.10	− .50	427.50	328.00	17,586
Oct	347.00	348.60	346.30	348.30	− .50	395.70	331.50	7,271
Dec	349.00	353.00	349.00	351.70	− .50	392.00	336.50	13,538
Feb87	354.50	355.00	354.40	355.20	− .50	397.50	337.30	11,716
Apr	357.00	357.00	357.00	358.30	− .50	405.00	346.30	8,147
June	360.00	360.70	360.00	361.60	− .50	409.00	350.50	7,368
Aug	....	....	....	365.10	− .50	408.50	356.00	6,472
Oct	368.70	366.70	366.70	368.70	− .50	420.00	361.00	4,973
Dec	372.00	372.00	372.00	372.60	− .50	399.40	367.00	1,666
Feb88	....	....	....	376.70	− .50	....	....	230
Est vol 27,000; vol Wed 33,678; open int 141,056, +3,142.								
PLATINUM (NYM)—50 troy oz.; $ per troy oz.								
Apr	428.70	430.50	425.00	427.90	− .80	444.50	264.50	544
July	430.50	435.00	425.50	431.10	+ .10	448.00	273.00	14,444
Oct	430.50	438.30	430.00	434.30	+ .50	450.00	303.50	2,374
Jan87	435.00	440.50	434.00	437.50	+ 1.00	450.00	347.00	835
Apr	437.50	442.50	436.00	440.70	+ 1.60	448.50	361.00	494
Est vol 4,985; vol Wed 5,703; open int 18,695, +743.								
PALLADIUM (NYM) 100 troy oz.; $ per troy oz.								
Apr	....	....	....	105.75	− .30	114.00	106.00	2
June	106.25	107.80	106.25	106.75	− .30	119.30	91.50	4,238
Sept	108.25	109.00	108.25	108.15	− .30	119.00	91.70	1,139
Dec	110.00	110.00	109.75	109.55	− .30	120.00	94.25	576
Mar87	111.75	111.75	111.75	110.95	− .30	127.50	90.00	145

Reprinted by permission of *Wall Street Journal* (Europe), © Dow Jones & Company, Inc., April 10, 1986. All rights reserved.

among others. When a commodity is traded on more than one exchange, it is repeated with the abbreviation for the exchange in parentheses after the commodity name. Wheat, for instance, is listed three times because it trades on the Chicago Board of Trade (CBT), the Kansas City Board of Trade (KC), and the Minneapolis Gains Exchange (MPLS). These abbreviations are explained in a key at the bottom of the quotation section. Next to the commodity names are the standard contract size, such as 5,000 bushels for corn, and the unit of quotation, such as cents per bushel.

At the top of the columns of quotations are the following headings:

- *Open:* The price at which each contract opened.
- *High/Low:* The high and low prices of the day.
- *Settle:* The price at which the contract closed.
- *Change:* The difference between the closing prices of this day and the previous day.
- *Lifetime High/Low:* The highest and lowest prices at which the contract has traded in its lifetime to date.
- *Open Interest:* The total number of futures contracts (purchases or sales) that have not been offset by an opposite transaction or fulfilled by delivery.

Example: In Figure 3-1, the size of a corn contract on the CBT is 5,000 bushels and the price quotes represent cents per bushel. Five yearly corn contracts settle on the same months: May, July, September, December, and March. As soon as a March contract for one year expires, a new contract begins trading for July of the next year on the CBT.

The May contract opened at 228½ ($2.285) per bushel. During the trading day, the highest price was 229½ ($2.295), and the lowest was 227 ($2.27). It closed at 228 ($2.28), which represents a ¼-point change from the previous day's close. Since the contract began trading, the highest price has been 291¼ ($2.9125) and the lowest, 222½ ($2.225). There are 33,049 positions (buys and sells) in the May contract that have not been offset by an opposite transaction or by delivery.

Expiration months tend to be standardized even from one exchange to another.

Example: Silver, which is traded on the CBT and COMEX, has identical expiration months on either exchange.

Open Interest and Volume

After the listing for each commodity in Figure 3-1 are figures for volume and open interest.

Volume is the number of contracts that were traded during the day, whether the transactions opened or closed positions. The previous day's volume is included as a point for comparison of the current day's trading.

Open interest is the total number of open contracts, whether buys or sells, *as of* the close of trading.

Volume and open interest do not necessarily increase or decrease in relationship to each other. Heavy volume during a trading day, for example, could leave open interest almost unchanged from the previous day if the opening and closing transactions are roughly equal in number. Or volume could increase from one day to the next—but decrease open interest if most of the trades closed positions.

MARGIN

To ensure that member firms have enough funds to cover their positions in the market, clearing corporations require members to deposit and maintain margin against their positions. Margin in futures trading is roughly analogous to margin in stock and bond trading.

But only roughly. The margin differs in several ways. Whereas margin for a securities transaction is at least 50% for a futures trade it is typically less than 10% (it varies from one exchange to the other). In securities, buying on margin is optional, but all futures trades are on margin. Perhaps the most crucial difference is in the purpose of margin. In the purchase of a stock or bond, margin is partial payment; the remainder of the purchase is financed by the brokerage firm. In futures transactions, margin is a *performance bond,* or *earnest money;* it ensures that purchasers and sellers will live up to their contractual obligations. Because the margin is not partial payment, the brokerage firm makes no loan and no interest is paid, as in the case of margin purchases of securities.

There are two kinds of margin in futures trading: initial margin and maintenance margin.

Initial Margin

Initial or original margin is the money deposited for each contract upon the purchase or sale of the contract, usually 10 percent of the total worth of the contract. The exchanges set initial margin, depending on the volatility of the commodity and of the futures market itself. Brokerage houses usually ask their customers for a slightly higher margin than that set by the exchange.

Example: If an exchange requires initial margin of 10% on its orange juice contracts, a member brokerage firm might require 15%. If the cash price of orange juice is $0.9500 per pound and a contract consists of 15,000 pounds, then the value of the contract is $14,250 (15,000 pounds times $0.95). The brokerage firm will require an initial margin deposit of $2,187.50 (15 percent of $14,250).

Original margin can be posted in any of the following ways—or in any combination of them:

1. Cash (usually in the form of bank-issued margin certificates).
2. Stock in the clearing corporation.
3. Interest-bearing obligations of the federal government (T bills, T bonds, T notes, and the like).
4. Letters of credit from an approved commercial bank.

Maintenance Margin

Maintenance (or *variation*) *margin* is additional margin required on an established position as a result of a decline in the value of the contract. It is calculated by the exchange clearing house at the end of the trading day. Retail clients are asked by their brokerage houses to put up more margin or have their positions sold out.

Most exchanges set the total amount of margin required in relation to the net short or long position that each member holds in each contract.

Example: A member holds a long position (the buy side) in 15 silver contracts and a short position (the sell side) in 10 silver contracts, and delivery for all the contracts is in the same month. The total margin required is for the net long position of 5 silver contracts.

Some exchanges and many independent clearing corporations seek additional protection by requiring maintenance margin on all long and short positions even when they can be offset by other contracts held by other members.

NORMAL AND INVERTED MARKETS

Refer to Figure 3-1, specifically the settle prices for copper. Notice that the prices for the near months are lower than the months farther out. The market for copper is said to be a *normal,* or *carrying charge,* market—that is, the distant months sell at a premium over near months. The premium is attributed to a carrying charge that is added to the value of the contract and that represents a collective value for insurance, warehousing, and cost of money to "carry" the commodity. The more distant months cost more because they entail greater carrying charges.

In a normal market, the maximum that a distant month can sell over a near month is the total of the carrying charges. If a price included more than these charges, the arbitrageurs would sell the distant month short and take delivery with the nearer, cheaper month, thus locking in a profit whether or not the more distant month's price rose or fell.

An *inverted market* is the opposite of a normal market; that is, the distant months sell at lower prices than near months. In Figure 3-1, the market for corn is inverted, with May contracts trading at a higher price than all others. The implication of an inverted market is that the commodity is in short supply. Buyers are bidding up the price of the near months to the extent that these months' prices more than offset the carrying charges included in the prices of contracts for the distant months.

In an inverted (or "discount") market, each contract that is further out in time trades at a lower price than one closer in. Whereas in a normal market the prices of the further-out contracts are limited by the carrying charges, *there is no limit to the amount that a near contract can trade over a more distant contract* in an inverted market. Inverted markets usually occur in spurts of extreme bullishness.

MARKET PARTICIPANTS

Those who trade commodities may be categorized as either hedgers or speculators.

Today the consumer of commodities, if not as large as, say, General Mills, is considerably larger than the local miller of yesteryear. This consumer–processor must figure out its commodity costs months in advance. Like the farmer in our example, the corporate food processor can fix its commodity costs by hedging—that is, by buying a number of contracts equal to its consumption need. The processor is thereby hedged against an unexpected price rise caused by crop shortages.

The main interest of hedgers is therefore to protect their business against sudden adverse price fluctuations. In traditional agricultural futures, the hedger is usually a producer or processor. Financial futures are traded by large financial institutions, such as banks or insurance companies. Large portfolio managers deal in stock index futures. The speculator may also trade any or all of these futures. *Speculators*, assuming the hedgers' risk, hope to profit through the astute buying and selling of contracts prior to expiration.

The distinction between hedgers and speculators, however, is not always hard and fast. Today's producer/consumers may "lift" (that is, offset) their hedge positions by buying or selling other futures contracts to close their initial purchase or sale. Eliminating the hedge entails risk, even though the large producers have the resources to estimate the size and profit of yearly crops more accurately than most speculators. When they lift their hedge positions, producer/consumers temporarily assume the role and risk of speculators. (As a result, futures exchanges also function as alternate cash marketplaces, because many producers and consumers prefer to deliver or take delivery over risking lifting their hedges at what seems to be a profitable time.)

Both hedgers and speculators benefit the futures marketplace. One of the biggest benefits of hedging is that it results in lower prices for the ultimate consumer. Without hedging, both producers and processors would have to add an extra amount to the price to counterbalance the risk of adverse price change.

Contrary to popular misconception, speculators create neither volatility nor risk in futures markets. In fact, they lessen volatility and *assume* the risk that is already inherent in futures markets and that would otherwise be borne by the producer/consumer. Speculators also enhance liquidity by concentrating risk capital at a central location and putting it at the service of producers and consumers.

LIMITS

Trading on futures exchanges is conducted within the restraints of several types of limit:

1. Position limits.
2. Reportable positions.
3. Trading limits.

Position Limit

A *position limit* is the maximum number of contracts a trader may hold in a commodity. The limit is set by the exchange for the broker, depending on the broker's individual capital structure. In the United States, the Commodity Futures Trading Commission (CFTC) approves the exchange's limits.

Reportable Positions

A *reportable limit* is the number of contracts at which traders must report their total positions by delivery month to the authorized exchange or, in the United States, the CFTC. In the U.S. for most commodities, the reportable limit is 25 contracts, a criterion set by the CFTC. Traders who hold 25 or more contracts, either long or short, are said to be *large traders.*

Both position and reportable limits apply only to large traders. Because of their economic needs, hedgers are not limited in the number of contracts that they may hold at one time. Notice, however, that position limits are considerably higher than reportable positions. If a reportable position is 40 contracts, the position limit may be 400 or even 600, depending on the commodity.

Trading Limit

A *trading limit* is the maximum price movement that an exchange allows for a commodity in one trading session.

Example: COMEX gold may move 2,500 points above or below the prior day's settlement.

(Sometimes the term *trading limit* is used to mean *position limit.*)

In a trading session, the market can be "limit up" or "limit down." When the market is *limit up* (or *bid limit*), all participants want to buy, and no one wants to sell. In such a situation, the bids to buy are at the top of the daily allowable limit move, with no offers to sell at that price. In a *limit down* market, participants are looking to sell, and no one wants to buy.

The trading limit is established to prevent panic. On stock exchanges, trading may be suspended until catastrophic news has time to be accepted. On futures exchanges, there may be a series of limit up or limit down days, but losses are curtailed.

FINANCIAL FUTURES CONTRACTS

Financial futures fall into two categories, both traded by speculators and hedgers: currencies and interest rate futures. Hedging is conducted primarily by *commercials*, which are large businesses and financial institutions seeking to protect themselves against radical swings in currency or interest rates.

Such institutions used to—and to some extent still do—hedge their currency needs by trading *forward contracts* in the foreign currency, or *forex*, market. Like its agricultural counterpart, the financial forward contract is tailor-made to the hedger's needs. It is not standardized, nor is there trading in a secondary market. Futures trading in foreign currencies is a more standardized and liquid market than that of forward contracting.

Background

In the early 1970s the Bretton-Woods Agreement of fixed currency parities was finally abandoned and the U.S. dollar started a free-floating ride that soon led to very volatile foreign exchange rates against the dollar. In response, the Chicago International Monetary Market (IMM), a division of the Chicago Mercantile Exchange, introduced the first financial futures contracts on foreign exchange in 1972.

Over the same period and throughout the 1970s, interest rate policies were liberalized in the United States. As a new school of monetarist economics emerged, monetary policy aims gradually became geared towards managing targeted monetary aggregates as opposed to direct management of the interest rate level. This development and the more erratic foreign exchange rate movements among the major convertible currencies made interest rates more volatile than before and led to the introduction of the first interest rate futures contracts on the Chicago Board of Trade (CBOT) in the fall of 1975. The first contracts introduced were the Government National Mortgage Association (GNMA) certificate futures, which essentially were created to further the financing of domestic building activities in the United States and very shortly after U.S. Treasury Bill futures contracts were engaged on the futures trading floor.

Since then, financial futures contracts have been developed on several other exchanges within the North American continent—such as the New York Futures Exchange (NYFE), the Kansas City Board of Trade (KCBOT), and the Toronto Stock Exchange (TSE), to mention some. Following several years of successful operation in North America the concept of trading financial futures contracts has gone into a phase of internationalization. In September 1982 the London International Financial Futures Exchange (LIFFE) was inaugurated. The exchange initially introduced three interest futures contracts on three-month pound sterling time deposits, pound sterling long gilts, and Eurodollar three-month time deposits plus foreign currency contracts for all major currencies against U.S. dollars.

Hence the market enabled traders to get direct access to pound sterling interest futures, which in the U.S. market would require engagements in both U.S. dollar interest rate contracts and currency contracts against pound sterling. LIFFE is also looking into the possibilities of introducing interest rate futures contracts in the other European currencies, such as Deutsche mark, and the European currency unit (ECU)—the latter becoming increasingly important in the European interbank market.

More recent developments of financial futures markets have taken place in Singapore, Hong Kong, and Sydney in cooperation with some of the U.S. and European exchanges, thereby expanding financial futures trading into other time zones. The Singapore International Monetary Exchange (SIMEX) opened for trading in futures contracts in September 1984. The introduction of the financial futures contracts was done in close cooperation with the Chicago Mercantile Exchange. SIMEX offers three financial futures contracts in Eurodollars; Deutsche marks and Japanese yen which are all interchangeable with the equivalent futures contracts of the CME. The link between the CME and the SIMEX has opened up for longer trading hours in the futures contracts (close to 24 hours), an issue which becomes an increasingly important consideration to many futures traders. In October 1986, the Sydney Futures Exchange (SFE) similarly joined forces with the LIFFE in trading U.S. Treasury bond and Eurodollar interest rate futures, and other international trading links are currently being investigated. Financial futures trading is becoming more and more international due to the improved communication systems, which enable dealings to be carried out in distant overseas markets.

New futures markets continue to be opened. In October 1985 the Tokyo Stock Exchange (TSE) launched a Japanese government bond futures contract and thereby opened up for the first futures contract traded in Japan. During 1986, the French government's attempts to revitalize the financial markets gave birth to the Paris Financial Futures Exchange's (Marché à terme d'instruments financier or MATIF) trading in French government bond futures contracts. In the meanwhile, also, the Swiss banking community is looking into the possibilities of setting up its own financial futures market to underscore Switzerland's status as a major financial center. Pending the success of LIFFE and the other new ventures, the late eighties and early nineties might well see more financial futures exchanges develop in other major currency areas.

Market Developments and Practices

The emergence of many different financial futures exchanges has created a wide variety of financial futures contracts available for trading. Financial futures contracts on interest rates are now traded on the GNMA mortgage certificate, the 90-day Treasury bill, Treasury notes, long-term U.S. government bonds, 90-day certificates of deposits, commercial paper, three-month Eurodollar deposits, 90-day pound sterling time deposits, pound sterling gilts and Dutch, Canadian, Australian, New Zealand, Japanese, and French government issues. Concurrently, financial futures contracts on foreign exchange are traded in pounds sterling, Deutsche marks, French francs, Swiss francs, Japanese yen, Canadian dollars, Mexican pesos, and European currency units, all traded against the U.S. dollar.

The most recent development in the financial futures markets has been the introduction of stock index futures contracts. The Kansas City Board of Trade began trading a Value Line Composite Average Index contract in February 1982. The Chicago Mercantile Exchange introduced the Standard & Poors 500 index contract in April 1982 and in May 1982 the New York Futures Exchange launched a NYSE Composite Index contract. In September 1986, LIFFE introduced a Financial Times–SE 100 ("footsie") share index contract, and also stock exchanges in Japan, Singapore, Switzerland, Sweden, and Spain are experimenting with stock index futures contracts. Forces to promote a market for a commodity price index contract have also been mobilized more recently and ideas of futures index contracts for property insurance policies and freight rates have been launched just to mention a few areas of applicability.

The rationale behind the creation of financial futures contracts on an exchange is that financial commitments are turned into a standard contract, the price of which is determined by the market's demand and supply forces. The conditions on an active exchange are very close to fulfilling the characteristics of the ideal economic state of perfect competition and hence the prices of the financial futures contracts very efficiently reflect the general expectations of the financial markets.

As in the case of commodities exchanges, each of the financial futures exchanges consists of members making the actual deals on the trading floor. The member dealers trade either for own account or for third parties against a commission fee. Memberships are purchased from the exchange, which pretty much functions as a private profit organization. The exchange will carry out a clearing function, or will engage an affiliated clearing agency, in order to settle all trades done by the exchange members during the day. Hence the direct counterpart, when trading financial futures contracts on a certain exchange, is usually the exchange itself or the clearing house and not the membership dealer. In most instances an institution that trades financial futures contracts will have to provide a cash advance of a certain size in order to do the transaction through the exchange. This provides the exchange with a safety margin to cover for potential losses if a counterparty might fail to meet its contractual obligations.

As each financial futures contract is developed to suit the specific conditions prevalent on the exchange on which it is traded, the characteristics of the futures contracts differ slightly from one exchange to the other. In other words the same type of financial futures contracts available in different exchanges are usually not completely compatible.

Benefits

The development of markets for financial futures contracts not only provides an efficient way of matching economic entities with differing financial exposures, but also enables them through trading of financial futures contracts to ameliorate the financial exposure. The fact that many dealers participate in the markets ensures that the necessary liquidity is always available in the market and that the counterparty risk of the inherent financial obligations is well diversified. The wide variety of financial futures contracts being initiated has created the necessary base for the further development of many other financial services to the institutional market.

The financial futures markets provide the means for institutions to neutralize price risks whether the exposure is brought about by interest rate gaps or by a mismatch in foreign exchange flows. Furthermore, the prices determined on the financial futures markets provide the dealers in the underlying cash markets with a valuable source of information on market trends. Information on exchange statistics and price developments on all the major financial futures contracts is available daily in the international newspapers. Figures 3-1, 3-2, and 3-3 show excerpts from the *Financial Times* and the *Wall Street Journal.*

The *Financial Times* provides information on the closing price, the highest and the lowest price quoted during the trading day, and the closing price of the previous trading day. This

Figure 3-2. Quotes on Financial Futures Contracts.

FINANCIAL FUTURES ▰▰▰▰

LONDON

THREE-MONTH EURODOLLAR $1m
points of 100%

	Close	High	Low	Prev
March	90.86	91.03	90 86	91.17
June	90.29	90.52	90.28	90.68
Sept	89.75	90.00	89.75	90.16
Dec	89.30	89.52	89.30	89.72
March	88.92	—	—	89.34

Est volume 10,402 (5,249)
Previous day's open int 13,271 (12,779)

THREE-MONTH STERLING £500,000
points of 100%

	Close	High	Low	Prev
March	87.87	88 06	87.70	88.16
June	88.68	88.90	88.65	88.98
Sept	89.05	89.05	88.90	89.18
Dec	89.30	89.35	89.20	89.50
March	89.25	89.30	69.25	89.50

Est volume 1,787 (3,068)
Previous day's open int 5,651 (5,554)

20-YEAR 12% NOTIONAL GILT £50,000
32nds of 100%

	Close	High	Low	Prev
March	103-08	103-29	103-08	104-05
June	103-08	—	—	104-02
Sept	106-23	—	—	107-17
Dec	106-14	—	—	107-08
March	106-03	—	—	106-29

Est volume 2,871 (2,872)
Previous day's open int 5,500 (5,755)
Basis quote (clean cash price of 13¾%
Treasury 2003 less equivalent price of
near futures contract) −10 to par
(32nds)

STERLING £25,000 $ per £

	Close	High	Low	Prev
March	1.1235	1.1237	1.1215	1.1245
June	1.1155	1.1155	1.1140	1.1165
Sept	1.1108	—	—	1.1120

Est volume 842 (851)
Previous day's open int 3,956 (4,767)

DEUTSCHE MARKS DM 125,000 $ per DM

	Close	High	Low	Prev
March	0.3160	0.3163	0.3164	0.3166

Est volume 33 (8)
Previous day's open int 187 (187)

SWISS FRANCS SwFr 125,000 $ per SwFr

	Close	High	Low	Prev
March	0.3722	—	—	0.3761
June	0.3754	—	—	0.3783

Est volume nil (nil)
Previous day's open int 121 (111)

JAPANESE YEN Y12.5m $ per Y100

	Close	High	Low	Prev
March	0.3910	0.3910	0 3905	0.3933
June	0.3936	0 3936	0.3932	—

Est volume 106 (nil)
Previous day's open int 116 (116)

FT-SE 100 INDEX £25 per full index point

	Close	High	Low	Prev
March	126.50	127.75	126.45	127.75
June	127.00	127.35	127.00	128.00
Sept	127.40	—	—	128.40

Est volume 451 (461)
Previous day's open int 1,207 (1,132)

U.S. TREASURY BONDS 8% $100,000
32nds of 100%

	Close	High	Low	Prev
March	72-14	73-02	72-14	73-13
June	71-13	72-00	71-20	72-11

Est volume 2,880 (2,260)
Previous day's open int 2,072 (1,847)

CHICAGO

U.S. TREASURY BONDS (CBT)
8% $100,000 32nds of 100%

	Latest	High	Low	Prev
March	90.78	91.00	90.76	91.07
June	90.28	90.50	90.22	90.57
Sept	89.72	89.96	89.66	90.03
Dec	89.26	89.50	89.20	89.57
March	88.88	89.10	88.83	89.19
June	88.56	88.67	68.48	88.88
Sept	88.27	88.39	88.19	88.59

U.S. TREASURY BILLS (IMM)
$1m points of 100%

	Latest	High	Low	Prev
March	91.73	91.85	91.71	91.90
June	91.33	91.47	91.29	91.54
Sept	90.86	91.00	90.82	91.06
Dec	90.46	90.62	90.41	90.68
March	90.12	90.15	90.08	90.32
June	89.85	90.00	89.80	90.04
Sept	89.61	89.76	89.58	89.81
Dec	89.38	—	89.38	89.58

CERT. DEPOSIT (IMM)
$1m points of 100%

	Latest	High	Low	Prev
March	91.10	91.27	91.08	91.36
June	90.62	90.78	90.54	90.89
Sept	90.08	90.18	90.03	90.36
Dec	89.62	89.67	89.58	89.91

THREE-MONTH EURODOLLAR (IMM)
$1m points of 100%

	Latest	High	Low	Prev
March	72-14	72-29	72-10	73-0⸴
June	71-12	71-25	71-08	72-03
Sept	70-19	70-31	70-16	71-09
Dec	69-31	70-08	69-24	70-19
March	69-13	69-19	69-11	69-31
June	68-30	69-01	68-28	69-14
Sept	68-17	68-20	68-15	68-31
Dec	68-06	68-09	67-31	68-18
March	67-28	67-30	67-23	68-06
June	67-19	67-20	67-13	67 27

STERLING (IMM) $s per £

	Latest	High	Low	Prev
March	1.1145	1.1250	1.1125	1.1195
June	1.1070	1.1180	1.1055	1.1120
Sept	1.1025	1.1125	1.1010	1.1075
Dec	1.1000	1.1090	1.1005	1.1050

GNMA (CBT)
8% $100,000 32nds of 100%

	Latest	High	Low	Prev
March	69-04	69-18	69-04	69-21
June	68-15	68-25	68-15	69-00
Sept	67-27	68-01	67-27	68-12
Dec	67-09	—	—	67-26
June	66-10	66-16	66-10	66-27
Sept	65-29	66-03	65-29	66-15

Reprinted by permission of *Financial Times.*

Figure 3-3. Quotes on Financial Futures Contracts.

Financial Futures

	Open	High	Low	Settle	Chg	Yield Settle	Chg	Open Interest

EURODOLLAR (LIFFE)—$1 million; pts of 100%

	Open	High	Low	Settle	Chg	Yield Settle	Chg	Open Interest
Mar	90.76	90.81	90.75	90.75	+ .18	91.41	85.49	6,504
June	90.16	90.23	89.16	89.18	+ .21	90.92	85.66	4,940
Sept	89.64	89.66	89.61	89.61	+ .20	90.37	85.50	2,501
Dec	89.17	89.18	89.15	88.15	+ .21	89.90	88.74	470

Est vol 2,534; vol Fri 7,496; open int 14,517, −42.

STERLING (LIFFE)—£250,000; pts of 100%

	Open	High	Low	Settle	Chg	Yield Settle	Chg	Open Interest
Mar	87.25	87.25	86.88	86.95	− .62	90.86	86.35	2,853
June	88.36	88.44	88.17	88.26	− .42	90.60	86.80	2,100
Sept	88.85	88.85	88.65	88.77	−. .23	90.50	87.10	853
Dec	89.00	89.00	89.00	88.80	− .50	89.75	87.50	455

Est vol 3,318; vol Fri 2,184; open int 6,307, +104.

LONG GILT (LIFFE)—£50,000; pts of 100%

	Open	High	Low	Settle	Chg	Yield Settle	Chg	Open Interest
Mar	103-24	103-31	103-05	103-13	− 1-03	109-21	96-21	4,906
June	103-23	103-23	103-03	103-13	− 0-31	108-03	97-16	456

Est vol 3,321; vol Fri 2,802; open int 5,472, −255.

EURODOLLAR (IMM)—$1 million; pts of 100%

	Open	High	Low	Settle	Chg	Yield Settle	Chg	Open Interest
Mar	90.76	90.80	90.60	90.63	− .08	9.37	+ .08	46,734
June	90.15	90.22	89.95	90.02	− .11	9.98	+ .11	33,368
Sept	89.58	89.65	89.41	89.46	− .10	10.54	+ .10	12,633
Dec	89.11	89.17	88.96	88.99	− .08	11.01	+ .08	5,199
Mr86	88.73	88.77	88.59	88.61	− .06	11.39	+ .06	3,940
June	88.38	88.44	88.25	88.29	− .04	11.71	+ .04	2,798
Sept	88.09	88.14	87.99	88.01	− .02	11.99	+ .02	1,018
Dec	87.78	87.83	87.73	87.74	− .02	12.26	+ .02	232

Est vol 38,479; vol Fri 54,605; open int 105,922, −616.

GNMA 8% (CBT)—$100,000 prncpl; pts. 32nds. of 100%

	Open	High	Low	Settle	Chg	Yield Settle	Chg	Open Interest
Mar	69-14	69-19	69-12	69-17	+ 4	13.251	− .028	3,892
June	68-26	68-29	68-22	68-28	+ 4	13.400	− .029	1,231
Sept	....	....	....	68-08	+ 4	13.545	− .029	211
Dec	....	....	....	67-22	+ 4	13.676	− .029	284
Mr86	....	....	....	67-06	+ 4	13.794	− .030	398
June	....	....	....	66-23	+ 4	13.906	− .030	549

Est vol 600; vol Fri 942; open int 6,627, −113.

TREASURY BONDS (CBT)—$100,000; pts. 32nds of 100%

	Open	High	Low	Settle	Chg	Yield Settle	Chg	Open Interest
Mar	72-09	72-18	71-22	71-26	− 13	11.669	+ .069	137,187
June	71-08	71-16	70-21	70-24	− 14	11.852	+ .076	51,117
Sept	70-14	70-22	69-27	69-29	− 16	12.000	+ .088	9,978
Dec	69-26	70-03	69-07	69-08	− 17	12.118	+ .096	9,281
Mr86	69-08	69-14	68-22	68-22	− 17	12.220	+ .097	7,498
June	68-27	68-30	68-07	68-07	− 17	12.306	+ .097	4,964
Sept	68-07	68-07	67-26	67-26	− 17	12.382	+ .099	2,963
Dec	....	....	....	67-15	− 17	12.446	+ .099	1,313
Mr87	67-30	67-30	67-05	67-05	− 17	12.506	+ .101	865
June	67-06	67-07	66-28	66-28	− 17	12.559	+ .101	1,113
Sept	....	....	....	66-21	− 17	12.601	+ .107	1,173

Est vol 192,000; vol Fri 201,332; open int 227,452, +1470.

TREASURY NOTES (CBT)—$100,000; pts. 32nds of 100%

	Open	High	Low	Settle	Chg	Yield Settle	Chg	Open Interest
Mar	81-10	81-17	80-29	81-01	− 8	11.201	+ .048	28,987
June	80-16	80-22	80-04	80-08	− 8	11.354	+ .049	12,840
Sept	79-29	79-29	79-17	79-20	− 8	11.478	+ .050	1,884
Dec	....	....	....	79-03	− 8	11.584	+ .050	456

Est vol 9,000; vol Fri 12,374; open int 44,278, +1449.

TREASURY BILLS (IMM)—$1 mil.; pts. of 100%

	Open	High	Low	Settle	Chg	Discount Settle	Chg	Open Interest
Mar	91.73	91.78	91.69	91.71	....	8.29	....	20,482
June	91.31	91.39	91.25	91.27	− .02	8.73	+ .02	19,176
Sept	90.82	90.89	90.76	90.77	....	9.23	....	4,177
Dec	90.41	90.46	90.36	90.36	....	9.64	....	1,654
Mr86	....	....	....	90.01	....	9.99	....	1,090
June	89.78	89.79	89.72	89.72	....	10.28	....	970
Sept	89.51	89.53	89.49	89.49	+ .02	10.51	− .02	172

Est vol 10,539; vol Fri 17,915; open int 47,773, +8.

BANK CDs (IMM)—$1 million; pts. of 100%

	Open	High	Low	Settle	Chg	Yield Settle	Chg	Open Interest
Mar	91.06	91.12	90.96	90.99	− .06	9.01	+ .06	4,945
June	90.52	90.56	90.30	90.39	− .09	9.61	+ .09	2,894
Sept	....	....	....	89.86	− .07	10.14	+ .07	3,850
Dec	....	....	....	89.36	− .08	10.64	+ .08	1,278
Mr86	....	....	....	88.97	− .05	11.03	+ .05	182
June	....	....	....	88.65	− .03	11.35	+ .03	98

Est vol 2,075; vol Fri 536; open int 13,267, +74.

Currency Futures

	Open	High	Low	Settle	Change	Lifetime High	Low	Open Interest

BRITISH POUND (IMM)—25,000 pounds; $ per pound

	Open	High	Low	Settle	Change	Lifetime High	Low	Open Interest
Mar	1.1000	1.1005	1.0850	1.0920	− .0035	1.5170	1.0850	19,406
June	1.0900	1.0915	1.0740	1.0825	− .0045	1.3050	1.0740	2,877
Sept	1.0860	1.0870	1.0715	1.0780	− .0045	1.2850	1.0715	264
Dec	1.0845	1.0845	1.0760	1.0760	− .0045	1.2860	1.0680	245

Est vol 8,231; vol Fri 12,207; open int 22,792, +1,188.

CANADIAN DOLLAR (IMM)—100,000 dlrs.; $ per Can $

	Open	High	Low	Settle	Change	Lifetime High	Low	Open Interest
Mar	.7466	.7467	.7453	.7465	− .0015	.8050	.7443	8,227
June	.7441	.7443	.7429	.7443	− .0015	.7835	.7429	2,049
Sept	....	....	....	.7425	− .0016	.7585	.7416	853
Dec	.7419	.7419	.7398	.7416	− .0017	.7568	.7398	192

Est vol 1,503; vol Fri 2,284; open int 11,376, +47.

JAPANESE YEN (IMM) 12.5 million yen; $ per yen (.00)

	Open	High	Low	Settle	Change	Lifetime High	Low	Open Interest
Mar	.3845	.3847	.3826	.3839	− .0015	.4695	.3826	17,479
June	.3873	.3875	.3854	.3868	− .0014	.4570	.3854	1,629

Est vol 5,406; vol Fri 9,057; open int 19,216, −414.

SWISS FRANC (IMM)—125,000 francs-$ per franc

	Open	High	Low	Settle	Change	Lifetime High	Low	Open Interest
Mar	.3605	.3619	.3584	.3615	+ .0001	.5035	.3584	23,986
June	.3638	.3655	.3617	.3650	+ .0003	.4900	.3617	1,789

Est vol 17,592; vol Fri 15,322; open int 25,929, +1,585.

W. GERMAN MARK (IMM)—125,000 marks; $ per mark

	Open	High	Low	Settle	Change	Lifetime High	Low	Open Interest
Mar	.3078	.3079	.3056	.3070	− .0010	.4110	.3056	37,279
June	.3101	.3101	.3079	.3093	− .0010	.3710	.3079	5,167
Sept	.3119	.3120	.3104	.3118	− .0009	.3560	.3104	466
Dec	.3150	.3150	.3128	.3147	− .0010	.3620	.3128	72

Est vol 20,477; vol Fri 19,562; open int 42,985, +895.

Stock Index Futures

	Open	High	Low	Settle	Change	Lifetime High	Low	Open Interest

NYSE COMPOSITE FUTURES (NYFE) 500 Times Index

	Open	High	Low	Settle	Change	Lifetime High	Low	Open Interest
Mar	106.60	106.65	104.85	105.20	− 1.30	106.85	88.20	9,748
June	108.45	108.50	106.70	107.05	− 1.35	108.80	90.00	1,017
Sept	110.25	110.25	108.60	108.85	− 1.40	110.35	91.35	352

Est vol 14,727; vol Fri 11,097; open int 11,168, −309.

NYSE COMPOSITE STOCK INDEX
105.35 105.35 104.30 104.50 − .89 ....

S&P 500 FUTURES INDEX (CME) 500 Times Index

	Open	High	Low	Settle	Change	Lifetime High	Low	Open Interest
Mar	183.30	183.45	180.50	180.95	− 2.25	183.80	153.00	55,940
June	186.40	186.45	183.60	184.10	− 2.25	186.90	155.70	2,933
Sept	189.40	189.55	186.90	187.25	− 2.25	189.90	158.10	180

Est vol 64,343; vol Fri 56,455; open int 59,082, +1,697.

S&P 500 STOCK INDEX (Prelim.)
181.59 182.18 180.11 180.51 − 1.68 ....

MAJOR MARKET INDEX (CBT) $100 Times Index

	Open	High	Low	Settle	Change	Lifetime High	Low	Open Interest
Feb	256⅞	257	252¾	253⅛	− 3⅛	257¾	235⅛	8,008
Mar	257⅞	257⅞	253¾	254	− 3⅜	258⅞	236	8,830
Apr	258½	258½	255½	255½	− 3½	*260⅛	248¼	738

Est vol 18,000; vol Fri 16,398; open int 17,655, −38.

MAJOR MARKET INDEX (Prelim.)
256.39 256.48 252.78 253.36 − 3.03 ....

KC VALUE LINE FUTURES (KC) 500 Times Index

	Open	High	Low	Settle	Change	Lifetime High	Low	Open Interest
Mar	205.00	205.05	200.85	201.30	− 3.35	205.15	168.10	6,952
June	209.10	209.10	204.90	205.30	− 3.55	209.60	170.10	468

Est vol 4,420; vol Fri 3,924; open int 7,433, −319.

KC VALUE LINE COMPOSITE STOCK INDEX
199.98 200.05 198.58 198.97 − 1.00 ....

Reprinted by permission of *Wall Street Journal* (Europe), © Dow Jones & Company, Inc., February 12, 1985. All rights reserved.

information is given for each delivery period. Below the price quotations, the London market's trading volume for each futures contract is indicated with the previous trading day's volume added in brackets. Furthermore the total transaction volume and open interests are noted.

The *Wall Street Journal* presents information about price developments on the United Kingdom and United States exchanges. It also provides information on price changes from the last trading day and the maximum price fluctuations over the life of the contracts. Finally, it indicates the open interest for each delivery period and the total transaction volume of the day.

Types of Contracts

INTEREST RATE FUTURES

An *interest rate futures contract* is a standard agreement that provides the holder with a certain interest-bearing asset at a predetermined price at a future time. The contracts are standardized so that each type of future asset is well defined and offered in standard trading units on the exchange. The contracts can be delivered only at certain predetermined dates in the delivery months of March, June, September, and December.[1]

Pricing

The prices on short-term financial futures, such as the three-month Eurodollar deposits and the three-month U.S. Treasury Bills, are quoted on an index basis. That is the par value of 100.00 minus the annual discount rate of, say, 12.25% making up a quoted price of 87.75. With this pricing system, changes in the interest rate lead to a predictable change in the contract price. Hence the contract values are changed by a fixed minimum price for each basis point (0.01%) change in the discount rate. The minimum price change is called a *tick* and is the change in contract value per basis point change in the in-

Table 4-1. *Summary of Some Interest Rate Futures Contracts.*

Chicago Board of Trade (CBOT)	*International Monetary Market (IMM)*	*London International Financial Futures Exchange (LIFFE)*
Commodity (Trading Unit)	*Commodity (Trading Unit)*	*Commodity (Trading Unit)*
Commercial paper 30-day maturity (US$ 3,000,000)	—	—
Commercial paper 90 day maturity (US$ 1,000,000)	Three-month certificates of deposits (US$ 1,000,000)	Three-month sterling deposit (£ Stg. 250,000)
—	Three-month Eurodollar deposit (US$ 1,000,000)	Three-month Eurodollar deposit (US$ 1,000,000)
GNMA collateralized depository receipt (CDR) (US$ 100,000)	—	—
—	Three-month U.S. Treasury bills (US$ 1,000,000)	—
—	One-year U.S. Treasury bills (US$ 250,000)	—
U.S. Treasury notes, four-six years to maturity, 8% coupon (US$ 100,000)	U.S. Treasury notes, four years to maturity 7% coupon (US$ 100,000)	—
U.S. Treasury bonds, fifteen years to maturity, 8% coupon (US$ 100,000)	—	U.S. Treasury bonds, fifteen years to maturity, 8% coupon (US$ 100,000)
—	—	Twenty-year gilt (£ Stg. 50,000)

terest rate. In the case of a three-month Eurodollar deposit standard contract of U.S. $1,000,000, the value of a tick is:

$1,000,000 \times 3/12 \times 0.01/100 = \$25$

From this, you can see that, if the interest rate increases by 10 basis points (0.1%), the value of one three-month Eurodollar deposit contract will fall in value by U.S.$ 250.

Given this standard formula for computation, the value of a tick can be found for the major short-term interest rate futures contracts.

$$\text{Tick Value} = \begin{array}{c}\text{Nominal Contract} \\ \text{Value}\end{array} \times \frac{\text{Maturity period (days)}}{\text{Year (days)}} \times \frac{0.01}{100}$$

Trading Unit						*Tick Value*	
Three-month dollar instruments	$100,000 \times$	$\frac{90}{360}$	$\times$	$\frac{0.01}{100}$	=	US$	25.00
Three-month sterling deposit	£250,000 \times$	$\frac{90}{360}$	$\times$	$\frac{0.01}{100}$	=	£ Stg.	6.25
One year U.S. dollar instruments	$250,000 \times$	$\frac{360}{360}$	x	$\frac{0.01}{100}$	=	US$	25.00

Turning to financial futures contracts for longer-term assets, the described formula for computation of the tick value no longer applies. Therefore it has been conceptually determined that the tick value equals 1/32 of a percentage point of the nominal contract value. Hence the tick values can be calculated by means of the following formula:

Tick value = Nominal contract value $\times$ 1/32 $\times$ 1/100

Trading Unit						*Tick Value*	
U.S. Treasury bond futures contract	$100,000 \times$	1/32	$\times$	$\frac{1}{100}$	=	US$	31.25
Twenty-year gilt	£50,000 \times$	1/32	$\times$	$\frac{1}{100}$	=	£ Stg.	15.625

By convention, the minimum allowable price movement of any financial futures contract corresponds to the tick value.

Hence the profit or loss incurred from a change in financial futures prices is always calculated by the net change in ticks (plus or minus) multiplied by the tick value. This makes for a very manageable accounting system in the hectic atmosphere of the exchanges where a handy method of computation is imperative.

Price Limit

During the course of a trading day prices might fluctuate widely or show a strong trend. To prevent extreme volatility and to stabilize the quotation of contract prices, the futures exchanges have introduced the concept of a *price limit*, which is the maximum change in trading prices during any one day. When this limit is reached, the market will be suspended for a period, in some instances until the following business day depending on the exchange.

Margin

Any change in value position caused by price changes will be settled by cash on a day-to-day basis. When a trade is done on the financial futures exchange, the dealer will pay an *initial margin* to the exchange which he eventually will pass on to the client if he is trading on behalf of third party.

The size of the margin varies from contract type to contract type and from exchange to exchange but usually ranges from 2 to 3% for both short-term and long-term financial futures. The rationale behind the initial margin is that the sum total of all cash margins will reduce the immediate risk of default to the exchange's clearing operation if one counterparty cannot fulfill its obligations.

The changes in the value of a trader's position is calculated currently and is settled in cash on a daily basis through a *variation margin*, which then represents the client's profit or loss for that day. The current cash settlement procedure also reduces the potential impact of the inherent counterparty risk. For the customer trading in the financial futures market, the daily cash settlement procedure has cash flow implications that ought to be evaluated before engaging in any dealings.

Conversion Factor

The U.S. Treasury bond futures contract has been traded very actively on the Chicago Board of Trade exchange for several years. To transfer the availability of a futures contract carrying the similar characteristics into the European time zone, an equivalent futures contract was introduced on the London International Financial Futures Exchange during 1984.

The problem with the U.S. Treasury bond futures contract, as well as the U.S. Treasury note futures and the sterling gilt contract for that matter, is that the underlying cash markets trade these securities with very different maturity profiles and with different coupons. Therefore no single security acts as a "natural" standard trading unit for a financial futures contract to be offered on the exchange. To circumvent this problem, the exchanges have introduced the concept of a conversion factor whose function is to bring any eligible security into a standard tradeable value.

For the U.S. Treasury bond futures contract, the unit of trading is the par value of a US $ 100,000 notional 15-year U.S. Treasury bond with an 8% coupon. The contract standard determines that an eligible security for delivery under the futures contract is any U.S. Treasury bond that matures at least 15 years from the first day of the contract, and if the security is callable, then the earliest call date must be at least 15 years from the first day of the contract month.

Settlement Price

When a futures contract is exchanged between buyer and seller on the exchange, the contract amount involved is the principal amount plus the accrued interest. The principal amount is reached by multiplying the exchange delivery settlement price by a conversion factor:

Principal amount = Exchange delivery settlement price × Conversion factor

The *exchange delivery settlement price (EDSP)* is determined by the current market price of the contract at a given time on the exchange. The *conversion factor* is simply the par value multiplier, which determines the discount/premium value of a security with different maturity or coupon from the standard trading unit.

Example: A 15-year security with a 7% coupon will be sold at a discount value of 91.44% to give a yield of 8%. For this type of security the conversion factor is .9144. Or a 20-year security with a 7% coupon will be sold at a discount value of 90.18% to give a yield of 8%, hence for this type of security the conversion factor is .9018.[2]

As these examples show, the conversion factor decreases when the coupon *decreases* and when the maturity *increases*.

The par value conversion factor ensures that all securities eligible for the contract standard will obtain a comparable evaluation. Thus it provides for an efficient way of dealing with contracts on securities of nonhomogenous characteristics.

Comparing Contracts

As already mentioned, each financial futures exchange might well have distinct market procedures which make the price development of two apparently equivalent financial futures contracts hard to compare. A good example is, again, the U.S. Treasury bond futures contract as traded on the Chicago Board of Trade and the London International Financial Futures Exchange:

- The price limit rules on the two exchanges differ. On the Chicago exchange the trading ceases for the remainder of the day unless prices return within the limit, but a progressive scale of price limits is triggered by successive days' excess of the initial price limit. On the London exchange the trading is suspended for an hour if the price limit is reached and then continues without any price limits for the remainder of the day.

- The Chicago exchange has several levels of initial margins, whereas the London exchange only has two initial margins.

- On the Chicago exchange the exchange delivery settlement price is determined by the last trading price before the close of trading on a given trading day, which is 3:00 p.m. (CST). The London exchange determines the exchange delivery settlement price as the average of the contract prices during the minute preceding 3:00 p.m. (London time).

This is to mention but a few of the things that must be taken into consideration when comparing prices at different exchanges and that require detailed procedural knowledge to interpret satisfactorily.

CURRENCY FUTURES

A *currency futures contract* is a standard agreement which provides the holder with a certain amount of foreign currency at a predetermined foreign exchange rate at a future time.

The contracts are standardized so that each contract specifies the same amount of foreign currency. Like interest rate futures, the currency futures contracts are deliverable at specified dates, namely the third Wednesday in March, June, September, and December on the International Monetary Market and on the second Wednesday in the same months on the London International Financial Futures Exchange.

Pricing

Financial futures contracts on currencies are usually quoted in U.S. dollars and cents per unit of the foreign currency as the trading units are determined as a certain amount of the foreign currency.

Example: A financial futures contract in Deutsche marks might be quoted as .3185, meaning that the price on the futures exchange for one Deutsche mark contract is U.S. $39,812.50 = (DM 125,000 × .3185 US$/DM).

Table 4-2. *Summary of Some Currency Futures Contracts.*

International Monetary Market (IMM)	London International Financial Futures Exchange (LIFFE)
Commodity (Trading Unit)	Commodity (Trading Unit)
Swiss Francs (Sw. Frc. 125,000)	Swiss Francs (Sw. Frc. 125,000)
Mexican Pesos (Mx. Ps. 1,000,000)	—
Deutsche Marks (DM 125,000)	Deutsche Marks (DM 125,000)
Canadian Dollars (CAN$ 100,000)	—
Pound Sterling (£ Stg. 25,000)	Pound Sterling (£ Stg. 25,000)
Japanese Yen (Y 12,500,000)	Japanese Yen (Y 12,500,000)
French Francs (F. Frc. 250,000)	—

On the international foreign exchange markets the exchange rate is normally quoted against the U.S. dollar as the amount of foreign currency per unit of the U.S. dollar, except Commonwealth currencies, which are quoted similar to the currency futures contracts.

On the International Monetary Market in Chicago the contract sizes have been determined so as to obtain the same tick value of US$ 12.50 for all the currency futures contracts with the exception of the Canadian dollar and the Mexican peso contracts, which have a tick value of US$ 10.00.

The *tick size,* which also indicates the minimum acceptable price fluctuation of the currency contract, is usually denominated in cents per unit of the foreign currency, as is the price of the futures contract. The tick value is calculated by using the following formula:

Tick value = Nominal contract value x Tick size

By using this formula, you can, for example, calculate the tick value of the Deutsche mark contract as:

DM 125,000 × .01 cents/DM = US$ 12.50

On the London International Financial Futures Exchange, the tick value of all the currency futures contracts traded is also US$ 12.50, except the pound sterling contract, whose tick value is calculated as (£ Stg. 25,000 × .01 cents/£ Stg.) = US$ 2.50. Consequently, this value is different from the tick value of the International Monetary Market's pound sterling contract.

Foreign Exchange Spot Market

The underlying cash market for the currency futures contracts is the foreign exchange spot market where the exchange rate at a given time is determined by the supply and demand forces in play for that currency. In the foreign exchange market, a future foreign exchange rate can be determined by engaging in money market transactions in the two currencies in question.

Example: U.S. dollars are borrowed, exchanged for Deutsche marks in the spot market, and the marks are deposited for say, three months. During that time, the holder of the marks sells the over-the-counter three-month future foreign exchange contract on Deutsche marks at the equilibrium price, against a premium to cover transaction costs.

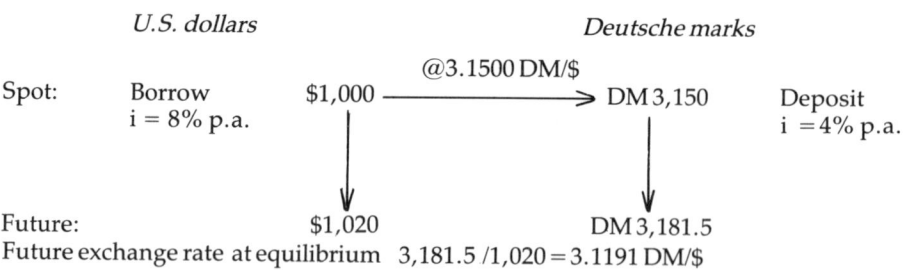

	U.S. dollars			Deutsche marks	
			@3.1500 DM/$		
Spot:	Borrow	$1,000	⟶	DM 3,150	Deposit
	i = 8% p.a.				i = 4% p.a.
		↓		↓	
Future:		$1,020		DM 3,181.5	

Future exchange rate at equilibrium 3,181.5 /1,020 = 3.1191 DM/$

This example focuses on the fact that prices on the currency futures always must tie into the relative interest rates of the currencies traded. If this were not so, riskfree arbitrage would be initiated and would flourish until the prices had adjusted to the equilibrium future price. This illustrates the interest parity theorem which is expressed in its theoretical form by the following formula.[3]

$$F = S \times \frac{1 + N_{f,t}}{1 + i_{\$,t}}$$

where

F = Future foreign exchange price (DM/US$).
S = Spot foreign exchange price (DM/US$).
$i_{f,t}$ = Interest rate in the foreign currency area.
$i_{\$,t}$ = U.S. dollar interest rate.
t = the time period (in our example three months).

From this example, we can deduce the following basic rules of thumb:

> The currency of the lower interest rate area will sell at a forward premium in terms of the higher interest currency. Conversely, the currency of the higher interest rate area will sell at a forward discount in terms of the lower interest currency.

Note, however, that these rules assume a free flow between currencies, which can take place only in unrestricted capital and foreign exchange markets. This also implies that the interest

Table 4-3. *Summary of Some Stock Index Futures Contracts.*

Kansas City Board of Trade (KCBOT)	Chicago Mercantile Exchange (CME)	New York Futures Exchange (NYFE)	London International Financial Futures Exchange (LIFFE)
Commodity (Trading Unit)	Commodity (Trading Unit)	Commodity (Trading Unit)	Commodity (Trading Unit)
Value Line Average (US$ 500)	Standard & Poors 500 (US$ 500)	New York Stock Exchange Composite (US$ 500)	Financial Times SE 100 (£ Stg. 25)
—	Standard & Poors 100 (US$ 200)	—	

rate parity theorem is valid only for nonregulated and economically stable currency areas. Note also that the real world can deviate slightly from the theory because of internal market procedures of the financial futures exchanges where settlement practices might deviate from those in the underlying cash markets for foreign currency.

INDEX FUTURES

A *stock index futures contract* is a standard agreement that provides the holder with a given index at a predetermined price at a future time. At the Chicago Mercantile Exchange the settlement day is the third Friday of March, June, September, and December.

The stock index futures contract is the latest development on the financial futures exchanges. The Kansas City Board of Trade introduced the Value Line Average index contract in February 1982 and other exchanges soon followed suit.

Pricing

The prices of the index futures contracts are determined by supply and demand in the market. Like other financial futures, the contracts are offered on the exchange through general outcry and an equilibrium market price is reached. The price of the index contract on the day of settlement is calculated as the trading unit times the value of the underlying index. The index is determined by the average (or weighted) price movement of a predefined portfolio of stocks.

Example: The underlying portfolio of the index consists of three stocks, and the base year for comparing the price movement is 1980. The index is calculated as follows:

	1980			*1985*		
	No. of Stocks Outstanding	*Price*	*Value*	*No. of Stocks Outstanding*	*Price*	*Value*
Stock 1	100	35	3,500	150	40	6,000
Stock 2	200	25	5,000	200	50	10,000
Stock 3	175	40	7,000	300	20	6,000
Total market value			15,500			22,000

Index Value   22,000/15,500 = 1.4194

Settlement value: Trading unit × Index value

$$US\$ \ 500 \ \times \ 1.4194 \ = \ US\$ \ \ 709.70$$

Settlement Value

As you can see, the settlement value is sensitive to the way the index is calculated, which again is a function of the underlying composition of the stock portfolio. Hence there is no guarantee that the various indexes will follow each other over time. Yet, in general, the more diversified and the more comprehensive the underlying stock portfolio is, the better the index will reflect the overall trend of the stock market.[4] The indexes used for the standard index futures contracts are well diversified, but due to the different composition of the underlying stock portfolios neither of these indexes fluctuate in a fully correlated manner.[5]

The settlement value of a stock index contract represents the average current value of the market's stocks; there is no directly related cash market for the stock index. As a result, the exchanges have developed a procedure of cash settlement at the maturity of the contracts. In this procedure the buyer and the seller of a specific contract exchange cash through the clearing house at delivery equal to the difference between the settlement value, representing the actual price of the contract at that day, and the price originally agreed to on the futures contract.

COMMODITY FUTURES

Commodity futures contracts deserve a brief mention because these contracts have been traded in the Chicago markets since the latter half of the nineteenth century. The commodity futures markets were created initially to reduce the impact of price fluctuations on producers and users of the commodities, whose availability is very often seasonal. As discussed earlier, commodity futures exchanges are the forerunners for the financial futures markets.[6]

Commodity futures are still very actively traded on several exchanges in North America.[7] A special segment of the com-

Table 4-4. Summary of Some Commodity Futures Contracts traded on the Chicago Mercantile Exchange.

Commodity	Trading Unit
Live cattle	40,000 lb.
Feeder cattle	44,000 lb.
Live hogs	30,000 lb.
Pork bellies	38,000 lb.
Fresh white eggs	22,500 doz.
Fuel oil	1,000 barrels
Leaded gasoline	1,000 barrels

Table 4-5. Summary of Some Precious Metal Futures Contracts.

Chicago Mercantile Exchange (CME)	Chicago Board of (Trade (CBOT)	London Metal Exchange
Commodity (Trading Unit)	Commodity (Trading Unit)	Commodity (Trading Unit)
Gold futures contract (100 troy oz.)	—	Gold futures contract (10,000 troy oz.)
Silver futures contract (5,000 troy oz.)	Silver futures contract (1,000 troy oz.)	—

modity futures markets is the futures contracts for precious metals. Due to their durability and "scarcity value," precious metals have always served as a safekeeper in times of economic distress, as well as a means for portfolio investments and therefore can be traded in conjunction with the true financial futures contract. In many ways the price development on the markets for precious metals have close ties to the developments in the real economy. So studying their market developments can give valuable hints to moves in the international economy.

Hedging With Financial Futures

The purpose of trading in the commodity futures markets, as well as in the financial futures markets, is to reduce or eliminate risk. By buying or selling "forward" what is needed or what is in surplus in, say, nine months, you can eliminate the uncertainty of the price level at the time of delivery, and you can rely on profitability calculations with full certainty—at least as far as prices are concerned.

In the commodity futures market the contracts more often result in the physical delivery of the goods of the contract. This is rarely the case in the financial futures markets. What is special about financial futures is that the commodities traded are financial obligations. Due to the daily mark-to-market (the variation margin), the net gain or net loss will be fully compensated in cash at the time of delivery, which is what most market participants are looking for. Usually, a seller of a futures contract will purchase a similar contract, and a buyer will sell a similar contract on or before the last trading day before delivery. As a result, the position will square out, that is, there will be no delivery of the underlying financial asset. This procedure, often called *closing out*, can be performed at any time during the trading period. Physical delivery of the financial asset of a financial futures contract can take place and does occasionally take place, although it is more the exception than the rule.

What drives the financial futures market is the fact that there is a difference between the future contract price agreed to and the contract price at the time of delivery. The contract price at the time of delivery will usually be equal to the going cash market price.

Example: A market participant sold a contract at a future price of $110, and the actual contract price at the last trading day before delivery is $100. That trader made a profit of $10 by closing out the position.

This principle applies to both speculative participants in the market who expect to incur a long-run profit by taking a position in the market, as well as to hedgers who offset changes in foreign exchange or interest rate expense by a capital gain or loss on the financial futures contracts.

Example: (See Figure 5-1.) In March, the actual cash market price for the contract is $95. Our view, as investors, is that the price in nine months, in December, will be $90. Yet the December financial futures contract currently trades at $105 on the futures exchange.

If our view is more correct than the market's indication, we could sell the December futures contract in the expectation

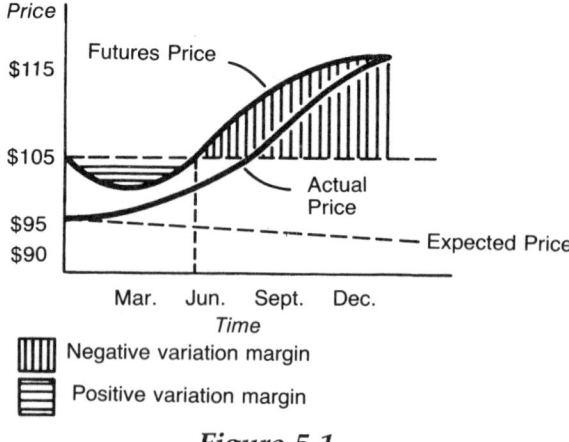

Figure 5-1

of a profit at delivery. (Futures price of $105 less the expected price of $90 is greater than zero.) In June the actual cash market price increases and continues to do so over the remainder of the year to finish at $115 at the time of delivery in December. In this case the investor would incur a loss because the market moved against our expectations. (The futures price less the actual price at delivery is less than zero.) Because the futures price initially dropped and remained below the futures price we settled for until June, the variation margin is positive and there is a cash inflow on the settlement account. From June onward, the futures price increases, resulting in a negative variation margin and a cash outflow from the settlement account.

Note that the price of the December financial futures contract converges towards the contract price in the underlying cash market to finally be equal at delivery date. This illustrates the phenomenom of *convergence.* In general the closer we get to the delivery date, the less will be the impact of market expectation. This does not mean, however, that one may assume a stable convergence.

This example is presented from an investor's point of view. It could equally well be seen from a hedger's point of view. For example, a buyer of the commodity who fears that the price will increase could then buy a futures contract. In this case he will sell at the higher cash market price against a purchase at the lower futures price which was settled at the purchase of the futures contract. He will thus make a profit (the actual price at delivery less the futures price is greater than zero). This profit would offset the increased cost from the actual purchase of the goods in the cash market. The hedger will end up with a positive variation margin, and the profit would be available in cash in the settlement account at the delivery date.

INTEREST RATE HEDGES

Consider an institution that has a twelve-month asset of $20,000,000 on its books at a return of say 12%. To fund this, the institution has acquired a nine-month liability at a rate of

10% p.a. Looking ahead, a liquidity gap of $20,000,000 will, of course, appear during the three-month period from month 9 to month 12 with funding costs at that time being unknown.

Balance Sheet

	Assets	*Liabilities*
3 months	$20,000,000 (12%)	$20,000,000 (10%)
6 months	$20,000,000 (12%)	$20,000,000 (10%)
9 months	$20,000,000 (12%)	$20,000,000 (10%)
12 months	$20,000,000 (12%)	(Funding requirement)

Assuming that interest is paid at maturity, the institution must provide interest payments in cash at the end of the nine-month period of:

$$\$20,000,000 \times .10 \times 9/12 = \$1,500,000$$

That is, the funding requirement in the fourth quarter is not $20,000,000 but $21,500,000—namely principal plus interest on the nine-month loan that has just expired. Hence the break-even cost of a three-month loan in the fourth quarter is:

$$\frac{\$20,000,000\ (.12 - .10 \times 9/12)}{\$21,500,000} \times 400 = 16\frac{3}{4}\%$$

But, who knows what will happen over the next nine months?

A less plausible way of closing the interest rate gap would be to obtain a twelve-month liability, preferably at a cost below 12% p.a. and acquire a nine-month asset preferably at a return above 10% p.a. The asset and liability positions would be fully matched in maturities, but total footings will have increased from $20,000,000 to $40,000,000, with whatever impact this has on leverage and profitability ratios.

Another possible avenue would be to find a counterparty with exactly the opposite interest rate gapping or an investor who is interested in putting the inverse position on his books—that is, accept a future obligation. This type of search, however, is an arduous process, and why go through it when the financial futures markets deals with financial obligations of exactly this nature? The interest gap can be effectively closed by selling three-month Eurodollar deposit contracts for delivery nine months hence, preferably at a rate below 16¾% (that is, a contract price in excess of 83.25 = (100 − 16.75). The financial futures market thus represents an efficient way of accessing counterparties in futures contracts—without affecting the balance sheet.

Short Interest Rate Hedges

Short interest rate hedges generate a profit when interest rates increase above the market's expected future rate, and they are therefore used by borrowers to lock in the future funding cost. The future loan could be an existing loan that is to be rolled over for an extended period, or it could be a completely new loan that is intended to cover expected cash outflows.

Example: In May, a loan of $10,000,000 is to be obtained for a six-month period with three months rollover periods from September this year to February the following year. If the effective borrowing rate is very close to the U.S. domestic certificate of deposit rate, the borrower could lock in the borrowing cost by selling ten three-month certificate of deposit contracts for delivery both in September and December.

The interest rate was 10% in May and the borrower is worried that interest rates will increase. The three-month CD contracts for delivery in September and December both trade for a price of 89.00, that is, implying a future interest rate of 11% p.a. By selling the financial futures contracts, the future funding cost will be locked in at the 11%.

In September the three-month interest rate has increased to 12%, so that a three-month CD contract is acquired on the futures exchange at a price of 88.00. For each contract sold at the already settled futures price of 89.00, there will be a price gain of 100 ticks. The total capital gain incurred from the sale of futures contracts will count against the increased interest cost on the loan, resulting in a net expense on the loan corresponding to the 11% interest rate.

Three-Month Loan September-December

Price of futures contract	89.00
Cash price of futures contract	88.00
Price gain per contract sold	1.00 = 1.00/0.1 = 100 ticks
Profit per contract sold	100 × $25 = $2,500
Actual interest expense	$300,000
September-December (12%)	
US$ 10,000,000 loan	
Profit from sale of 10 futures contracts	$ 25,000
Net cash expense on loan	$275,000

Corresponding to an effective interest rate of 11.00% p.a.

In December the three-month interest rate has increased to 13%, that is, the cash price for the futures contract now amounts to 87.00 leading to a price gain of 200 ticks per futures contract sold. Again the net interest expense on the loan corresponds to an 11% effective interest rate.

The Three-Month Loan December-February

Price of futures contract	89.00
Cash price of futures contract	87.00
Price gain per contract sold	2.00 = 2.00/0.1 = 200 ticks
Profit per contract sold	200 × $25 = $5,000
Actual interest expense	$325,000
September-February (13%)	
US$ 10,000,000 Loan	
Profit from sale of 10 futures contracts	$ 50,000
Net cash expense on loan	$275,000

Corresponding to an effective interest rate of 11.00% p.a.

The quotes on the futures exchanges will reflect the average interest rate expectation of the market participants themselves. In this example the market expected an interest rate increase from 10% to 11%, and the borrower could fix the future funding cost at the market's future expected interest rate—namely 11%. It turned out to be a very wise decision.

In our example, the market expected an increase in the interest rates, and the actual interest rate level turned out to be in excess of the market's expectations. But what happens if the actual interest rate movement turns out to follow a declining trend due to some unforeseeable economic developments?

Example: The actual three-month CD rate in September has fallen to 10%. The three-month CD futures contract for September delivery would therefore have a cash price of 90.00, and we would be losing 100 ticks for the sale of each contract.

Three-Month Loan September-December

Price of futures contract sold	89.00
Cash price of futures contract	90.00
Price loss per contract sold	1.00 = 1.00/0.1 = 100 ticks
Loss per contract sold	100 × $25 = $2,500
Actual interest expense	$250,000
September-December (10%)	
US$ 10,000,000 loan	
Loss from sale of 10 futures contracts	$25,000
Net cash expense on loan	$275,000

Corresponding to an effective interest rate of 11.00% p.a.

So, no matter what direction the interest rate level takes, the interest rate has been effectively locked in at 11% p.a.

> *A borrower can fix the future cost of funding by **selling** a suitable number of interest futures contracts.*

In the above example the funding cost was fully correlated to the CD rate and we therefore obtained a 100% hedge. Such, however, is not always the case. In the example, the time loan periods also corresponded exactly to the maturities of the futures contracts, which made the hedging exercise relatively simple. Yet, often the real world is not so favorable.

Example: In May we foresee that we have to fund ourselves for a six-month period from July to December through a floating rate loan of $10,000,000, with interest payable at the end of each month at the going one-month CD rate. We would like to hedge the loan against an increase in the interest rate level. As in the previous example, the floating rate loan is hedged through the sale of twenty three-month CD financial futures contracts, of which ten are to be delivered in September and ten are to be delivered in December.

Six-Month Loan July-December

Month	Principal	One-Month CD Rate	Interest Amount	Futures Settling Account	Net Cash Outflow
July	$10,000,000	11.0% p.a.	$ 91,667	—	$ 91,667
August	$10,091,667	11.5% p.a.	$ 96,712	—	$ 96,712
September	$10,188,379	12.0% p.a.	$101,884	+ $25,000	$ 76,884
October	$10,290,263	12.5% p.a.	$107,190	—	$107,190
November	$10,397,453	13.0% p.a.	$112,639	—	$112,639
December	$10,510,092	13.5% p.a.	$118,238	+ $50,000	$ 68,238
	$10,246,309	12.25% p.a.	$628,330		$553,330

Corresponding to an average interest rate of 10.8% p.a.

These calculations imply that, through hedging, the average funding cost was reduced from 12.25% to 10.8% p.a. However, the example also illustrates some of the problems occurring in more complex borrowing situations. As we cannot be sure that the three-month CD rate will correspond to the average of the one-month CD rate over the corresponding three-month period, the future funding cost cannot be locked in 100%, and the timing of the financial futures contracts does not necessarily fit the time schedule of the borrowing program. So in general more skill is required in arranging the appropriate hedging program for a more complex borrowing scheme of the real world. Nevertheless, the following axiom holds true in general:

> *Institution can hedge against increasing interest rates by **selling** interest futures contracts.*

Long Interest Rate Hedges

Long interest rate hedges generate a profit when interest rates fall below the market's expected future rate. They are therefore used by lenders and investors to lock in the return on future loans or investments.

Example: An institution foresees a cash inflow of US$ 20,000,000 in three months, which it intends to place in one-year U.S. Treasury bills for a twelve-month period. The future return on this investment could be locked in by buying 80 U.S. Treasury bill contracts for delivery in three months. Presently the return on one-year Treasury bills is 11.50% p.a., but the market expects the rate to fall to 11% in three months (as implied by a futures contract price of 89.00). Fearing that rates might move further down, the institution would like to lock in the future return of 11% p.a. and so it buys 80 futures contracts at 89.00.

Three months later, the one-year U.S. treasury bill rate has dropped to 10.50%, and so the futures contract now trades at a price of 89.50. The futures contracts, acquired at a price of 89.00, can be sold at a profit.

A Twelve-Month Investment

Cash price of futures contract	89.50
Price of futures contract bought	89.00
Price gain per contract bought	.50 = .50/0.1 = 50 ticks
Profit per contract bought	50 × $25 = $1,250
Actual return	$2,100,000
12 months (10.5%)	
US$ 20,000,000 investment	
Profit from purchase of 80 contracts	$ 100,000
Net return on investment	$2,200,000

Corresponding to an effective interest rate of 11.00% p.a.

Had the return on one-year Treasury bills instead remained unchanged at the 11.50% p.a., then the institution would have lost money on the futures contracts because the futures contract bought at a price of 89.00, would sell at 88.50.

A Twelve-Month Investment

Cash price of futures contract	88.50
Price of futures contract bought	89.00
Price loss per contract bought	.50 = .50/0.1 = 50 ticks
Loss per contract bought	50 × $25 = $1,250
Actual return	$ 2,300,000

12 months (11.5%)
US$ 20,000,000 investment
Loss from sale of 80 contracts $ 100,000
Net return on investment $ 2,200,000

Corresponding to an effective interest rate of 11.00% p.a.

Again we see that the return on the investment has effectively been fixed at the expected futures rate of 11% p.a. Again we know that this 100% locked-in return is obtained only because the actual return on the Treasury bills was fully correlated to the return of the corresponding futures contracts, based on the assumption that the date of delivery could be completely matched to our timing of the cash inflow. Therefore the best that can be said is:

> *Institutions can hedge against falling interest rates by **buying** interest futures contracts.*

When using a specific market like the one-year Treasury bill futures contracts, you should understand how the underlying cash market works in order to get a feel for the interest rate developments in this market. For instance, intimate knowledge about the Federal Reserve auctioning practice on the one-year Treasury bills becomes crucial. You might ask what impact will the auction timing (an auction every 28 days) have on interest rate movements, etc.? Hence understanding the related cash market is important in order to stay in touch with what you are trying to hedge and how the hedge itself functions in connection with that specific market.[1]

Hedging Investments in Long-Term Securities

Let's look at this strategy from the investor's point of view.

Example: In early January, $10,000,000 has been invested in fifteen-year 8% coupon U.S. Treasury bonds. At year end, in twelve months, the investor will either sell the securities or have to put the going market value of the securities on the balance sheet, thereby registering an equivalent loss or gain on the income statement for the year. The investor is worried that their initial expectation of an interest rate drop will not hold true so that the year-end discount values of the securities would incur a loss either because the translation values are low or because the actual sale took place at an unfavorable price.

In this case, the investor has to hedge against an increase in the interest rate level, and the rule of thumb says that this can be done by selling interest futures contracts. So if the investor sold 127 fifteen-year U.S. Treasury bond futures, corresponding to the nominal amount of the investment, it would represent a hedge. The securities were bought at a market rate of 11% p.a., corresponding to a discount purchase price of $78^{14}/_{32}$. The market expects the future Treasury bond rate to be $11\frac{1}{2}$%, that is, the corresponding U.S. Treasury bond futures contracts for December delivery are traded at a price around $75^{16}/_{32}$.

In December the Treasury bond rate turns out to be 12%. The investor therefore gains on the contracts sold at the futures price of $75^{16}/_{32}$ because the current price of the contract in December has dropped to $72^{24}/_{32}$.

Twelve-Month Investment in U.S. Treasury Bonds.[2]

Price of futures contract sold	$75^{16}/_{32}$
Cash Price of futures contract	$72^{24}/_{32}$
Price gain per contract sold	$2^{24}/_{32} = 2^{24}/_{32} / {}^{1}/_{32} = 88$ ticks
Profit per contract sold	$88 \times \$31.25 = \$2,750$
Actual return	$173,000
$10,000,000 investment in Treasury bonds	
(Nominal Value $12,700,000)	
Profit from sale of 127 contracts	= $349,250
Net return on investment	= $522,250

Corresponding to an effective return of 5.25% p.a.

If instead the interest rate had dropped to $10\frac{1}{2}$% in December, the investor would lose on the contracts sold at the futures price of $75^{16}/_{32}$ because the current price of the contract in that case would increase to $81^{17}/_{32}$.

Twelve-Months Investment in U.S. Treasury Bonds.[3]

Price of futures contract sold	$75^{16}/_{32}$
Cash Price of futures contract	$81^{17}/_{32}$
Price loss per contract sold	$6^1/_{32} = 6^1/_{32} / ^1/_{32} = 193$ ticks
Loss per contract sold	$193 \times \$31.25 = \$6.031.25$
Actual return	$1,262,660.00
\$10,000,000 investment in Treasury bonds	
(Nominal value \$12,700,000)	
Loss from sale of 127 contracts	= \$(765,968.75)
Net return on investment	= \$496,691.25

Corresponds to an effective return of 4.99% p.a.

The hedge is such that the income from the Treasury bond investment has been adapted to the market's expected future rate of 11.5%.

The reason for the unbalanced gain/loss position relates to the fact that the price change for a given change in the interest rate level is smaller at a higher interest rate level than it is at a lower interest rate level. In the preceding example, note:

- An increase in the interest rate level from 11% to 11.5% on a fourteenth-year 100 nominal security will cause a loss of 2.85 due to a drop in the market price from 79.05 to 76.20.

- Yet a fall in the interest rate from 11% to 10.5% will cause a capital gain of 3.02.

The return on the investment itself over the one-year period is a negligible 5% p.a., which might appear less than satisfactory. Compare this result to the same situation without a hedge, which would bring a return of only 1.75% had the interest rate increased to 12%. So in this context 5% looks reasonable.

The example also illustrates the common characteristic of a futures hedge, namely that it covers for the downside risk but at the same time excludes profit taking from a more favorable interest rate development. In the end whether or not the hedge should be pursued, given the economic outlook, must depend on how strongly the investor feels that the interest rate level will exceed the expected market rate of 11.5%.

Why not sell more contracts to improve the net return on the investment in an increasing interest rate environment? In Example 1, where the interest rate increases to 12% in December, the sale of 371 Treasury bond futures contracts, as opposed to the present sale of only 127 contracts, would have brought the investor a net return on the investment of 12% p.a. However, had the interest rate dropped to 10.5%, as in Example 2, then the investor would have lost $975,000. So if you buy contracts in excess of the nominal exposure of the long-term investment portfolio to be hedged, a gapping position is opened and a complete hedging position no longer pertains.

The situation could also be presented in a different interest rate environment.

Example: The futures market expects the Treasury bond rate to fall to 10.5% by December, that is, the futures contracts for December delivery are traded at $81^{17}/_{32}$. Yet the investor does not agree, thinking rather that a stable or perhaps a slightly increasing interest rate level is the more likely outcome over the next year. In this situation the investor could lock in the gain from the market expectations by selling 127 Treasury bond futures contracts at the future price of $81^{17}/_{32}$. Let us assume that the investor was right in that the Treasury bond rate in December turned out to be 11.5%, that is, it went through a half-percent increase instead of the expected half-percent reduction. The investor was able to lock in the future rate at 10.5%, despite the adverse rate development in the cash market.

Twelve-Month Investment in U.S. Treasury Bonds.

Price of futures contract sold	$81^{17}/_{32}$
Cash Price of futures contract	$75^{16}/_{32}$
Price gain per contract sold	$6^{1}/_{32} = 6^{1}/_{32} / ^{1}/_{32} = 193$ ticks
Profit per contract sold	$193 \times \$31.25 = \$6,031.25$
Actual return	$517,170.00
$10,000,000 investment in Treasury Bonds	
(Nominal value $12,700,000)	
Profit from sale of 127 contracts	= $765,968.75
Net return on investment	= $1,283,138.75

Corresponding to an effective return of 12.88% p.a.

The applicability of a financial futures hedge on a long-term securities portfolio, therefore, very much depends on the prevalent interest rate environment, which must be evaluated thoroughly before engaging in a futures position. Another possibility would be to perform a partial hedge to reflect management's uncertain outlook on the future interest rate development.

Example: The view is that there is a 50% chance that the interest rate level will increase by one percentage point and a 50% chance that the interest rate will drop by one percentage point. The investor could then hedge half the investment portfolio against the effect of an interest rate increase by selling only 63 Treasury bond futures contracts. In case the interest rate increases, the portfolio will be partially hedged. If the interest rate drops, the investor will incur a fair share of the upside capital gain associated with the increase in the market price of the securities portfolio.

Including a long-term instrument in a short-term investment portfolio, where the instruments are not to be held to maturity, obviously in itself represents an interest rate gapping situation. Here the investor tries to take advantage of an unexpected favorable movement in the interest rate level. In this situation, as we have seen, the financial futures can help reduce the loss if the interest moves against the initial outlook, or they can help lock in a gain if the market expectation is bullish.

Hedging New Issues of Long-Term Securities

In North America and overseas on the Eurocurrency markets, investment bankers have a long established procedure of underwriting new issues of long-term securities. At the closing date of the underwriting agreement the investment banker commits to forward a fixed amount of money in return for the securities to be sold in the securities market by the investment banker. Hence the banker carries the full risk of the securities not being sold in the market at the predetermined price.

The underwriter's problem is that the interest rate might increase to a level exceeding what was committed to the borrower at the closing of the underwriting agreement. The securities would then have to be sold in the market at a lower price and would thus bring the underwriter a loss because he already has committed to a future cash payout to the borrower. Usually this risk will be carried throughout a period of a few days to five or six weeks at the worst.

Let's apply the rule of thumb. The risk of increasing interest rates could be hedged through the sale of a suitable number of interest futures contracts.

Example: **In August the investment banker has committed an underwriting of US$ 20,000,000 in fifteen-year 8% coupon Eurobond issue at an interest rate of 10.75%. That is a committed discount price of 79.74.[4] The Treasury bond futures contract for delivery in September is trading at $79^{24}/32$, implying that the market expects the interest rate to stay put. The investment banker would like to lock in this interest rate and does so by selling 200 Treasury bond futures contracts for delivery in September at the going futures price of $79^{24}/32$.**

It turns out that in September, when the investment banker is ready to sell the Euro securities, the interest rate actually has increased to 11%—one quarter of a percent up from the August forecast. However, the Treasury bond futures contract, for the same reason, trades at a price around $78^{6}/32$, and the investment banker will make a profit from selling the Treasury bond contracts at the future price of $79^{24}/32$.

One-Month Underwriting Commitment[5]

Price of futures contract sold	$79^{24}/32$
Cash price of futures contract	$78^{6}/32$
Price gain per contract sold	$1^{18}/32 = {}^{18}/32 / {}^{1}/32 = 50$ ticks
Profit per contract sold	$50 \times \$31.25 = \$1,562.50$
Loss from Eurobond issue	$= \$307,562.71$
Profit from sale of 200 contracts	$= \$312,500.00$

As you can see, the profit from the sale of the Treasury bond futures contracts is approximately equivalent to the loss incurred from the Eurobond issue in our example and the interest rate gap has been effectively closed.

CROSS HEDGING

As implied by the previous examples, a hedge is performed by trading the number of futures contracts that match up to the face value of the financial obligation to be hedged.

Example: Ten three-month certificate of deposit contracts were sold to hedge a future three-month loan of US$ 10,000,000.

The general principle adhered to in this process is:

The change in the value of the futures contract should match the change in the interest income/expense of the cash instrument to be hedged.

A special problem occurs when the portfolio to be hedged differs in maturity from the maturity of the futures contract.

Example: A one-month dollar investment is hedged by buying three-month interest futures. The value of a one basis point change in the interest rate on a $1,000,000 one-month investment is $8.33, against the tick value of a three-month futures contract of $25.00. Therefore financial futures contracts should be bought to match one-third of the principal investment. Conversely, when three-month futures contracts are used to hedge a six-month investment, interest contracts should be bought to match twice the principal investment. The value of a one basis point change in the interest rate on a $1,000,000 six-month investment is $50, against the tick value of $25 on the three-month futures contract.

If there is a maturity mismatch between the futures contract and the cash instrument to be hedged, the number of futures contracts traded should be inversely related to the maturities of the cash instrument and the futures contract.

$$\text{Number of futures contracts traded} = \frac{N}{F} \cdot \frac{M_c}{M_f}$$

where:
N = Nominal value of the cash instrument.
F = Value of the futures contract.
M_c = Maturity of the cash instrument.
M_f = Maturity of the futures contract.

Example: To hedge a one-month dollar investment of $15,000,000 with three-month interest futures contracts, buy five contracts:

$$\frac{\$15,000,000}{\$\ 1,000,000} \times \frac{1}{3} = 5$$

In previous examples, one was always able to find a financial futures contract that completely matches the cash instrument to be hedged because they had the same denominations and maturities, and because the interest rates of the two financial instruments were always fully correlated. Obviously this is far from the case at all times. So a method is called for that can tell us, in case no corresponding futures contract exists, how many of the available futures contracts to trade in order to obtain a full hedge.

Example: An investor wants to hedge a portfolio of $20,000,000 Eurobonds with a 7% coupon rate and 20 years to maturity by applying the U.S. Treasury bond futures contract.

We may no longer assume that the interest rate movements of the two dollar-denominated securities are fully correlated. In fact, they *may* be correlated to some extent inasmuch as the two instruments often appeal to the same institutional investors' and the two securities are close substitutes. However, from the investor's point of view there is a major difference between the two—namely, the credit risk. For a domestic U.S. investor a credit to the U.S. Treasury must be considered virtually riskless, whereas a Eurobond represents a loan to an international corporate entity or a sovereign borrower and therefore represents a slightly higher credit risk. On top of this, changes in the regulatory environment in the U.S. and changes in monetary regulations will also cause a situation in which interest rates do not move in complete unison over time.

For the hedger, it is interesting to know how the two interest rates have developed historically, and to what extent the two time series represent a correlated pattern of movements. This can be investigated by calculating the *regression coefficient:* This is a single number that indicates how much a change in the interest rate of the one security has "induced" an interest rate change in the other security and vice versa.

For a given period, the daily interest rates of the Eurobond and the cheapest deliverable bond[6] under the U.S. Treasury bond futures contract is plotted. (See Figure 5-2.) In this diagram the development in the Eurobond interest rate is presented as a function of the development in the Treasury bond interest rate.

The regression analysis assumes that a linear relationship can be applied to describe the covariation of the two interest rates, and the regression coefficient is calculated by applying the standard formula:[7]

$$b = \frac{\text{sum } (E_i \times F_i)}{\text{sum } (F_i^2)}$$

where $i = 1, 2, \ldots n$ represent all observations plotted into the diagram.

Example: Assume that, in our analysis, for different reference periods, the regression coefficient was calculated to be 1.15. In that case, for a one basis point change in the Treasury bond rate, the historical interest rate pattern indicates that there will be a 1.15 basis point change in the Eurobond interest rate. A one basis point change in the yield corresponds to a $10,250 price change on the $20,000,000 Eurobond portfolio and a price change of $11,200 on the corresponding portfolio of notional Treasury bonds.[8] Say the cheapest deliverable bond under the Treasury bond futures contract turned out to be the 8% coupon rate bond with 20 years to maturity and that the conversion factor to apply to bring this bond into the standard contract is

0.9010. Then we can calculate the hedging ratio by using the following formula:[9]

$$\frac{\text{Hedging}}{\text{Ratio}} = \frac{\text{Regression}}{\text{Coefficient}} \times \frac{\text{Eurobond Price Change}}{\text{Treasury Bond Price Change}} \times \frac{\text{Conversion}}{\text{Factor}}$$

$$0.9483 = 1.15 \times \frac{10,250}{11,200} \times 0.9010$$

With a ratio of 1, we should buy 200 U.S. Treasury bond futures contracts in order to hedge the investment corresponding to the nominal value of $20,000,000 Eurobonds. Now apply the rule that the change in the value of the futures contracts should match the change in the value of the cash instruments to be hedged: The number of $100,000 Treasury futures contracts to sell is 190 ($20,000,000/$100,000 × .9483 = 189.66).

CURRENCY HEDGING

Transactions involving the exchange of currencies are usually the ones registered on the official balance of payments statistics. That is, they are payments for trade transactions involving delivery of goods and services across national borders or capital transactions involving the extension of cross-border credits and debt service payments on the outstanding foreign loans. Within these wide categories of foreign exchange transactions, one could think of a myriad of examples where different institutions would be interested in locking in the future foreign exchange rate. Here we will focus only on a few trade transactions in order to show how to hedge by using financial futures contracts. The same hedging principles, however, apply to any situation involving the exchange of foreign currencies.

Example: In April an American company has shipped goods for delivery to a corporation in Switzerland, and the price has been settled in Swiss francs. The payment of Swiss francs 10,000,000 is expected in mid-June. The present spot exchange rate is quoted at 2.8852 Sw. frc./US$ (.3466 US$/Sw. frc.). Given the past U.S. dollar exchange rate development, the American exporter is worried that he will see a weakened Swiss franc in

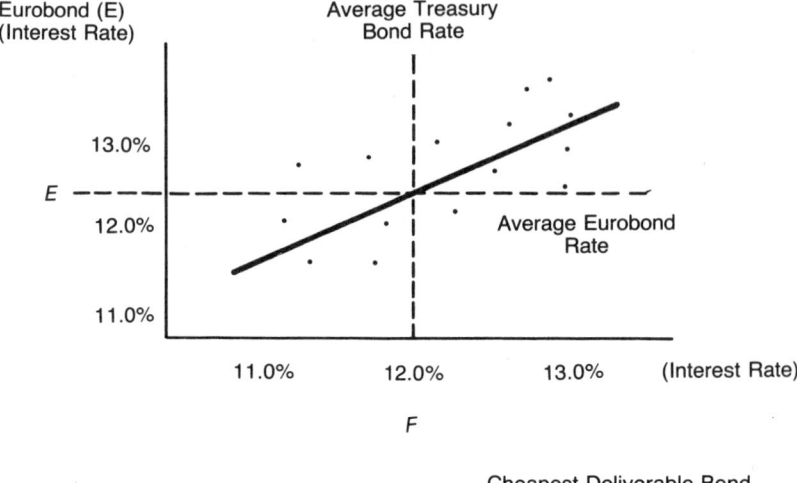

Eurobond (E)
(Interest Rate)

Average Treasury
Bond Rate

13.0%

E

12.0%

Average Eurobond
Rate

11.0%

11.0%   12.0%   13.0%   (Interest Rate)

F

Cheapest Deliverable Bond
under the Treasury Bond
Futures Contract (*F*).

Figure 5-2. *Eurobond and U.S. Treasury Bond Interest Rates.*

two months, meaning that he will receive at that time fewer dollars for the incoming number of Swiss francs.

The Swiss franc futures contract with delivery in June is quoted on the futures exchange at .3400. The American exporter finds this rate attractive because it is higher than his own two-month forecast for the exchange rate. To lock in this foreign exchange rate, he sells 80 Swiss franc futures contracts for delivery in June. In June it turns out that the exporter's worst guesses were correct, the spot exchange rate has increased to 2.9851 Sw. frc./US\$ (.3350 US\$/Sw. frc.). Yet the loss made in the cash exchange market is compensated for by the profit gained on the sale of the futures contracts.

Price of futures contract sold	.3400
Cash price of futures contract	.3350
Price gain per contract sold	.0050 = .0050/.0001 = 50 ticks
Profit per contract sold	50 × \$12.50 = \$625
Loss on spot sale of Swiss Franc	\$ (50,000)
10,000,000 (.3350 − .3400)	
Profit from sale of 80 futures contracts	\$ 50,000

Now assume, on the other hand, that the not unlikely event that the exporter's two-month foreign exchange forecast was off the mark as the June spot rate hit 2.8571 Sw. frc./US$ (.3500 US$/Sw. frc.). Then the exporter would gain on the spot exchange of the Swiss Francs but would correspondingly lose on the sale of the financial futures contracts.

Price of futures contract sold	.3400
Cash price of futures contract	.3500
Price loss per contract sold	.0100 = .0100/.0001 = 100 ticks
Loss per contract sold	100 × $12.50 = $(1,250)
Gain on spot sale of Swiss franc	$100,000
10,000,000 (.3500 − .3400)	
Loss from sale of 80 futures contracts	$(100,000)

In other words, the future exchange rate has been effectively locked in at the futures market's expected future exchange rate of .3400 US$/Sw. Frc.

By going through a similar example with the applicable calculations, one can be convinced that an American importer who pays for the import in the exporter's currency can lock in the future exchange rate by buying futures contracts.

Example: An American importer must make a payment of 10,000,000 Swiss francs by mid-June. He would hedge this by buying 80 Swiss franc contracts at the market price of .3400. In June the Swiss franc spot rate was .3500; so he will have to pay more dollars for the francs on the spot market but will gain from the purchase of the futures contracts.

Price of futures contract	.3500
Price of futures contract bought	.3400
Price per contract bought	.0100 = .0100/.0001 = 100 ticks
Profit per contract bought	100 × $12.50 = $1,250
Loss on spot purchase of Swiss franc	$(100,000)
10,000,000 (.3400 − .3500)	
Profit from purchase of 80 futures contracts	$ 100,000

The previous examples and calculation exercises lead then to the following rule, which holds true in general:

*A U.S. resident who receives payments in a foreign currency hedge by **selling** futures contracts of that currency.*

and

*A U.S. resident who makes payments in a foreign currency hedge by **buying** futures contracts of that currency.*

How does such a hedge work in the case of a non-U.S. resident?

Example: A German exporter who is exporting to the U.S.A. and receives payment in U.S. dollars. In October the exchange rate was quoted at 3.4305 DM/US$ (0.2915 US$/DM). Yet the German exporter is afraid from past experience that this rate might decrease, that is, the DM might strengthen. So he will get less DM in December when his receivable of US$ 5,000,000 comes due. Since the DM futures contract for December delivery is trading at 0.2910, he is willing to lock in this rate by buying 40 Deutsche mark contracts for December delivery. In December the exchange rate turned out to be 3.1746 DM/US$ (.3150 US$/DM), so the German exporter got less DMs for the dollar receivables but instead made an equivalent gain from the purchase of the futures contracts.

Cash Price of futures contracts sold	.3150
Cash Price of futures contracts bought	.2910
Price gain per contract sold	.0240 = .0240/.0001 = 240 ticks
Profit per contract bought	240 × $12.50 = $3,000
Loss on spot purchase of DM 5,000,000 (.2910 − .3150)	$(120,000)
Profit from 40 contracts bought	$120,000

Had the German resident instead been importing goods from the U.S.A. to be paid in U.S. dollars, the dollars payable could be hedged by selling the Deutsche mark contracts.

Example: Using the same data as in the previous example, we can perform the following calculation:

Price of futures contracts sold	.2910
Cash price of futures contracts	.3150
Price loss per contract sold	.0240 = .0240/.0001 240 ticks
Profit per contract sold	240 × $12.50 = $3,000
Gain on spot sale of Swiss franc 5,000,000 (.3150 − .2910)	$120,000
Loss from sale of 40 Deutsche Mark futures contracts	$(120,000)

This reasoning enables us to formulate the following rules of thumb:

*A non-U.S resident receiving payments in U.S. dollars can hedge by **buying** futures contracts of the home currency.*

and

*A non-U.S. resident making payments in U.S. dollars can hedge by **selling** futures contracts of the home currency.*

CROSS CURRENCY HEDGING

In a situation in which U.S. dollars are not directly involved, hedging becomes slightly more complicated when using the traditional currency futures contracts.

Example: A French producer is exporting to an English importer. In mid-August the producer has shipped the goods and is expecting pound sterling payments of 5,000,000 when the goods have safely arrived in the U.K. in mid-September. In mid-August the pound sterling exchange rate is 1.0668 US$/£ Stg., and the French franc exchange rate is 10.4810 Fr. Frc./US$ (.0954 US$/Fr. frc.), thus implying a cross rate of 11.1811 Fr. Frc./£ Stg. The present market expects the pound to strengthen slightly against the dollar because of an improvement in the international spot price on crude oil. The franc is expected to drop slightly in value against the U.S. dollar, as indicated by the values of the September futures contracts for pounds and French francs of 1.0750 and 0.0952, respectively, implying a cross rate of 11.2920 Fr. Frc./£ Stg.[10]

Now, the French importer has experienced the volatile foreign exchange markets of the recent past and is worried that the favorable exchange rate development might reverse before receipt of the payments in pounds. However, by selling 200 £ Stg. contracts and buying 225 French franc contracts, he can hedge the value of his foreign currency receivables. If the exporter's worries were justified—that is, if the spot exchange cross rate in mid-September turned out to be, for example, 11.1996 Fr. Frc./£ Stg.—he would receive fewer French francs in the cash spot exchange of the pounds sterling receivables. However, the gains from trading the franc and pound futures contracts will make up for this loss.

Price of £ Stg. contract sold	1.0750
Cash price of £ Stg. contract	1.0718
Price gain per contract sold	0.0032 = 0.0032/0.0005 = 6 ticks
Profit per £ Stg. contract sold	6 × $12.50 = $7,500
Cash price of Fr. Frc. contract	0.0957
Price of Fr. Frc. contract bought	0.0952
Price gain per Fr. Frc. contract bought	0.0005 = 0.0005/0.00005 = 10 ticks
Profit per Fr. Frc. contract bought	10 × $12.50 = $125.00
Loss on spot sale of £ Stg. against Fr. Frc.	$(44,213.40)
(11.2920 – 11.1996) 5,000,000 × 0.0957	
Profit from sale of 200 £ Stg. contracts	$15,000.00
Profit from purchase of 225 Fr. Frc. contracts	$28,125.00
Total profit from futures contracts	$43,125.00

In this example, the hedge was very close to being complete but was, however, slightly less advantageous than the straightforward rates indicated. Due to the standard size of the futures contracts, rarely is a 100 percent hedge possible. In the preceding example 200 £ Stg. contracts were sold, perfectly hedging the £ Stg. 5,000,000 conversion into U.S. dollars. However, the purchase of 225 Fr. Frc. contracts lock in the dollar conversion of Fr. Frc. 56,250,000, thus leaving Fr. Frc. 210,000 unhedged (5,000,000 × 11.2920 − 56,250,000).

Cross currency hedging can be formalized in the following rules of thumb:

*A non-U.S. resident receiving payments in a foreign currency can hedge by **selling** futures contracts of the foreign currency against dollars and **buying** futures contracts of the domestic currency against dollars.*

*A non-U.S. resident making payments in a foreign currency hedge by **buying** futures contracts of the foreign currency against dollars and **selling** futures contracts of the domestic currency against dollars.*

INTEREST RATE HEDGING IN OTHER CURRENCIES

Example: A German institution, in the end of February, is running a short interest rate gap: It has on its books a six-month fixed yield Deutsche mark asset of DM 10,000,000, which is funded by a three-month fixed rate Deutsche mark liability at 6.4% p.a. On the present day, no future contract on Deutsche mark financial instruments is available on a futures exchange. However, one is able to create a Deutsche mark interest rate hedge by employing a swap transaction and access the futures market by trading a suitable number of say, three-month Eurodollar deposit contracts and the Deutsche marks futures contracts.

The three-month Eurodollar deposit contract for March delivery is trading at 90.70, implying a three-month Eurodollar offer rate of 9.3% p.a. The June contract is trading at 90.00, that is, the market expects the three-month Eurodollar rate to be 10% p.a. three months from now.

The Deutsche mark contract for March delivery is trading at 0.3070, thus implying a spot DM exchange rate of 3.2573 DM/US$. Since the DM contract for delivery in June is trading at .3093, the futures market expects the DM exchange rate to be around 3.2331 DM/US$ by June. By putting the Eurodollar offer rate of 9.3% p.a. into the interest rate parity formula we see that the corresponding three-month DM bid rate must be around 6⅜% p.a.

$$i_{f,t} = F/S \, (1 + i_{\$,t}) - 1$$

$$= 3.2331 \, / \, 3.2573 \, (1 + \frac{0.093}{4}) - 1$$

$$= 0.0159 \quad (= 6.36\% \text{ p.a.})$$

The DM futures contract for September delivery is trading at 0.3118, implying a future spot exchange rate of 3.2072 DM/$. In other words, the market continues to believe in a strengthening of the mark against the U.S. dollar.

So what we want to accomplish is to:

- Borrow the funds in U.S. dollars at 10% p.a. for three months from June to September.
- Convert the amount into Deutsche marks in June at the future rate of 3.2331 DM/US$.
- Convert it back into dollars in September at the future exchange rate of 3.2074 DM/US$.

The expected strengthening of the DM exchange rate from June to September reflects an interest rate differential in favor of the Deutsche mark, whose interest rate can be found by applying the interest rate parity theory.

$$i_{f,t} = 3.2072 \, / \, 3.2331 \, (1 + \frac{0.10}{4}) - 1$$

$$= 0.01679 \, (= 6.7\% \text{ p.a.})$$

So, by adhering to this strategy and given that the future dollar interest rate and the Deutsche mark exchange rate can be completely locked in, we have created a future three-month DM loan at a rate of 6.7% p.a.

We also want to hedge against (1) an increase in the Eurodollar interest rate and (2) a decrease in the Deutsche mark exchange rate in June and an increase of it by September.

Example: We accomplish the first hedge by selling three three-month Eurodollar deposit contracts (10,000,000 × .3070/1,000,000 = 3.07). For the second, we buy 80 Deutsche mark futures contracts for June delivery and sell another 80 for September delivery (10,000,000/125,000 = 80). Now in the cash market the three-month Eurodollar rate went up to 10⅛% p.a. by June. The Deutsche mark exchange rate fell to 3.2279 by June and increased to 3.2410 DM/US$ by September. The whole scenario is laid out in the following table:

	March Actual	Financial Futures (June)	June Actual	Financial Futures (Sept.)	September Actual
Foreign Exchange Rate (DM/US$)	3.2573	3.2331	3.2279	3.2072	3.2410
DM financial futures price (US$/DM)	0.3070	0.3093	0.3098	0.3118	0.3085
Three-Month Eurodollar financial futures price	90.70	90.00	89.87	—	—
US$ interest rate (p.a.)	9.30%	10.00%	10⅛%	—	—

We will pay more for the three-month U.S. dollar loan, get less DM at the June conversion, and have to pay more DM at the September conversion in the cash markets. However, what is lost on the transactions in the cash market is offset by the profit made on the financial futures trading.

Price of three-month Eurocurrency futures contract sold	$90.00
Cash price of three-month Eurocurrency futures contract	$89.87
Price gain per contract sold	$ 0.13 = 0.13/0.01 = 13 ticks
Profit per contract sold	13 × $25 = $325

Cash price of DM futures contract in June 0.3098
Price of DM June futures contract bought   0.3093
Price gain per DM contract bought   0.0005 = 0.00005/0.0001 = 5 ticks
Profit per DM contract sold   5 × $12.50 = $62.50

Price of September DM futures contract sold   0.3118
Cash price of DM futures contract in September 0.3085
Price gain per DM contract sold   0.0033 = 0.0033/0.0001 = 33 ticks
Profit per DM contract sold   33 × $12.50 = $412.50
Loss on increased funding cost
(10,000,000/3.2279 × (0.00125/4) = $ 968.12
Loss on $-DM conversion in June
(3,097,990 × (3.2331 – 3.2279)/3.2279) = $ 4,990.72
Loss on DM-$ conversion in September
(3,176,407.87 × (3.2410 – 3.2072)/3.2410) = $33,126.38
Total loss from cash market transaction $39,085.22
Profit from sale of three Eurocurrency contracts $ 975.00
Profit from purchase of 80 June DM contracts $ 5,000.00
Profit from sale of 80 September DM contracts $33,000.00
Total profit from financial futures transactions $38,975.00

Like the cross currency hedge, this hedge is not 100% because the standard size of the financial futures contracts will not allow such a perfect matching of the exposed amounts. Yet the hedge in this case is very close to being complete.

HEDGING A STOCK PORTFOLIO

For a portfolio manager the risk attached to holding stocks is primarily linked to stock price fluctuations as the return on a stock is made up by dividend payments and capital gains and losses.

The price fluctuation of a stock is impacted by two distinct risk factors. The *systematic risk* is linked to changes in the interest rate level of the economy as a whole. The other risk factor, often termed the *unsystematic risk,* is stock-specific and relates to the circumstances of the business sector and the specific corporation's financial performance.

The *price variance* of a given stock portfolio is the weighted sum of the covariances among all the individual categories of stocks. As the number of individual categories of stocks increases, the weight attached to each covariance is vastly reduced thus reducing the overall price variance of the stock portfolio. In other words, by increasing the number of stocks added to the stock portfolio, the unsystematic risk can be reduced.[11] This phenomenon is usually termed *risk diversification.*

The systematic risk of a stock portfolio, however, is not reduced through diversification, and traditional portfolio theory gives no answer as how to hedge against this risk factor. Stock index futures are one response to this exposure.

The unsystematic risk factor is often quantified in an expression termed the *beta coefficient,* which provides a standardized measurement of how a specific category of stock fluctuates with the general price movement of the whole stock market. The beta coefficient is found by calculating the price covariance between the category of stock in question and the general stock market. The expression is standardized by dividing by the price variance of the general stock market:

$$\text{Beta}_i = \frac{\text{cov}\ (P_i,\ P_m)}{\text{var}\ (P_m)}$$

where:

P = Stock price.

i = A specific category of stock.

m = The total stock market.

Hence a low-risk stock has a beta coefficient close to zero because the covariance with the market is small, and a more risky stock has a coefficient higher than one, showing that it fluctuates with the market but in a more volatile manner. The incorporation of the beta coefficient as a risk measure explaining the average return on a stock is contained in the well known *capital asset pricing model* (*CAPM*). The higher the beta coefficient (risk), the higher is the average return of the stock.

Example: A portfolio manager holds a sample of industrial stock in the investment portfolio with a total market value of US$

10,000,000. Now, the fear is that the interest rate level in general will increase over the next three-month period. Yet it is found more opportune to hold the stock investment over the next three months as opposed to liquidating the position up front, provided a proper hedge against a price decrease can be established. Hence the portfolio manager approaches the Chicago Mercantile Exchange to trade in the S&P 500 stock index futures contract.

The three-month S&P 500 futures index is quoted at 180.95, that is, the value of the futures contract amounts to $90.475 ($500 × 180.95). The beta coefficient of the stock portfolio has been calculated over the past six months to be 1.45, that is, the stock portfolio is more volatile than the general market represented by the Standard & Poors 500 index. To compensate for this excess price volatility, additional index futures contracts should be sold in a ratio of 1.45:1.00. Hence the total number of contracts sold is equal to 160 (1.45 × $10,000,000/$90,475).

If the prices on the stock market decrease, the financial futures sold have been locked in at a higher price. So the loss incurred on the stock portfolio is offset by a capital gain on the index futures position. An element of uncertainty in this type of hedge is that the coefficient calculated for the previous six-month period will not necessarily correspond to the beta coefficient during the three-month period being hedged. However, despite this obstacle, an index futures position will provide the portfolio manager with a reasonable hedge against stock price fluctuations.

BASIS RISKS

As discussed, a precondition for obtaining a full hedge using financial futures contracts is that the financial futures price converts to the cash market price before the delivery date of the futures contract. To discuss this requirement further, we define the *basis* to be the numerical value of the difference between the cash market price and the price of the corresponding financial futures contract:

Basis = | Financial futures price − Cash market price |

As has become apparent in the previous examples, the basis is not always zero and so, to the extent that this is *not* the case, the hedge will be less than perfect. Consequently the outright risk of the position we want to hedge has been converted into a *basis risk* (namely, the risk that the financial futures price will not convert to the cash market price before the delivery date of the financial futures contract) and thus corresponds to the risk of *not* obtaining a full hedge.

To obtain a measure of the size of the basis risk, compare the development of the cash market price and the price of the financial futures contract on the last trading day before delivery of the contract, which is the last price available for closing in the futures position without taking delivery. In general the more closely the two move together over time, the smaller the basis risk is. The correlation of the two time series can be quantified statistically by calculating the correlation coefficient as defined in the following standard formula:[8]

$$r = \frac{1}{n-1} \, \text{sum} \, \frac{X_i - \overline{X}}{S_x} \cdot \frac{Y_i - \overline{Y}}{S_y} = \frac{\text{sum} \, (X_i - \overline{X}) \, (Y_i - \overline{Y})}{\sqrt{\text{sum} \, (X_i - \overline{X})^2 \, \text{sum} \, (Y_i - \overline{Y})^2}}$$

where $i = 1, 2, \ldots n$ corresponds to each set of observations.

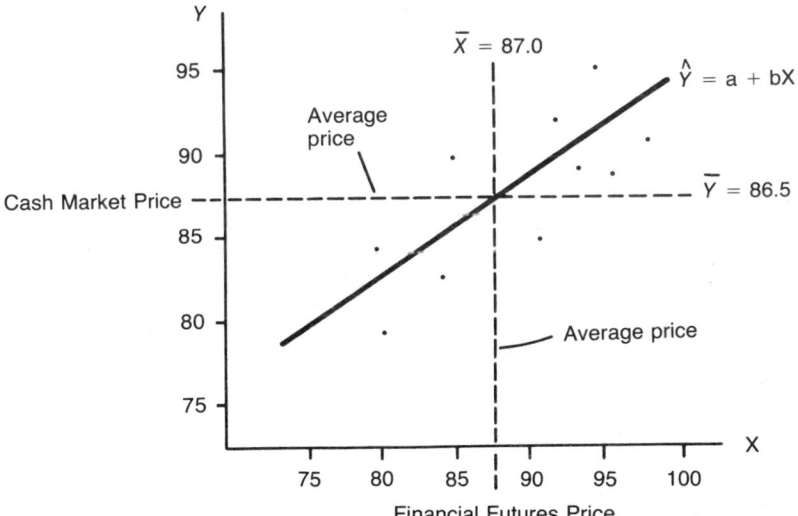

Figure 5-3. *Illustration of the Correlation Coefficient and Regression Equation.*

The correlation coefficient measures the average covariation of the two variables X and Y, and the coefficient is put on a standard comparable basis by dividing by the standard deviation of the two variables. Hence the correlation coefficient will always vary between minus one and plus one. If the numerical value is one, there is full correlation between the two variables. As the numerical value moves toward zero, the less significant is the correlation between the two variables. The correlation coefficient is a measure of the *linear* relationship between the two variables being investigated and thus corresponds closely to the linear regression coefficient (b) discussed earlier in the example of cross hedging. This relationship is expressed in the following standard equation:

$$r = b\frac{S_x}{S_y} = b\sqrt{\frac{\text{sum } (X_i - \overline{X})}{\text{sum } (Y_i - \overline{Y})^2}}$$

When we want to do cross hedging, we can find out what the potential effectiveness of the hedge is by squaring the correlation coefficient to get the coefficient of determination *(R)*.

$$R = r^2 = \frac{\text{sum } (\hat{Y}_i - \overline{Y})^2}{\text{sum } (Y_i - \overline{Y})^2} \qquad \text{where } \hat{Y}_i = a + bX_i$$

As implied by the formula the coefficient of determination tells us to what extent the regression analysis explains the variation of the two variables, in that the variation explained by the regression equation is put in relation to the total variation of the variable. Similarly will the coefficient of determination, calculated on the financial futures price on the last trading day, and the corresponding cash market price tell us how potentially effective the financial futures hedge is going to be.

Example: The regression coefficient has been calculated to 0.91. The coefficient of determination is 0.83 (0.91^2). That is, by using the financial futures contract there is a potential that 83% of the outright risk will be hedged.

It is only "potential" because all statistical analysis of this nature is based on historical data. In this analysis we assume that the financial markets in the future will continue to perform as they have in the past, but we have no guarantee that this will be the case. Therefore if one expects market performance to change in the future, that outlook should be incorporated into the evaluation of the statistical coefficients calculated.

The farther away we are from the last trading day of the financial futures contract, the more unpredictable and volatile will be the basis. This is because the financial futures price, by its very nature, is influenced by future expectations on price movements. The interest rate expectation of the market is reflected in the term structure of interest rates in the cash market.

The *term structure* of interest rates in the cash market is derived by plotting the effective yield of different investment alternatives of similar risk at different maturities.

In a *normal market*, the yield curve has a positive slope. Liquidity can be acquired short term at a cheaper rate and can be invested longer term at a higher rate, thus earning a positive spread for the mitigater. This is often termed a *positive carry market*. We know that for a given security the capital gain or loss from a change in the interest rate level will be relatively higher for the longer maturity asset. Hence in the neutral situation, when interest rate movements follow a random walk, risk-averse investors would prefer shorter-maturity securities in their portfolios. This would lower the interest rates of shorter-term securities against the longer-term securities and the yield curve would be upward sloping.

When the market expects future interest rates to be higher, the risk-averse investors would be even more inclined to invest

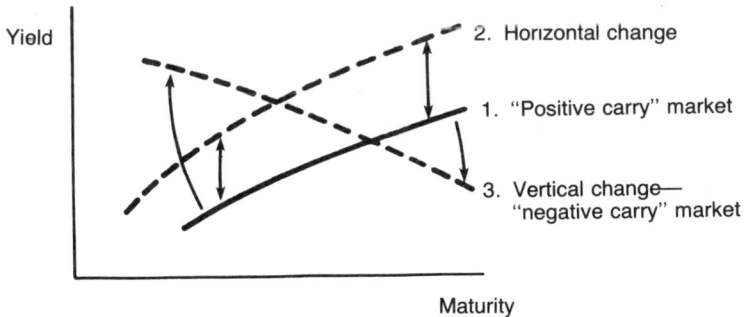

Figure 5-4. Yield Curves.

short-term and the yield curve would show a steeper positive slope.

When the market expects future interest rates to decline, the capital gain on longer-term securities will be bigger than that of the shorter-term securities. Hence investors are more inclined to invest in longer-term securities which will reduce the interest rate on the longer maturity securities. Hence we will witness a downward sloping yield curve, often termed a *negative carry market.*

We can define two types of changes in the yield curve. One, termed a *horizontal change*, corresponds to a change in the general interest rate level (the change from 1 to 2 in Figure 5-4). This could be caused by a temporary change in liquidity which, through substitution effects, will impose an effect on financial assets of all maturities. The other, called a *vertical change*, relates to a change in the slope of the yield curve (the change from 1 to 3 in the graph). As already discussed, this will be affected by changes in market expectations.

A yield curve can also be construed on the financial futures market by plotting the contract prices of financial future contracts on securities of different maturities. The futures yield curve will reflect the market's expectation of the future shape of the cash market term structure of interest rates. As in the cash market, the futures yield curve changes its shape as market conditions and future expectations change.

Once we have taken a position on the futures market we are locked in to the future price of that contract. Until the contract matures the underlying cash market and the financial futures market might go through sharp changes due to changes in market conditions and market expectations. (See Figure 5-1.) Under these circumstances, you might take the view that it pays off to close in the futures position before the last trading day of the futures contract. However, if you decide to do so, do not forget that the hedge is eliminated for the period remaining until the maturity of the contract and that the cash market might still move against you.

In general we see that a change in the basis of interest rate futures contracts is determined by changes in the yield curve on the cash market and by changes in the term structure of

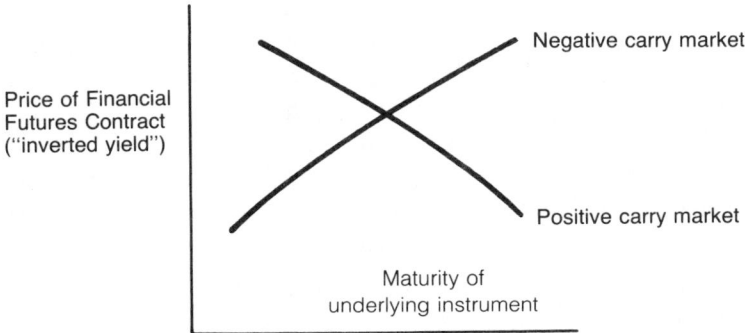

Figure 5-5. *Term Structure of Interest Rates.*

interest rates in the financial futures market. The farther we are away from the last trading day of the financial futures contract, the higher the volatility of the basis. Conversely the closer we get to the maturity date of the financial futures contract, the more the futures market will convert toward the cash market and the less will be the impact of market expectations.

CONCLUSION

The application of financial futures contracts for hedging purposes requires substantial planning. Initially the open position to hedge must be properly identified and an appropriate hedging program established in accordance with the management board's view on the size of the exposure risk that is acceptable to the institution. Once the hedging program is implemented it is essential that a central function in the financial controls department monitors the development of the hedge and ties it into the planning strategy of future hedging programs to be implemented.

When planning a hedging program, pay attention to the timing of the cash flows on the settlement account at the futures exchange clearing house and the underlying income steam to be hedged. The potential cash implication appearing from the principle of the daily mark to market should be investigated in the planning phase of the hedging program. An intimate knowledge of the mechanics of the financial futures market entered into will always put the hedger in a stronger position, and an understanding of the underlying market forces in the financial futures markets will enable the hedger to take advantage of favorable market conditions that might develop.

An essential precondition for successful hedging through the financial futures markets is that the income or loss incurred from the futures contract position by the tax authorities is treated in the same way as is the income flows it is hedging. Consequently it is very important to investigate the current tax treatment of income and losses emanating from financial futures trading. For the management board and for financial analysts in general another interesting and important area of concern is the accounting treatment of financial futures contracts.

Usually financial futures contracts are not recorded on the balance sheet before actual delivery of contracts, and unrealized gains and losses are not registered on the profit and loss account. However, it has been suggested that open financial futures positions be valued at the difference between the entered contract price and the current price of closing out at the date the accounts are settled. Hence the realized profit or loss would be registered on the profit and loss account. If the correlation between the hedged asset or liability and the financial futures contract is very high, the conditions for a perfect hedge are present. In this case it appears reasonable that the unrealized gains and losses also be recorded on the profit and loss account. However, there are no uniform rules regarding the accounting treatment of financial futures contracts in different countries and consultation with local auditors is strongly recommended before engaging in financial futures trading.

When using financial futures contracts for hedging purposes, realize that it does *not* guarantee a full hedge. Also the financial futures market provides the hedger with a limited time horizon. Financial futures contracts can usually be traded for delivery only up to twelve months ahead. This obviously limits the time horizon of a financial futures hedge. If the open position to hedge has a maturity exceeding the twelve-month period, the whole period of the gap cannot be closed through this type of hedging technique. However, accessing the financial futures markets usually enables the institution to hedge within the coming accounting year, which to many institutions is suffi-cient.

The financial futures markets, as witnessed in this chapter's examples, offer many hedging applications. The financial fu-tures exchanges are efficient markets that can be accessed by making only a minimal initial payment, and that can provide institutions with a variety of off-balance-sheet hedging oppor-tunities.

PART **III**
OPTIONS

The Option Contract

Options were first introduced on the international stock exchanges, and stock options have been quoted on these exchanges for many years. On the other hand, the currency and interest rate options are relatively new inventions introduced by the futures and options exchanges in the early 1980s. For this reason the original theory on options was developed against a background of stock options. This theory has since been adapted to the analysis of currency and interest rate options. To get a feel for the chronological development of the options markets and the initial theory on options, this chapter will take a discussion of the market for stock options as its starting point.

Today, options are actively bought and sold on a number of United States exchanges and in the over-the-counter market. In addition to stock options, there are options on indexes, debt instruments, and foreign currencies. To get an idea of the scope of options trading, buy a copy of the *Wall Street Journal* or the *New York Times* and turn to the section containing options quotations. Notice how many different individual options series, with different expiration months and exercise prices, can be connected on one underlying security.

STOCK (EQUITY) OPTIONS

The *stock option* has been a common feature of the major stock exchanges in North America and Europe for several decades. However, an organized trading floor for standardized stock options was first introduced in the United States in April 1973 through the creation of the Chicago Board of Options Exchange (CBOE). Several other markets have since then developed on the major stock exchanges in North America and Europe.

An *option* is the right, but not the obligation, to purchase or sell a stated number of shares at a specified price (the *exercise price*) within a predetermined period. The option to purchase stock is known as a *call option* in that it gives the holder the right to *buy* the underlying security. A *put option* entails the right to sell the security. Either type of option can be traded in the market or exercised by the holder.

Let us begin by defining the basic components of an options contract (see Table 6-1):

1. The *underlying security* is the stock that the option holder is entitled to buy or sell.
2. The *expiration date* is the date after which the contract is worthless.
3. The *strike (or exercise) price* is the specified price at which an option contract may be exercised.

Options are usually exercisable into 100 shares of their underlying related stock, the normal round lot unit of trading.

An "MP Feb 40 call" is a call option that gives the owner:

1. The right to *buy* (it's a call).
2. One hundred shares of MetPath Lines (MP) stock (the underlying and, in this case, fictitious stock).
3. At $40 per share (40, the strike price).
4. By the third Friday in February (Feb., the expiration date).

Table 6-1. *Basic Components of a Stock Option Contract.*

Component	Example
Underlying stock	100 shares (to be adjusted as necessary for stock dividends or splits)
Expiration month	Three fixed cycles: 1. January/April/July/October 2. February/May/August/November 3. March/June/September/December For example, in January options may be written for expiration only in April, July, or October. In May, they may be written only for August, November, and February. For certain very active stocks, three nearly monthly expiration dates are permitted. For example, in March, options may be written for April and May, as well as for March itself.
Expiration day	The option must be exercised by 5:30 P.M. New York time, on the Friday before the third Saturday of the expiration month. If not offset or exercised by this time, it expires worthless.
Strike price	• 2½ points up to $25 per share. • 5-point intervals above $25, such as 35-40-45. • 10-point intervals above $200.

An "MP Feb 40 put" is a put option that entitles the owner to *sell* 100 shares of MetPath stock at $40 per share by the third Friday in February.

If either the put or the call is not *exercised* (that is, bought or sold) by the expiration date, then it expires worthless.

OPTIONS CLEARING HOUSE

Perhaps as great an innovation as the standardized contract is the Options Clearing house. The Options Clearing house has the following three primary functions:

1. After payment of the cost of the option to the original seller, the Options Clearing house assumes the opposite side of each options transaction—that is, the Clearing House issues and guarantees each options contract. The cost of an option is referred to as the *premium*.

2. The Options Clearing house clears all trades in listed options.

3. The Options Clearing house assigns exercise notices.

By acting as the issuer of each options contract, the Clearing House ultimately steps between the original buyer and seller. Once the order is executed, the Option Clearing house *clears* it. At that point, the original buyer and seller have no further responsibility to each other. Their relationships are now with the Option Clearing house: If buyers choose to exercise; they rely on the clearing organization, not on the sellers, for performance. Thus, the Option Clearing house guarantees performance to all participants.

The Option Clearing house also handles the assignment of options exercise notices submitted by buyers. Although most writers and holders close their positions with offsetting purchases or sales by selling or covering their options, a writer should not be surprised to be notified that some holder has exercised his or her option and that the writer has been assigned the obligation of delivering stock (which is known as being a *call writer*) or purchasing it (being a *put writer*). Holders of calls may elect to *buy* the stock at the strike price, and put holders may choose to *sell* it at the strike price. In either case, option holders simply notify their brokerage firm. The firm notifies the Option Clearing house, which then assigns an exercise notice to an Option Clearing house member brokerage firm that has options writers identical to the one exercised. The assignment obligation is then assigned to one of those option writers, almost always to the oldest options first (FIFO—first in, first out).

The Options Clearing house takes it from there. For every buyer of a given option, there must be a writer on its books. The Option Clearing house finds a member firm in its records that has written an MP Mar 40 call and assigns it as the firm against which the option is to be exercised. The selection is usually made at random. Upon receipt of the exercise notice, the firm must assign the exercise notice to one of its customers who has written such a call. That customer then has to honor the exercise notice and deliver the stock: 100 shares at $40.

TRADING OPTIONS

Short and Long

Option investors are said to "open" or "close" their positions. Buying an option is an *opening* (or *initial*) *transaction* by which the holder takes a *long* open position. Writing an option is also an opening transaction in which the seller is considered to create an open *short* option position. A *closing transaction* reduces (or closes) an open options position. A closing purchaser reduces (or closes) a prior opening sale, and a closing sale closes a previous opening purchase.

Going long or short is an indicator of investors' expectations. Those who buy calls (long) or sell puts (short) are generally regarded as bullish. They will profit if the underlying stock's price rises. By writing calls or buying puts, investors present themselves as bearish. They expect the stock's value to decline and will profit if it does so.

Writers

Option writers have one basic aim: to earn income. A writer may be classified as "covered" or "uncovered" (naked). To illustrate this point, let's examine the following:

1. Covered call writing.
2. Naked call writing.
3. Put writing.

Covered Call Writing. An option is *covered* when the writer owns enough of the underlying stock to meet the requirements of the contract if it is exercised. In such a case, a covered call writer is not required to pay any initial margin costs. A writer is also covered by owning another call of the same class that has a lower strike price.

Example: Investor Smith writes an MP May 35 call, which represents 100 shares of MetPath. Because Smith owns 100 shares of MP, the call is covered.

The covered call writer, by pocketing the premium, gives up the right to any increase in the value of the stock beyond the strike price. (Call writers are usually neutral to bearish on the stock). At the same time, they retain the risk that their stock might decline in price.

Example: If MetPath is trading at $30 a share when Smith writes his Mar 30 call as a covered writer, the contract is at parity.

If MetPath stock declines to a price below $30, the option holder will not exercise. The premium income Smith received for selling the call will offset, or cushion, Smith's stock portfolio loss up to the amount received.

If MetPath increases in value to $35 per share before expiration, then Smith (assuming the probability of his being exercised against) has limited his share of this increase to the premium.

Naked Call Writing. When the option writer does not own shares of the underlying stock to meet the requirements of an exercise notice, the contract is said to be *uncovered,* or *naked.*

Example: Smith writes an MP 30 call, but he does not own 100 shares of MetPath. The call is naked, or uncovered. Because it is the equivalent of a short sale, Smith must pay initial margin as collateral.

Writers of naked calls face the possibility of a theoretically unlimited loss. As the market price of the underlying stock increases beyond the options strike price, the writer's loss grows.

Example: MetPath's stock increases to a price above $30 (to $34 per share, for example) just before expiration, and Smith receives an exercise notice from his broker. He is forced to buy 100 shares of MetPath in the open market at its current price of $34 and deliver it to the option exercising holder at $30 for a loss of $4 per share, which is only partially offset by the premium income.

Put Writing. The risk to a put writer is that the price of the underlying stock will decline. (Put writers are generally bullish on the security.)

Example: Smith sells an MP Mar 40 put for $2 ($200) when MetPath stock is trading at $40. Because the put is at the money and because (for this example) MetPath is not considered to be a volatile stock, the premium represents pure time value.

Over the next few weeks, during the life of the option, MetPath declines to $32, and Smith gets an exercise notice. He must buy the stock from the holder at $40 per share even though its market value is only $32. Only the $2 premium eases some of the $8 loss ($40 less $32).

Note. All these examples illustrate events that can make writing an option unprofitable. Needless to say, whenever the market moves in the direction that writers expect, they see their contracts expire worthless to the holders—and they keep the premiums.

Buyers

People and institutions buy options for a number of reasons. Some need to hedge a position or otherwise manage their risk by locking in a stock's appreciation in value or protecting a position in some other way. Others are speculators who are trading simply in the pursuit of profit.

Advantages. Buying options has two main benefits: (1) limited loss, and (2) great leverage.

The potential loss that an option holder faces is limited to the premium paid. If the underlying stock does not move as expected, the holder simply lets the contract expire and tries again.

Perhaps the greater benefit of the two, however, is *leverage:* By buying options, an option holder can control a great deal more stock than by buying the stock outright.

Example: Smith and Phelps have $3,000 each to invest. Phelps buys 100 shares of MetPath now trading at $30 ($3,000 total). She controls 100 shares. Smith buys 10 MP Mar 30 calls ($3,000 total). He controls 1,000 shares (10 contracts, 100 shares each).

Over the next 60 days, MetPath stock rises to $33. Phelps enjoys a $300 increase in the value of her stock. Smith, if he exercises his calls, can collect a gross profit of $3,000. He buys 1,000 shares at the strike price of 30 ($30,000) and resells them right away at 33 ($33,000).

Option holders thus use their funds to purchase the *right* to buy or sell a security, not the security itself. Because the option costs less than the underlying stock, a holder can control a great deal more shares than in an outright purchase of the stock.

Drawbacks. Owners of stock might be a "little wrong" about their purchases; that is, if the stock does not increase in value as expected, they can wait a little longer if they still feel confident about their purchase.

Not so with options, which are wasting assets. To enjoy a profit, option buyers must be right about three things: price direction, magnitude, and timing.

1. *Direction:* They must forecast whether a stock's price is going up or down and by how much. Then they must purchase an appropriate put or call—in, at, or out of the money.
2. *Magnitude:* They must also be sure that the price will move far enough in the right direction to make the option profitable.
3. *Timing:* Finally, they must be certain that the price will move before expiration.

If any of these forecasts is wrong, the investment may be rendered worthless at expiration.

Example: With Phelps holding her 100 shares and Smith his 10 MP calls, MetPath stock falls by 5 points to 25. At expiration, the options are still deep out of money.

Phelps gets the bad news and decides to hold the stock for another 60 days.

Smith takes a short-term capital loss of $3,000.

So, although one of the benefits of buying options is that all you can lose is the premium, one of the drawbacks is that you *can* lose all of the premium if you are not right on all three points.

MARGIN

Investors may borrow money, referred to as *margin*, from their brokerage firms to purchase stock. Options, however, cannot be purchased on margin. With options, *margin* is the money or stock that the naked (uncovered) call writer must deliver to the brokerage firm and that assures the writer's performance. (Because option holders must pay premiums in full, they do not come under any margin requirements.)

How much collateral a writer has to put up is set by Regulation T in the United States, but the brokerage firms often require even more than the exchanges do.

READING OPTIONS QUOTATIONS

Figure 6-1 shows an excerpt from the options section of the *New York Times*'s financial news, and Figure 6-2 similarly gives some examples of stock options from the *Wall Street Journal* and the *Financial Times*.

Underlying Stock

In Figure 6-1, the first column lists the underlying stocks in alphabetical order. Below the name of each company is the day's closing price on the exchange on which the stock is traded. The closing price is repeated for each option series traded on the stock.

Trading in Stock Options

WEDNESDAY, MARCH 5, 1986

MOST ACTIVE OPTIONS

Chicago

CALLS

	Sales	Last	Chg.	N.Y. Close
SP100 Mar220	73012	1 3/8	+ 1-16	214.79
SP100 Mar215	60377	3 3/8	+ 3/8	214.79
SP100 Mar210	26724	6 7/8	+ 3/8	214.79
SP100 Mar225	20760	1/2	− 1-16	214.79
SP100 Apr220	17243	4	+ 1/8	214.79

PUTS

	Sales	Last	Chg.	N.Y. Close
SP100 Mar210	59105	1 1-16	− 1/4	214.79
SP100 Mar215	47491	2 15-16	− 7-16	214.79
SP100 Mar205	25188	5-16	− 1-16	214.79
SP100 Mar200	13863	1/8	....	214.79
SP100 Mar220	10011	5 7/8	− 7/8	214.79

American

CALLS

	Sales	Last	Chg	N.Y Close
MMIdx Mar320	13066	1 1/4	− 1-16	7.72
MMIdx Mar315	10414	2 3/8	+ 1/8	7.72
MMIdx Mar305	7012	7 3/4	+ 3/8	7.72
MMIdx Mar310	6401	4 3/4	+ 3/8	7.72
Texaco Apr30	4280	1 1-16	+ 1-16	29 1/8

PUTS

	Sales	Last	Chg	N.Y Close
MMIdx Mar305	5443	2 3/8	− 3/8	7.72
MMIdx Mar310	4825	4 1/8	− 1 1/8	7.72
MMIdx Mar300	3494	1 1-16	−11-16	7.72
MMIdx Mar295	2675	1/2	− 3-16	7.72
MMIdx Apr270	1236	1-16	....	7.72

Philadelphia

CALLS

	Sales	Last	Chg.	N.Y Close
AnheusB Mar45	2748	2 1/8	+ 1 1/8	46 1/2
AldSig Jun50	2518	2 3/4	− 1/4	49 7/8
VL Idx Mar230	1759	2 1/2	....	229.44
McDln May17 1/2	1757	1 1/8	+ 3/8	16 7/8
AnheusB Jun45	1629	4	+1 1-16	46 1/2

PUTS

	Sales	Last	Chg.	N.Y Close
F N M Jun30	1449	1 3/4	+ 1/4	31 1/2
VL Idx Mar225	1203	5-16	− 7-16	229.44
Waste May40	892	7/8	+ 3-16	43
McDln May15	813	3/8	− 1/4	16 7/8
PhibroS Apr40	740	1-16	....	50 7/8

Pacific

CALLS

	Sales	Last	Chg.	N.Y Close
Unocal Apr25	2070	3-16	....	22
KeyPh Mar12 1/2	1897	2 3/8	− 3/8	15
A M D Mar30	1478	1	− 1/8	30
Hasbro Apr40	1436	3 3/8	....	42
Wendy Jun17 1/2	1375	1 7/8	+ 1-16	18

PUTS

	Sales	Last	Chg.	N.Y Close
DataGn Mar40	2240	2 3/8	+ 9-16	38
DataGn Mar35	648	3/8	+ 1-16	38
KeyPh Mar15	530	1/2	− 1-16	15
DataGn Jun35	501	1 3/4	+ 5-16	38
A M I Mar20	493	3-16	....	21

Figure 6-1

Reprinted by permission of *Wall Street Journal* (Europe), © Dow Jones & Company, Inc., March 5, 1986. All rights reserved.

LISTED U.S. OPTIONS

Thursday, April 11, 1985
3:00 p.m. New York Time

Prices of all options. Sales unit usually is 100 shares. Security description includes exercise price.

CBOE

Option & 3:00 p.m.	Strike Price	Calls-Last Apr	Calls-Last Jul	Calls-Last Oct	Puts-Last Apr	Puts-Last Jul	Puts-Last Oct
Alcoa	30	r	r	6¼	r	r	r
34⅜	... 35	⅜	1 9-16	2⅝	1	1⅝	2⅛
34⅜	... 40	r	⅜	13-16	r	r	r
AT&T	... 15	6⅜	r	r	r	r	r
21⅜	... 20	1⅜	1⅞	2¼	r	7-16	⅝
21⅜	... 25	1-16	3-16	7-16	r	r	r
Atl R	45	4⅛	r	r	r	11-16	1⅛
49	 50	¼	1 9-16	2¼	1	2½	r
49	 55	r	⅜	¾	r	r	r
Avon	 20	1¼	1⅞	2⅜	1-16	r	1
21¼	... 25	1-16	3-16	½	r	r	4¼
BankAm	.15	4¼	r	4⅜	r	r	¼
19¼	... 20	1-16	9-16	15-16	13-16	1¼	1½
19¼	... 25	r	1-16	⅛	r	r	r
Beth S	.. 15	r	r	r	1-16	⅛	r
17¾	... 25	r	1-16	r	r	r	r
Burl N	.. 45	8¼	8¼	s	1-16	r	s
52½	... 50	2⅝	4¼	r	⅛	1⅛	1⅞
52½	... 55	¼	1 13-16	3⅛	2⅝	r	r
52½	... 60	r	11-16	r	r	r	r
ChiNw	...20	½	1¾	r	¾	r	r
19½	... 25	r	r	⅝	r	r	r
CIGNA	..45	r	r	r	1-16	11-16	r
49⅜	... 50	¼	2	r	r	2½	r
Citicp	... 35	10¼	11	r	r	⅛	r
45⅝	... 40	5⅝	6½	7¼	r	⅜	r
45⅝	... 45	⅞	2⅝	3⅜	5-16	2	r
45⅝	... 50	r	⅝	1⅜	r	r	r

Total call vol. 30,465 Call open int. 881,083
Total put vol. 12,024 Put open int. 241,524
r—Not traded. s—No option offered. o—Old.
Last is premium (purchase price).

OPTIONS

3-month call rates

Industrials	p		
Allied-Lyons	16	Midland Bk	30
BAT	32	NEI	8
BOC Grp	25	Nat West Bk	60
BSR	16	P & O Dfd	36
BTR	52	Plessey	17
Babcock	14	Polly Peck	26
Barclays	48	Racal Elect	18
Beecham	32	RHM	11
Blue Circle	45	Rank Org Ord	32
Boots	15	Reed Intnl	50
Bowaters	20	Sears	8
Brit Aerospace	33	TI	20
Brit. Telecom	11	Tesco	20
Brown (J.)	3	Thorn EMI	35
Burton Ord	39	Trust Houses	13
Cadburys	14	Turner Newall	10
Comm Union	19	Unilever	85
Courtaulds	12½	Vickers	19
Debenhams	17½	**Property**	
Distillers	28	Brit Land	12
Dunlop	6	Cap Counties	18
FNFC	8½	Land Secs	25
Gen Accident	45	MEPC	28
Gen Electric	17	Peachey	22
Glaxo	85	Samuel Props	14
Grand Met	25		
GUS 'A'	60	**Oils**	
Guardian	60	Brist. Oil & Min	4
GKN	17	Brit Petroleum	42
Hanson Tst.	17½	Burmah Oil	18
Hawker Sidd	38	Charterhall	6
Hse of Fraser	30	Premier	5
ICI	60	Shell	60
'Imps'	18	Tricentrol	18
Jaguar	28	Ultramar	19
Ladbroke	24		
Legal & Gen	50	**Mines**	
Lex Service	28	Charter Cons	18
Lloyds Bank	45	Cons Gold	44
Lucas Inds	25	Lonrho	14
Marks & Spencer	11	Rio T Zinc	56

A selection of Options traded is given on the London Stock Exchange Report Page.

Figure 6-2. *Quotes on Stock Options.*

Reprinted by permission of Financial Times.

Strike Price

The second column lists the strike prices. Notice how they occur in multiples of 5—and, in some cases, in multiples of 2½. Note also how the strike prices approximate the closing price of the underlying stock.

Calls and Puts

The next six columns reflect the current expiration cycles for calls and puts. The figures under these column headings are the premiums as of the close of business for the days. In most cases, they reflect a dollar value that has to be multiplied by 100 to arrive at the dollar cost of the option.

Example: The Alcoa Jan 25 call closed at 4¼, or $4.25. To get the dollar total of the premium, multiply by 100: $4.25 times 100 equals $425 for the total cost of the call.

The letter symbols in the price columns are explained at the bottom of the newspaper page:

- "r" means "restricted."
- "s" means "no option offered."
- "o" means "old."

Example: Look at a few of the entries in Figure 6-1.
- The Alcoa Mar 40 call has an intrinsic value of 2⅞ (stock price of 42⅞ less the strike price of 40). Yet its last trade was at 3⅝. The ¾ point is time value.
- The AT&T Jun 22½ put is ⅛ point in the money (strike price of 22½ less stock price of 22⅜). Its premium of 1¼ point is almost purely time value. The AT&T June 30 put is not traded (r), and the September is not even offered (s).

Volume and Open Interest

At the bottom of all the listings for each exchange are tabulations of volume and open interest for puts and calls.

- *Volume* is the total number of contracts, puts or calls, trading on the exchange for the day.
- *Open interest* is the total number of open positions at the close of trading, which have not been closed either by exercise or covering purchases.

PRICING

A number of factors affect the purchase price (the premium) of an option. They are the following:

1. The relationship of the market price of the underlying stock to the options strike price.
2. The time remaining to the expiration date (that is, the life of the option).
3. The volatility of the underlying stock.
4. Interest rates.
5. Cash dividends on the underlying stock.

Market Price of the Underlying Stock

The relationship between the stock's current market price and the option's strike price determines whether or not the option has an actual value, which is referred to as the *intrinsic value.* This relationship also establishes whether the option is either in the money or out of the money. An option is said to be *in-the-money* if it can be exercised profitably. A call is in-the-money if the stock is selling at a price higher than the strike price.

Example: An MP 40 call is in-the-money because MetPath stock is trading at 41⅛. The call holder may exercise the option, buy 100 shares of MetPath at 40, and resell it profitably at 41⅛. An MP 45 call, with the stock at 41⅛, has no intrinsic value and is at the same time out of the money. No holder of MP 45 would exercise and pay $45 per share for a stock currently at 41⅛.

A put is in-the-money if the stock is trading below the strike price.

Example: An MP 45 put is in-the-money because the stock is at 41⅛. The holder of the put may exercise the option and sell the 100 shares of MP stock at $45 per share. At the same time, an MP 40 put is out of the money. With the stock at 41⅛, no holder of MP 40 would exercise, which would require the holder to sell 100 shares of MetPath at $40 per share.

Example: In the case of the MP 40 call, the intrinsic value is 1⅛ (41⅛ less 40), or $1.125. For a standard 100-share contract, the intrinsic value is $112.50 ($1.125 times 100).

The intrinsic value of the put is 4⅞ (45 less 41⅛), which amounts to $487.50 ($4.875 times 100).

An option is said to be *at-the-money* if the stock's market price is equal to the strike price.

Example: Assume that MetPath stock is currently trading at $40 per share. Any MP option—put or call—with a strike price of 40 is at the money.

An at-the-money option is said to have no intrinsic value. Were it to be exercised, it would yield no profit.

An option is *out-of-the-money* if exercising it would result in a loss. A call is out of the money when the stock's price is lower than the strike price.

Example: Assume that MetPath is trading at 39½. An MP 40 call is out of the money by ½ point, or $50 ($40 less $39.50 equals $0.50 times 100).

For a put to be out of the money, the strike has to be higher than the stock's price.

Example: An MP 40 put is out of the money when MetPath stock is trading at 41. The out-of-the-money amount is $100 ($41 less $40 equals $1 times 100).

Out-of-the-money options have zero intrinsic value, obviously not a negative value.

An options premium is said to be at *parity* when it is trading at a dollar amount equal to its intrinsic value alone, without any additional charge for time value or volatility.

Example: An MP Mar 40 call is at parity when the market price of MetPath stock is 43 and the options premium is $3.

Life of the Option (Time Value)

An option is a security with a limited and relatively short life span. If it is not exercised, liquidated, or covered by the expiration date, it ceases to exist. It becomes worthless. As a result, an option is considered a *wasting asset.* As the day of expiration nears, the contract is worth less and less because of the diminishing time of its life span.

Time value is often reflected in the current price of an option, or the premium, as an amount in excess of the option's intrinsic value.

Example: An MP Feb 40 call, with MetPath trading at 43, is in the money by 3 points ($300). That is, its intrinsic value is $3. Yet in early December the premium is $5. The difference of $2 between the call's intrinsic value ($3) and the actual trading price ($5) is the call's time value.

By mid-January, with MetPath still trading at 43, the February call is selling for $4. Its premium is lower, even though the intrinsic value is unchanged. The time value has decreased as the expiration date has approached.

Time value plays more of a role in what are known as "American" options, as opposed to "European" options. An *American option* may be exercised at any time up to expration; all U.S listed stock options are of this kind. A *European option* may be exercised only *at* expiration.

Time value theoretically follows a fairly predictable pattern during the life of an option, decreasing as time passes.

Experience has shown that investors are almost always willing to pay more than the intrinsic value of a option. Because an option represents, a right and not an obligation, it can never have a value below zero. So, for a *call:*[1]

$$\begin{matrix} \text{Market price} \\ \text{of a call} \end{matrix} > \begin{matrix} \text{Intrinsic} \\ \text{value} \end{matrix} = \left(\begin{matrix} \text{Market price} \\ \text{of stock} \end{matrix} - \begin{matrix} \text{Exercise} \\ \text{price} \end{matrix} \right) \times \begin{matrix} \text{Number of} \\ \text{stocks} \end{matrix} > 0$$

This relationship is often illustrated graphically as in Figure 6-3.

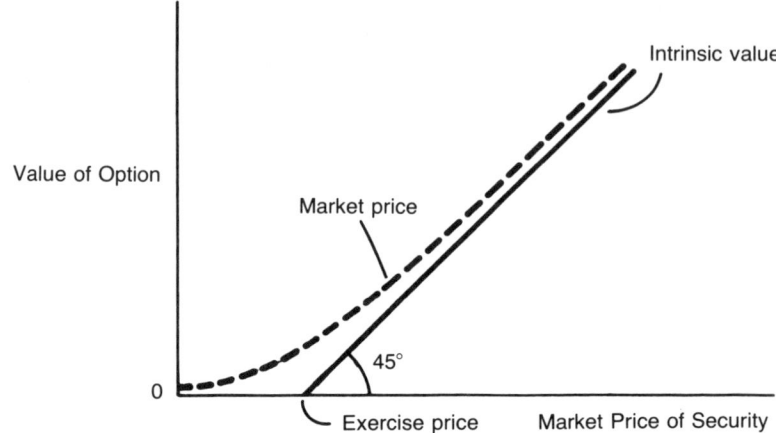

Figure 6-3. *Relationship of Market Value to Theoretical Value for a Call Option.*

Why is an investor willing to pay more than the intrinsic value? The reason has to do with the very nature of an option: It provides the holder with a future chance to make money by exercising the contract under favorable conditions. If the price of the underlying stock historically has shown a positively sloping trendline, then the likelihood of making a future profit is increased. Similarly if the price movements of the underlying stock are volatile, then the chance of finding an opportune moment to make more money through exercise is enhanced. Hence the price of the call is also a function of the price variance of the underlying stock, as illustrated in Figure 6-4.

The longer the time to maturity, the higher is the chance that the investor can exercise the call at an optimal profit. So in general the longer the time to maturity, the higher will be the market price of the option. Conversely, the closer we get to the maturity date, the closer the price of the contract will get to the contract's intrinsic value.

Volatility of the Underlying Stock

When the underlying stock is considered *volatile*—that is, capable of dramatic and rapid price changes—the premium tends to be higher than for nonvolatile stocks.

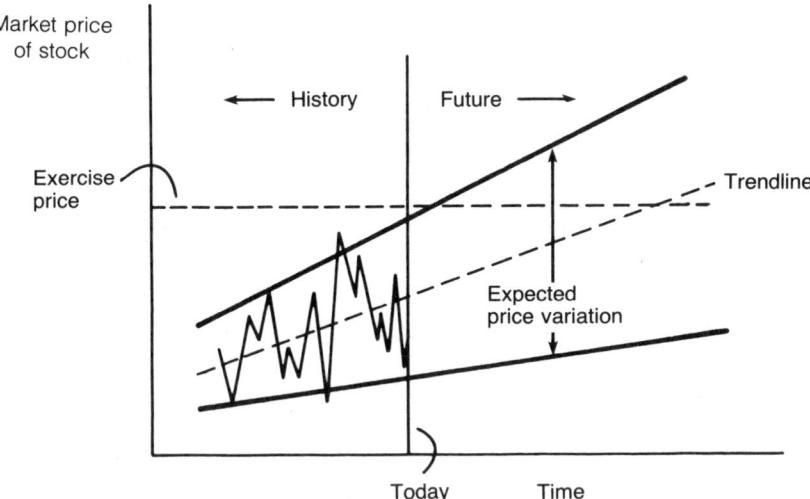

Figure 6-4. *Price as a Function of the Underlying Security.*

Example: An MP Feb 40 call is selling for $5, with $3 of that premium consisting of intrinsic value. The other $2 is considered pure time value because MetPath historically moves no more than ⅛ to ¼ point at a time.

Laser Hi-Tech (a fictitious stock), on the other hand, is a growing firm whose stock can move 2 to 5 points in a morning or afternoon of trading. For this reason, it is considered to be a highly volatile stock. Given a $3 intrinsic value and a "reasonable" $2 worth of time value, Hi-Tech calls should be selling for $5. Instead, they are selling for $6.50.

The rationale for the added $1.50 premium value is that a volatile stock is very likely to move into the money more quickly than a more stable stock. (Of course, a volatile stock could also move far out of the money.) It is for this reason that options are said to be instruments to transfer the underlying stocks' volatility to themselves.

Interest Rate Level

It can be argued that the market price of the option relates to the interest rate level. If the market price of the call option is fully correlated with the market price of the underlying stock, then a fully hedged (riskless) investment can be made in the stock by concurrently writing a suitable number of options on that stock.

If the price of the stock increases, the investor will incur a capital gain on the long position in the stock but will lose money on the short position in the call option because he is obliged to sell at the exercise price even if the market price is higher. Conversely, if the market price of the stock falls, the investor will incur a loss on the long position in the stock, but there will be no exercise of the option, the value of which will be zero. The investor who sold the call option can retain the full premium paid by the buyer.

Given that the price of the call is determined efficiently no matter what the stock price does, the investor will end up with a return on the investment equal to what can be termed a risk-free rate. Hence the argument is that, when the risk-free rate increases, so will the price of the call, whereas a decrease in the risk-free rate induces a lower price on the option.

The argument therefore is that, if the risk-free part of the return from a stock portfolio increases, then the investor will be willing to pay more for the option to purchase the stock at a given price. This is not intuitively clear because an increase in the general interest rate level would cause the stock prices to drop, thus reducing the value of the call option. However, the following theoretical example might clarify the argument.

Example: Initially we invest in a zero dividend stock with a value of $100. Assume that only two events are possible: (1) The stock price can increase to $105, or (2) The stock price can decrease to $95. Also assume that probabilities can be attached to each event. Because the stock doesn't pay a dividend, the return on the investment relates solely to an increase in the market value of the stock. For this reason we assume that there is a likelihood of 60% that the stock price will increase and only a 40% chance that the stock price will decrease. (See Figure 6-5.) The expected value of the investment at the end of the period is (.6 × $105) + (4 × $95) = $101, amounting to a 1% return on the investment during the period.

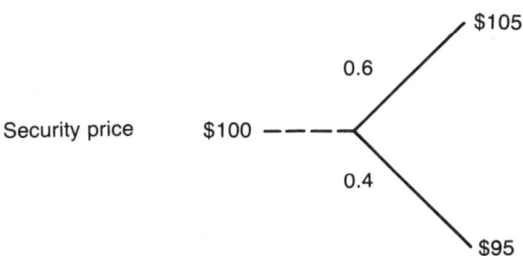

Figure 6-5

To hedge this investment a certain number of options must be written in the same stock. The number to issue can be found by dividing the maximum fluctuation of the stock price by the fluctuation in the price of the option during the period:

$$\text{Number of contracts} = \frac{\$105 - \$95}{\$5 - \$0} = \frac{10}{5} = 2$$

So two contracts are issued with an exercise price of $100. In situation 1, the investor will incur a capital gain of $5 on the stock portfolio. On the other hand, the two options will be exercised at a total cost of $10 ($2 × $5), leaving the investor with an end-of-period net worth position of $95 ($100 – $5).

Let us further assume that the riskless rate in this period amounts to .50%. We can then calculate the price of the option that secures the risk-free return on the fully hedged investment. The net worth position at the beginning of the period equals the initial investment minus the price incurred from the sale of the contract, and the initial net worth position plus the risk-free return should equal the end-of-period net worth position. Hence:

$$(\$100 - 2w)\,1.0050 = 95$$

$$\text{Option Price} = \frac{100.50 - 95}{1.0050} \quad /2 = \$\,2.7363$$

Initial net worth position $100 - 2 \times 2.7363 = 94.5274$

We see that the return on the investment exactly equals the risk-free return:

$$\frac{95 - 94.5274}{94.5274} \times 100 = .50\%$$

If the market price of the option differs from the equilibrium price, investors would be able to increase the return above the risk-free rate through positioning. Such transactions would force the equilibrium price back into force.[2]

If we assume an increase in the risk-free rate from .50% to .75%, we can recalculate the new option price using the same principle:

$$(\$100 - 2w) \quad 1.0075 = \quad 95$$

$$w = \frac{100.75 - 95}{1.0075} \quad /2 \quad = \$2.8536$$

Initial net worth position: $100 - 2 \times 2.8536 = 94.2928$.

Again it is seen that the return on the investment equals the risk-free return:

$$\frac{95 - 94.2928}{94.2928} \times 100 = .75\%$$

An increase in the risk-free rate from .50% to .75% per period hence will induce an increase in the price of the call option from $2.7363 to $2.8536, given that the options are efficiently priced.

Cash Dividend Rate

Another determinant of the stock option price is the cash dividend rate of the underlying stock, which can be particularly influential on high-yield stocks. The relationship has to do with the fact that stock prices vary with the dividend payment dates. The stock price increases as the dividend payment date approaches, and the ex-dividend stock price is usually reduced by the amount of the cash dividend payout. In general the larger the stock dividend is, the lower will be the option price. This is so because, if the market price increases as the dividend date approaches, then the intrinsic value of a call option in the money will decrease correspondingly.

Black-Scholes Formula[3]

All these factors can be summarized in a single expression:

$$C = g\ (P, E, s^2, T, r_f)$$

where g indicates a relationship function and

C	$=$	Price of the call option.
P	$=$	Market price of the underlying stock.
E	$=$	Exercise price of the option.
s^2	$=$	Annual price variance of the underlying stock.
T	$=$	Time to expiration date (as percentage of a year).
r_f	$=$	The risk-free rate.

The mathematical relationship among these variables has been approximated by Black and Scholes in the following formula for the price of a European-type option, which is used both by professional option traders as well as by researchers to explore the developments in the market prices of call options. The experience with the pricing model vis-a-vis stock options has concluded that it estimates the true option price with a satisfactory accuracy.

$$C = P \cdot N(X_1) - e^{-r_f \cdot T} \cdot E \cdot N(X_2)$$
$$X_1 = (\ln P/E) + [r_f + (s^2/2) \cdot T] / (s \cdot \sqrt{T})$$
$$X_2 = (\ln P/E) + [r_f - (s^2/2) \cdot T] / (s \cdot \sqrt{T})$$

$\ln$	$=$	Natural logarithm.
e	$=$	2.71828
$N(\cdot)$	$=$	Cumulative normal probability of a normally distributed variable with a mean value of 0 and a standard deviation of 1

The risk-free rate is often approximated by the interest rate on medium-term government securities. An area of dispute can occur when defining volatility of the underlying security's price: For which time period should the price variance be calculated? What is the impact of future expectations on price volatility? And so on. This discussion will not be pursued further here: Suffice it to say that the Black-Scholes model forms the basis for the theoretical calculation of any type of option price.

The preceding discussion relates to the European type of option, but all the arguments apply as well to the American type of option. In general an American option is worth more than a European option because it provides the holder with a wider possibility of exercising the option at the opportune moment. Consequently an American option will trade at a higher price than the equivalent European option.

Pricing Puts

Similarly the price of a put stock option can be found. The theoretical value of the put is equal to the difference between the exercise price and the current market price of the underlying security times the number of securities the put entitles the holder to sell. The put holder will make a profit if the going market price of the security is lower than the exercise price. Because the put represents an option and not an obligation, it cannot have a negative value.

$$\frac{\text{Market price}}{\text{of a put}} > \frac{\text{Intrinsic}}{\text{value of a put}} = \left(\frac{\text{Market price}}{\text{of stock}} - \frac{\text{Exercise}}{\text{price}}\right) \times \frac{\text{Number of}}{\text{stocks}} \; >($$

This relationship is llustrated in Figure 6-6.

For the same reasons as in the case of calls, the market price of a put option exceeds that of its theoretical value. Further, although the Black-Scholes option pricing model applies only to call options, it can be adapted to the put option case due to the inherent relationship between a call and a put option.

A risk-free arbitrage position can be created by (1) buying the stock, (2) buying a put option, and (3) simultaneously selling a call option with the same exercise price as the put option. This transaction is often termed *conversion*.

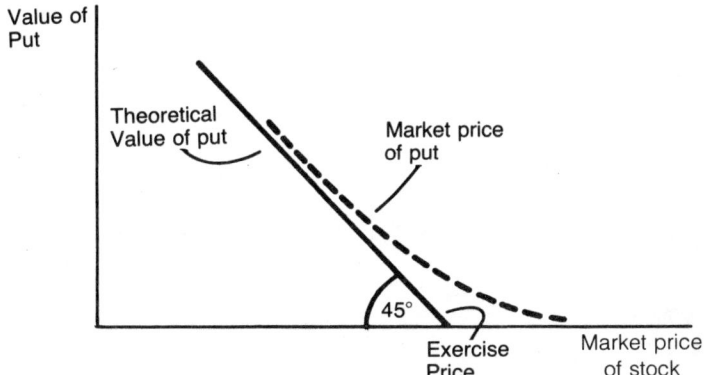

Figure 6-6. *Relationship of Market Value to Theoretical Value For a Put Option.*

If the stock price increases, the capital gain on the portfolio outweighs the loss from the exercise of the call option. If the stock price decreases, the gain from exercising the put option will outweigh the loss incurred on the stock portfolio. Hence it describes a risk-free transaction.

What is interesting in this context is that this conversion process indicates the relationship between call prices and the put price prevailing in an efficient option market.[4] The cost equation of the zero risk position is:

$$\frac{\text{Zero}}{\text{Risk (0)}} = \frac{\text{Put}}{\text{price}} - \frac{\text{Call}}{\text{price}} + \frac{\text{Price of}}{\text{stock}} - \frac{\text{Exercise}}{\text{price}} + \frac{\text{Cost of finance}}{\substack{\text{during life} \\ \text{of position}}}$$

or

$$\frac{\text{Put}}{\text{price}} = \frac{\text{Call}}{\text{price}} + \frac{\text{Exercise}}{\text{price}} - \frac{\text{Price of}}{\text{stock}} - \frac{\text{Cost of}}{\text{finance}}$$

If the stock pays a dividend during the period it should be included in the equation as well.

Due to the positive cost of finance, the price of a put option is usually lower than that of the equivalent call option price.

Chapter 7

Types of Contracts

For many years, options trading remained within the equities marketplace. The early 1980s, however, saw options trading begin on other "underlying interests," particularly:

- Currencies.
- Interest (debt) instruments.
- Indexes.

CURRENCY OPTIONS

Option contracts on foreign currencies were first introduced in North America in November 1982, at which time the Montreal Exchange (ME) introduced a Canadian dollar option on the trading floor. The Montreal Exchange started trading Canadian stock options back in 1975, and this market was used as a model in the introduction of new option contracts in the early 1980s. The success of the Canadian dollar option subsequently led to the introduction of currency options on pounds sterling, German marks, Swiss francs, and Japanese yen. The currency options on the Montreal Exchange are cleared and guaranteed by the International Options Clearing Corporation (IOCC) which

Table 7-1. Comparison of Types of Options.

Option	Underlying Interest	Contract Size	Exercise and Settlement	Strike Price	Premiums
Equity (listed)	Stocks	100 shares	Writer buys or sells stock at stock price	In dollars	In points
Foreign currencies	Pound, yen mark, franc, etc.	Varies by currency	Writer buys or sells currency at strike price. Delivery made in country of origin.	U.S. cents per unit of foreign currency (except for for Japanese yen)	U.S. cents per unit of foreign currency (except for yen)
Debt	Treasury securities	Bonds & notes: $100,000 in principal Bills: $1 million in principal	Writer buys or sells security at strike price	Bonds & notes: par value Bills: discount rate	Points & 32nd basis points
Index	Stock Indexes	Multiplier	Writer makes cash payment to holder	In dollars	In points

operates the Montreal Exchange, the Vancouver Stock Exchange (VSE), the Sydney Stock Exchange (SSE), and the European Options Exchange (EOE) in Amsterdam. The European Options Exchange also started trading a Dutch guilder option contract to follow up on the success of the already established currency options.

In December 1982 the Philadelphia Stock Exchange (PHLX) introduced a pound sterling option contract, which in early 1983 was followed by option contracts in the other major international currencies—German marks, Swiss francs, Canadian dollars, Japanese yen, and French francs. Other currencies, such as the Belgian franc, the Dutch guilder, and the Italian lira, are being considered for future introduction on the exchange. The options on the Philadelphia Stock Exchange are cleared by the Options Clearing Corporation. In terms of volume the Philadelphia Stock Exchange is the most active of the option exchanges, all of which have had an impressive growth rate in options transactions over the past couple of years. Partly induced by the immediate success of the introduction of currency options, the Chicago Mercantile Exchange decided to introduce an option on the German mark futures contract of the same exchange during January 1984. Option contracts in pounds sterling and Swiss francs soon followed. The German mark option has turned out to be very successful and, instead of taking away trade volume from the already established exchanges, the publicity of the new option has stimulated options trading activities in general. One explanation is that the new option contract provides the vast number of futures traders on the Chicago Mercantile Exchange with a suitable instrument to hedge their futures positions, an exercise that apparently was found more applicable with an option geared directly toward the futures contract of the exchange. At the same time it represented a new investment opportunity in an option contract available directly on that busy exchange.

During June 1985 LIFFE introduced its first currency option based on its financial futures contract in pounds sterling with a trading unit of £ Stg. 25,000. The futures and options contracts of the London International Financial Futures Exchange are cleared by the International Commodities Clearing Corporation.

In November 1985 the European Options Exchange (EOE) in Amsterdam successfully introduced the first option contract in the European currency unit with a denomination of U.S. $10,000, and several other exchanges have since introduced ECU options. In October 1985, the EOE introduced the world's first cross currency option, a pounds sterling/Dutch guilder contract in £ Stg. 10,000 denomination and consequently quoted in guilders.

Contract Size

The options contracts traded on the Montreal Exchange, the European Options Exchange, and the Philadelphia Stock Exchange are based on delivery of physical commodities, whereas options traded on the Chicago Mercantile Exchange and the London International Financial Futures Exchange are based on the delivery of the corresponding financial futures contract. Because the futures contracts also provide the physical delivery of the underlying currency, if required, the general features of the option contracts are very similar.

The contract size varies from one exchange to the other, but they are all initially related to the size of the corresponding financial futures contracts on the Chicago Mercantile Exchange. The contract size of the options on the Montreal Exchange at their initial introduction was one-fifth the size of the corresponding futures contracts on the Chicago Mercantile Exchange, whereas the contract size on the Philadelphia Stock Exchange has been half the size of the CME contracts.

During 1984 the Montreal Exchange carried out a market study to determine the optimal trading units for the option contracts traded on the exchange. As a result of this investigation the Montreal Exchange terminated the trading of the old contract denominations in December 1984 and instead implemented new trading units of Can. $ 50,000 and £ Stg. 100,000 on the two commonwealth currencies and trading units of U.S. $ 100,000 on the other currencies German marks, Japanese yen, and Swiss francs. This meant that the currency options would have a quotation similar to that prevailing in the foreign exchange markets. The Dutch guilder contract of the European Options Exchange follows the same principle of denomination and has a trading unit of U.S. $ 10,000. In early 1987, the London International Financial Futures Exchange also adopted the principle to follow the foreign exchange market quotation by introducing option contracts in £ Stg. and German marks with £25,000 and US $ 50,000 denominations on the two contracts.

Quotations

Currency option quotes are usually indicated in cents or dollars per unit of the contract amount of foreign currency.

Example: The PHLX £ Stg. June call option may be quoted at .45¢/£, and the premium is found by multiplying the contract amount by the option quote:

£ 12,5000 × .0045 $/£ = $56.25

Table 7-2. *Trading Units for Some Currency Option Contracts.*

	Montreal Exchange		European Options Exchange	Philadelphia Stock Exchange	Chicago Mercantile Exchange		London International Financial Futures Exchange	
	Old* Contracts	New Contracts			Option Contracts	Financial Futures	Options	Futures
Swiss franc (SF 25,000)	Swiss franc (SF 25,000)	Swiss franc (US$ 100,000)	—	Swiss franc (US$ 62,500)	Swiss franc (SF 125,000)	Swiss franc (SF 125,000)	—	Swiss franc (SF 125,000)
Pound sterling (£Stg. 5,000)	Pound sterling (£Stg. 5,000)	Pound sterling (£Stg. 100,000)	Pound Stg. /Hfl (£Stg. 10,000)	Pound sterling (£Stg. 12,500)	Pound sterling (£Stg. 25,000)	Pound sterling (£Stg. 25,000)	Pound sterling (£Stg. 25,000)	Pound sterling (£Stg. 25,000)
German mark (DM 25,000)	German mark (DM 25,000)	German mark (US$ 100,000)	—	German mark (DM 62,500)	German mark (DM 125,000)	German mark (DM 125,000)	German mark (US$ 50,000)	German mark (US$ 50,000 & DM 125,000)
Japanese yen (Y 2,500,000)	Japanese yen (Y 2,500,000)	Japanese yen (US$ 100,000)	—	Japanese yen (Y 6,250,000)	—	Japanese yen (Y 12,500,000)	—	Japanese yen (Y12,500,000)
Canadian dollar (Can. $50,000)	Canadian dollar (Can. $50,000)	Canadian dollar (Can. $50,000)	—	Canadian dollar (Can. $50,000)	—	Canadian dollar (Can. $100,000)	—	—
—	—	—	Dutch guilder (US$ 10,000)	—	—	—	—	—
—	—	—	—	French franc (FF 125,000)	—	French franc (FF 250,000)	—	—
—	—	—	European currency (US$ 10,000)	—	—	European currency (ECU 125,000)	—	—

*The old contracts were traded until December 1984.

With the implementation of the new trading units on the Montreal Exchange, the Swiss franc, the German mark, and the Japanese yen contracts will be quoted in units of foreign currency per U.S. dollar. Likewise the Dutch guilder contract will be quoted in Hfl or cents per U.S. dollar.

Example: If the Dutch guilder contract is quoted at 2.20 cents/ U.S. $, the premium is found to be Hfl 220 (.0220 × 10,000). Hence the option quotes correspond to the foreign exchange rate denominations prevalent in the interbank market.

Price quotations on currency option contracts can be found in the major international newspapers. The *Wall Street Journal* brings daily quotations on the currency options of the Philadel-phia Stock Exchange and the currency future option of the Chicago Mercantile Exchange (see Figure 7-1). The major Cana-dian newspapers convey quotations on the currency options of the Montreal Exchange, and the *Financial Times* brings daily quotations on the currency options traded on the European Options Exchange (see Figures 7-2 and 7-3). As it appears the quotations are presented in different ways, but they all contain the same basic information.

The *Wall Street Journal* presents the foreign exchange rate in cents per unit of the foreign currency, with the exercise price indicated by the addition to the "big figure." The closing prices on calls and puts are given for the different exercise (strike) prices traded on the exchanges with contract maturities pre-sented horizontally. The quotes are given as cents per unit of foreign currency. A summary statistic indicates the total number of contracts traded during the day (volume) on each exchange and gives the total number of open call and put option quotes made during the business day (open interest).

The *Montreal Gazette* presents the foreign exchange rates on Canadian dollars and pounds sterling in U.S. dollars per unit of the currency, whereas the Deutsche mark and Swiss franc exchange rates are indicated in currency amounts per U.S. dollar. The contract maturities are presented vertically, with the "series" indicating the contract month and the exercise price. For each series is given the total number of contracts traded

Currency Options
Philadelphia Exchange

Option & Underlying	Strike Price	Calls—Last			Puts—Last		
		Mar	Jun	Sep	Mar	Jun	Sep
12,500 British Pounds-cents per unit.							
BPound	105	r	r	r	0.50	2.20	r
109.71	.110	1.20	2.50	3.95	2.40	s	r
109.71	.115	0.30	1.10	1.80	6.00	7.40	r
109.71	.120	0.05	0.45	0.95	r	12.00	r
50,000 Canadian Dollars-cents per unit.							
CDollr	...74	r	r	r	0.23	0.67	r
74.74	...75	0.17	r	r	0.65	r	r
74.74	...76	r	0.21	r	1.32	r	r
62,500 West German Marks-cents per unit.							
DMark	.. 30	r	1.34	r	0.19	0.54	0.73
30.61	...31	0.27	0.86	1.26	0.60	1.00	s
30.61	...32	0.06	0.46	r	1.34	1.70	r
30.61	...33	0.02	0.26	0.58	2.40	r	r
30.61	...34	r	0.13	r	r	3.30	r
125,000 French Francs-10ths of a cent per unit.							
FFranc	.105	0.10	r	r	5.00	r	r
6,250,000 Japanese Yen-100ths of a cent per unit.							
JYen	... 38	r	r	1.62	0.23	r	r
38.27	...39	0.12	0.65	r	0.83	1.07	r
38.27	...40	0.03	0.34	0.73	1.74	r	r
38.27	...41	r	0.19	r	r	r	r
62,500 Swiss Francs-cents per unit.							
SFranc	..36	0.60	1.17	r	0.53	0.88	r
35.94	...37	0.21	0.72	r	1.24	1.55	r
35.94	...38	0.05	0.48	r	r	2.26	r
35.94	...39	r	0.19	r	r	r	r
35.94	...40	0.01	0.12	r	r	r	r

Total call vol. 8,746   Call open int. 159,821
Total put vol. 5,879   Put open int. 86,033
r—Not traded. s—No option offered. o—Old.
Last is premium (purchase price).

Currency Futures Options
Chicago Mercantile Exchange

W. GERMAN MARK (CME)—125,000 marks, cents per mark

Strike Price	Calls—Settle		Puts—Settle	
	Mar	June	Mar	June
29	....	....	0.03	0.24
30	0.82	1.35	0.12	0.47
31	0.25	0.82	0.54	0.92
32	0.07	0.47	1.36	1.55
33	0.02	0.22	2.30	2.36
34	0.008	0.12	3.29	3.24

Est. vol. 5,958; Fri vol. 9,854 calls, 3,624 puts
Open interest Fri; 46,127 calls, 22,521 puts

Figure 7-1. *Quotes on Currency Option Contracts.*
Reprinted by permission of *Wall Street Journal,* Europe © Dow Jones & Company, Inc. (April 12, 1985).

and the number of open quotes made during the day with an indication of the closing option price. For the untraded option contracts a listing provides information on the number of open quotes made in each series, with an indication of the bid and ask prices at the close of trading. Summary statistics indicate the total number of contracts closed and the total number of open quotes made during the business day.

In the *Financial Times,* for each exercise price and delivery month is given the total number of contracts traded, along with the option quotes at the close of trading. The option quotes are denominated in cents (.01 guilder). A last column presents the corresponding spot exchange rate at the end of the business day. Contract maturities are indicated horizontally.

Pricing

The values of foreign currency options rise and fall in reaction to the values of the underlying foreign currency.

```
IOCC  CURRENCY  OPTIONS        May 130p  0 00748  0 0763  1.2300    May 320   0 00160  00195  3.1310
CANADA—EUROPE—AUSTRALIA        Jun 130   50 0 0114  0 0130  1.2300   May 320p  0 0.0687  00922  3.1310
Distributed by The Canadian Press  Jun 130p  100 0 0874  0 0899  1.2300   Jun 320   0 0 0415  0 0465  3.1310
Series traded May 1            Jul 130   0 0.0172  0.0192  1.2300   Jun 320p  0 0 1214  0 1264  3.1310
                Op.  Currency   Jul 130p  0 0 0957  0 0981  1.7300   Jul 320   0 0.0564  0 0624  3.1310
Series        Vol. Int. Close Close  Sep 130  0 0 0270  0 0300  1.2300   Jul 320p  0 0 1423  0 1483  3.1310
CANADIAN  $—50,000 CANS IN US$  Sep 130p  0 0 1098  0 1128  1.2300   Sep 320   0 0 0805  0 0880  3.1310
Jun 72p   100  88 0 0021  0.7309   Dec 130  0 0 0389  0 0429  1.2300   Sep 320p  8 0 1809  0 1884  3.1310
Jun 73o   100  80 0 0068  0.7309   Dec 130p  0 0 1239  0 1279  1.2300   Dec 320   0 0 1033  0 1128  3.1310
Jun 74    10  351 0 0023  0.7309   May 135  0 0 0005  0 0010  1.2300   Dec 320p  0 0 2264  0 2359  3.1310
BRITISH  POUND—100,000 BP IN US$  May 135o  0 0 1223  0 1238  1.2300   U.S. DOLLAR—100,000 US$ IN CANS
Jul 120   15   0 0 0515  1.7300   Jun 135  0 0 0048  0 0058  1.2300   May 132   0 0 0485  0 0495  1.3800
GERMAN MARK—100,000 US$ IN DM   Jun 135o  0 0 1301  0 1326  1.2300   May 132p  0 0 0000  0 0005  1.3800
Jun 315   20  30 0.0642  3.1310   Jul 135  0 0 0087  0 0102  1.2300   Jun 132   0 0 0501  0 0516  1.3800
Total volume·  245             Jul 135o  0 0 1363  0 1393  1.2300   Jun 132p  0 0 0004  0 0012  1.3800
Untraded (Closing Quotations)  Sep 135  0 0 0163  0 0193  1.2300   Jul 132   0 0 0513  0 0533  1.3800
                Op.  Currency   Sep 135o  0 0 1477  0 1507  1.2300   Jul 132p  2 0 0010  0 0020  1.3800
Series       Int. Bid  Ask  Close  Dec 135  0 0 0265  0.0295  1.2300   Sep 132   0 0 0544  0 0569  1.3800
CANADIAN  $—50,000 CANS IN US$  Dec 135o  0 0.1593  0.1633  1.2300   Sep 132p  0 0 0021  0 0040  1.3800
Jun 70    0 0.0302  0.0312  0.7309   May 140  0 0.0001  0 0006  1.2300   Dec 132   0 0 0579  0 0614  1.3800
Jun 70o   0 0.0002  0.0006  0.7309   May 140o  0 0.1717  0.1737  1.2300   Dec 132p  0 0 0040  0 0065  1.3800
Sep 70    0 0.0307  0.0317  0.7309   Jun 140  0 0.0019  0.0029  1.2300   May 134   0 0 0289  0 0299  1.3800
Sep 70o   0 0.0022  0 0027  0.7309   Jun 140o  0 0.1765  0 1790  1.2300   Mai 134p  0 0 0003  0 0011  1.3800
Dec 70    2 0.0311  0 0321  0.7309   Jul 140  0 0.0042  0 0051  1.2300   Jun 134  40 0 0319  0 0336  1.3800
Dec 70p   20 0 0047  0.0057  0.7309   Jul 140p  0 0.1808  0 1838  1.2300   Jun 134o 375 0.0019  0 0031  1.3800
Jun 71    0 0.0202  0 0212  0.7309   Sep 140  0 0.0098  0 0118  1.2300   Jul 134  10 0 0340  0 0365  1.3800
Jun 71o  75 0.0009  0 0012  0.7309   Sep 140o  0 0.1893  0 1924  1.2300   Jul 134p  10 0 0032  0 0051  1.3800
Sep 71    3 0 0213  0.0223  0.7309   Dec 140  0 0.0181  0.0206  1.2300   Sep 134   0 0 0380  0 0415  1.3800
Sep 71o  33 0.0038  0.0045  0.7309   Dec 140o  0 0.1980  0.2020  1.2300   Sep 134p  1 0 0051  0 0086  1.3800
Dec 71    0 0.0229  0 0239  0.7309   GERMAN MARK—100,000 US$ IN DM   Dec 134   0 0 0428  0 0468  1.3800
Dec 71p   3 0 0072  0 0081  0.7309   may 290  0 0.2297  0.2332  3.1310   Dec 134o  0 0 0078  0 0113  1.3800
Jun 72   81 0.0124  0.0134  0.7309   May 290o  0 0.0008  0 0018  3.1310   May 136   0 0 0116  0 0131  1.3800
Sep 72  138 0.0149  0.0159  0.7309   Jun 290  0 0.2326  0.2376  3.1310   May 136o  50 0 0029  0 0044  1.3800

Jun 76  310 0.0001  0 0005  0.7309   May 300  0 0.1337  0.1372  3.1310   Dec 138p  0 0 0029  0 0270  1.3800
Jun 76o  77 0.0301  0.0311  0.7309   May 300p  0 0.0061  0.0076  3.1310   May 140   0 0 0002  0 0010  1.3800
Sep 76   17 0 0016  0 0021  0.7309   Jun 300  0 0.1491  0 1541  3.1310   May 140o  0 0 0317  0 0327  1.3800
Sep 76o  10 0.0339  0.0349  0.7309   Jun 300o  0 0.0282  0 0322  3.1310   Jun 140  20 0 0021  0 0036  1.3800
Jun 77   J 0.0000  0 0004  0.7309   Jul 300  0 0.1602  0.1663  3.1310   Jun 140o  0 0 0318  0 0338  1.3800
Jun 77p   1 0 0400  0.0410  0.7309   Jul 300o  0 0.0450  0.0500  3.1310   Jul 140  20 0 0039  0 0059  1.3800
Sep 77    3 0 0008  0 0012  0.7309   Sep 300  0 0.1796  0.1871  3.1310   Jul 140o  20 0.0325  0 0345  1.3800
Sep 77p   0 0.0430  0.0440  0.7309   Sep 300o  0 0.0783  0.0858  3.1310   Sep 140   0 0 0073  0 0108  1.3800
BRITISH  POUND—100,000 BP IN US$  Dec 300  0 0.1985  0.2080  3.1310   Sep 140o  0 0.0332  0 0367  1.3800
May 115   0 0.0798  0.0818  1.2300   Dec 300o  0 0.1190  0.1285  3.1310   Dec 140   0 0 0121  0 0161  1.3800
Mai 115o  0 0 0018  0 0028  1.2300   May 305  0 0.0917  0.0952  3.1310   Dec 140o  0 0.0349  0 0390  1.3800
Jun 115   0 0.0852  0.0877  1.2300   May 305o  0 0.0142  0.0167  3.1310   Total open interest:  4483
```

Figure 7-2. *Quotes on Currency Option Contracts.*

Source: *The Gazette,* Montreal (May 2, 1985). Reprinted with permission.

EUROPEAN OPTIONS EXCHANGE

Series		Aug. Vol.	Last	Nov. Vol.	Last	Feb. Vol.	Last	Stock
GOLD C	$300	5	23	12	32	—	—	$315.75
GOLD C	$320	1	10.90	—	—	—	—	"
GOLD C	$340	7	3.90	—	—	—	—	"
GOLD C	$360	1	1.50	10	6.50	—	—	"
GOLD P	$300	14	4	30	7.50	—	—	"
GOLD P	$320	—	—	10	13	—	—	"
		Sept.		**Dec.**		**March**		
SILVER C	$550	2	50	—	—	—	—	$616
SILVER P	$600	—	—	—	—	3	38	"
$/FL C	Fl.340	—	—	2	16	—	—	Fl.346.55
$/FL C	Fl.345	—	—	2	13.30	—	—	"
$/FL C	Fl.350	59	8.20	—	—	—	—	"
$/FL C	Fl.355	18	5.80	53	9.50	—	—	"
$/FL C	Fl.360	155	4.20	—	—	—	—	"
$/FL C	Fl.370	146	3	—	—	—	—	"
$/FL C	Fl.375	105	2.20	100	4	—	—	"
$/FL C	Fl.380	50	1.50	3	3	—	—	"
$/FL P	Fl.335	55	6	30	11.70 A	2	16 A	"
$/FL P	Fl.340	51	9 A	23	14.20 A	—	—	"
$/FL P	Fl.345	60	10.20	—	—	—	—	"
$/FL P	Fl.350	30	13.40	1	19.50 A	—	—	"
		Jul.		**Oct.**		**Jan.**		
ABN C	Fl.460	30	5.50	20	12.50	—	—	Fl.456.5
ABN P	Fl.440	31	1.50	64	8.10	—	—	"
ROBE C	Fl.77.50	—	—	3	1.60	20	3.30	Fl.76.50
UNIL C	Fl.360	56	1.60	36	7.20	21	9.50	Fl.350.50
UNIL P	Fl.340	33	1.20	34	4.80 B	—	—	"

TOTAL VOLUME IN CONTRACTS: 13,188

A=Ask   B=Bid   C=Call   P= Put

Figure 7-3. Quotes on Currency Option Contracts.
Source: The Financial Times (June 26, 1985). Reprinted with permission.

1. As the currency's price rises, call premiums go up and put premiums go down.
2. As the currency's price declines, so do call prices, whereas put prices increase.

Example: Unibank (a fictitious firm) has a call option and a put option on the British pound, each with a strike price of $1.40. The call entitles the bank to buy $1 million worth of pounds at $1.40 each; the put gives it the right to sell $1 million worth of pounds at $1.40. The pound is presently trading at $1.40.

Then the value of the pound decreases to, say, $1.35 — that is, the pound weakens with respect to the U.S. dollar. In this case, the call goes out of the money, and the put takes on an intrinsic value of $5.

If the pound gets *stronger*—that is, if its price rises to $1.50—then the call assumes an intrinsic value of $0.10, and the put goes out of the money.

Currency option prices (premiums) are calculated in U.S. dollars insofar as the contract amount is denominated in the foreign currency and the exercise price is quoted in dollars per unit of the foreign currency. (When the contract amount is denominated in U.S. dollars, the exercise price is quoted in units of the foreign currency per U.S. $ and the option premiums are calculated in the foreign currency amount.) In the case of an option to buy a foreign currency (or to buy dollars against a foreign currency), the premium denotes the amount of dollars (or foreign currency) that the market is willing to pay for the right to buy the contract amount of foreign currency (or dollars) at the agreed-upon exercise price. In the case of an option to sell a foreign currency (or to sell dollars against a foreign currency), the premium denotes the amount of dollars (or foreign currency) that the market is willing to pay for the right to sell the contract amount of foreign currency (or U.S. dollars) at the agreed-upon exercise price.

Expiration Dates

The currency options are usually deliverable with maturities three, six, and nine months, with the exception of new contracts available on the Montreal Exchange which are also delivered with maturities of one and two months. The expiration months correspond to the delivery months on the financial futures exchanges, namely March, June, September, and December. Within the months of maturity, however, there are certain differences among exchanges on the exact day of expiration, as well as on the last trading day. As in the financial futures market, option traders will pay an initial margin to clear the option trade through the exchange clearing house, although only option writers are required to pay margin (the size of which varies with the type of option strategy). The higher the potential risk of the position, the higher will be the initial margin, and, if rates move against the position holder, additional margins will be required.

Trading Limits

To regulate and stabilize the trading activities on the exchanges, certain rules are established with regard to exercise price intervals, minimum change in the option quotes (tick size), and, from time to time, limits. On all the exchanges with dollar-denominated trading units, the tick size is .01 cents ($.0001), which on the Chicago Mercantile Exchange, German mark option contracts have a tick value of $12.50 (DM 125,000 × .0001 $/DM), equivalent to the tick value of the corresponding financial futures contract. The tick value indicates the minimum change in the option premium. Due to the differing contract sizes the corresponding tick value on the Philadelphia Stock Exchange German mark option is $6.25 (DM 62,500 × .0001 $/DM), and on the Montreal Exchange the old contracts had a tick value of $2.50 (DM 25,000 × .0001 $/DM).

The exceptions to the tick size of .01 cents are the pound sterling option contract with a tick size of .05 cents and the Japanese yen option contract with a tick size of .0001 cents. The tick values following the Chicago Mercantile financial futures denomination are $12.50 (£ 25,000 × .0005 $/£) and $12.50 (Y 12,500,000 × .000001 $/Y), respectively, thereby bringing about the same tick value for all contracts traded on each exchange.

On the Montreal Exchange the tick sizes on the dollar-denominated pound sterling and Canadian dollar options are unchanged, but the introduction of new trading units has changed the tick value to U.S. $ 5.00 ($50,000 × .0001) on the pound sterling contract and to U.S. $ 10.00 ($100,000 × .0001) on the Canadian dollar contract. The tick sizes on the Deutsche mark, Swiss franc, and yen options are .01 pfennig, .01 centimes, and .01 Y, respectively, corresponding to the following tick values in the foreign currencies: DM 10 (10,000,000 × 0001), Sw. Frc. 10 (100,000 × .0001), and Y 1,000 (100,000 × .01), respectively.

As in the financial futures markets, an option position can be liquidated without actual delivery of the underlying commodity by incurring an offsetting option trade. If, for instance, a call option is bought and it turns out that the option price stays very far above its theoretical value as it gets closer to maturity, the option holder may sell the call option and thereby offset the initial purchase of the option. The excess price advantage can be taken as profit before the maturity of the contract.

INTEREST OPTIONS

Dept options are quite similar to equity contracts. They differ from equities in that their values respond much more quickly to changes in interest rates. When prevailing interest rates are on the rise, new issues of debt generally have increased yields. Old debt issues with lower yields lose value in the marketplace, and their prices drop. So the value of a debt instrument varies inversely with interest rates. That is, bond prices generally go down when interest rates are up, and they rise when interest rates are down.

Interest rates also affect, of course, the prices of debt options. Specifically:

- When rates increase, the market prices of the lower- yielding underlying instruments drop, call prices go down, and put prices go up.
- When rates decrease, underlying prices advance, call prices rise, and put prices drop.

Debt options are becoming increasingly popular and new instruments continue to be developed. The debt options are often tied into an underlying futures contract. For example, the fifteen-year U.S. Treasury bond futures contract of the Chicago Board of Trade is an actively traded financial futures contract. Tied to this is a U.S. Treasury bond future option contract, which is also actively traded.

Quotes on the Treasury bond option are in $\frac{1}{32}$nds, equivalent to the tick size of the underlying Treasury bond futures contract.

Example: A quote of 1-07 indicates that the option premium is equal to $1\frac{7}{32}$ percentage points of the contract amount, that is, U.S. $ 100,000 \times \frac{39}{32} \times .01 = \$1,218.75$. The minimum change

Table 7-3. *Summary of Trading Units for Some Interest Rate Option Contracts*

Chicaco Board Options Exchange	Chicago Board of Trade	London International Financial Futures Exchange
Option Contract	*Option Contract*	*Option Contract*
US Treasury Bond (US $ 100,000)	US Treasury Bonds (US $ 100,000)	US Treasury Bonds (US $ 100,000)
—	US Treasury Notes (US $ 100,000)	—
—	—	Three-Month Eurodollar (US $ 100,000)
—	—	UK Long Gilt (£ 50,000)

in the option premium is indicated by the tick size of $\frac{1}{32}$, which is equivalent to $31.25 ($100,000 × $\frac{1}{32}$ × .01).

Other U.S. Treasury issue options are traded on the Chicago Board Options Exchange, the Chicago Mercantile Exchange and the American Exchange, and most recently the London International Financial Futures Exchange, which also offers options on the pound gilt futures contract, but at somewhat lower volumes. Similarly, the Chicago Board of Trade, in cooperation with the London International Financial Futures Exchange, is trying to establish an interchangeable Eurobond futures and options contract. U.S. Treasury issue options are quoted daily in the *Wall Street Journal*.

As of May 10, 1985 the Philadelphia Stock Exchange started trading a Eurodollar three-month deposit option contract through a subsidiary, the Philadelphia Board of Trade (PBOT). The new contract has a trading unit of U.S. dollars 1,000,000 and, as all short-term contracts, it has a reference price denominated as 100 minus the p.a. interest rate of the contract. The tick size equals one basis point (.0001) with a tick value of U.S. $ 25.00 ($1,000,000 × $\frac{3}{12}$ × .01/100).

During the fall of 1985 LiFFE introduced its first interest rate option based on the actively traded $1,000,000 three-month Eurodollar deposit futures contract (tick value of $25.00).

Treasury Issue Options

For Notes and Bonds, decimals in closing prices represent 32nds; 1.1 means 1 1/32. For Bills, decimals in closing prices represent basis points; $25 per .01

Chicago Board of Trade

T-BONDS (CBT)—$100,000; points and 64ths of 100%.

Strike	Calls—Last			Puts—Last		
Price	Mar	Jun	Sep	Mar	Jun	Sep
68	3-49	3-24	3-24	0-01	0-44	1-32
70	1-51	2-03	2-22	0-02	1-21	2-26
72	0-18	1-07	1-32	0-32	2-24	3-34
74	0-01	0-36	0-62	2-14	3-52	....
76	0-01	0-16	0-38	4-14	5-28	6-32
78	0-01	0-07	0-22	6-14	....	....

Est. vol. 45,000, Fri vol. 1,938 calls, 948 puts
Open interest Fri; 19,958 calls, 5,484 puts

Figure 7-4. Quotes on U.S. Treasury Bond Options.

Reprinted by permission of *Wall Street Journal,* Europe
© Dow Jones & Company, Inc. (April 12, 1985).

INDEX OPTIONS

The introduction of the Standard & Poors 500 Stock Index future on the Chicago Mercantile Exchange and the introduction of the NYSE Composite Index future on the New York Futures Exchange during 1982 led both the exchanges to introduce option contracts on the two stock index futures. These index options have traded at significant volumes since their introduction, whereas the Standard & Poors 100 index has been trading at decreasing volumes.

Several other index options are traded on the exchanges including other stock index options like the NYSE Double Index contract, the AMEX Major Market Index contract, and the Value Line Index option of the Kansas City Board.

In conjunction with the introduction of the FT-SE 100 index futures contract, the London International Financial Futures Exchange also offered an option on the index future. Similar ventures are presently being pursued by various national stock exchanges in, for example, Sweden, Switzerland, and Spain.

Underlying Interest

An index option differs from all others in that it has no one underlying security. Instead, the underlying interest consists of an *index*, which is a measure of the value of a group of stocks. The New York Stock Exchange and Standard & Poors, for example, publish two such indexes—the value of the index, which is expressed as a dollar figure, serves as the "price" of the underlying interest.

The value of the index is also relative. When an index is first published, it is assigned an arbitrary *base value*. For example, on the first day of recording the index, the value may be established at 100 (the base value). From that day forward, all index values are expressed in terms of the 100 base value. (Other base values can be used, of course.) If the index declines on the next day, its value will be something less than 100. Should it advance, the value will be greater than 100.

The Multiplier

The link between the index value and the option's value is the *multiplier*, which does not change. To arrive at the dollar value of either the strike price or the underlying index value, multiply it by the multiplier.

Example: The OEX Index has a multiplier (not a base value) of 100. An OEX June 95 call has a strike price (expressed as a dollar value) of $9,500 ($95 strike price times the multiplier of 100).

Settlement

Index options are unusual in that settlement consists solely of a cash payment. No securities are involved. For either a put or a call, the writer is obligated to pay the holder the intrinsic value, which is the cash difference between the strike price and the index value.

Example: With the OEX index at 89, Barnes exercises his OEX Mar 80 put, which is 9 points in the money (index value of $89 less strike price of $80 equals intrinsic value of $9). The assigned writer must pay Barnes $900 (intrinsic value of $9 times the OEX multiplier of 100).

Example: With the OEX index at 95, Barnes exercises his OEX June 90 call, which is 5 points in the money ($95 index value less $90 strike price). The assigned writer must pay Barnes $500 ($5 intrinsic value times the multiplier of 100).

Quotations

The option index quotes are represented as a multiplicand to the contract amount.

Example: The Standard & Poors 500 Stock Index option is quoted at 5.55, and the option premium is equal to $2,775 ($500 times 5.55).

The option indexes are quoted daily in the *Wall Street Journal* and the *Financial Times*, as shown in Figures 7-5 and 7-6.

Options Indexes

CHICAGO MERCANTILE EXCHANGE

S&P 500 STOCK INDEX (CME)—$500 times premium.

Strike	Calls—Settle			Puts—Settle		
Price	Mar	Jun	Sep	Mar	Jun	Sep
170	11.10	15.00	....	.30	1.40	2.20
175	6.65	11.20	14.80	.80	2.50	....
180	3.50	8.00	....	2.60	4.15	....
185	1.50	5.55	8.80	5.50	6.40	....
190	.50	3.65	6.00	....	....	....
195	....	2.35	....	....	....	....

Est. vol. 7,150; Fri vol. 2,058 calls; 3,559 puts
Open interest Fri; 23,273 calls; 14,639 puts

NEW YORK FUTURES EXCHANGE

NYSE COMPOSITE INDEX (NYFE)—$500 times premium

Strike	Calls—Settle			Puts—Settle		
Price	Mar	Jun	Sep	Mar	Jun	Sep
100	5.40	7.95	10.00	.25	1.05	1.50
102	3.75	6.50	8.60	.60	1.55	2.00
104	2.40	5.20	7.25	1.25	2.20	3.35
106	1.40	4.05	6.10	2.20	3.05	4.20
108	.75	3.10	5.05	3.50	4.05	5.25
110	.40	2.35	4.15	5.10	5.25	6.35

Est. vol. 1,323, Fri vol. 439 calls, 409 puts
Open interest Fri; 3,936 calls, 3,309 puts

CHICAGO BOARD

S&P 100 INDEX

Strike	Calls—Last			Puts—Last		
Price	Feb	Mar	Apr	Feb	Mar	Apr
150	28⅛	....	....	1/16	1/16	....
155	22⅞	23	....	....	....	⅛
160	17¾	18½	20¼	1/16	1/16	3/16
165	12¾	13⅞	15½	1/16	⅛	½
170	7¾	9¼	11¼	1/16	½	1⅛
175	3	5⅜	7½	⅜	1 11/16	2 9/16
180	⅜	2 13/16	4⅞	2 11/16	4⅛	4⅞
185	1/16	1¼	2-15/16	7½	7⅞	8¼
190	1/16	½	1 9/16	....	13½	10½

Total call volume 249,083 Total call open int. 616,375
Total put volume 145,094 Total put open int. 599,080
The index: High 180.05; Low 177.32; Close 177.70, −2.35.

Figure 7-5. *Quotes on Stock Index Option Contracts.*
Reprinted by permission of *Wall Street Journal,* Europe © Dow Jones & Company, Inc. (April 12, 1985).

A variety of stock index option contracts have been developed over the recent years, such as those based on the S&P 500, the NYSE Composite, and the FT-SE 100 stock indexes, a development that continues on a global basis. The Chicago Mercantile Exchange (CME) and the Chicago Board Options Exchange (CBOT) are looking into ways of establishing futures and options trading on an index of international securities, which should become increasingly interesting for many insitutional investors. Other types of index contracts have been established over the years. Index contracts are currently being traded in areas such as oil and gas prices and future freight rates, and various exchanges have been planning to introduce trading of a commodity price index option, to mention but a few of the innovations in the growing market for index futures and options contracts.

Chapter 8

Profitability Patterns

In Chapter 5, we saw how future foreign exchange rates and interest rates could be locked in by positioning in the appropriate financial futures contracts. Neglecting the basis risk, this means that the rates are fixed once and for all, making future financial variables certain, to the benefit of the business planner. The benefits of selling U.S. dollars against Deutsche marks at 3.6550 when the actual spot exchange rate has moved down to 3.2550 are easy to see. Not as easy to accept, however, is a locked-in exchange rate of 3.6550 when rates have moved to a level of 3.8550 DM/US$ because the upside potential of the gain is eliminated. Options, as opposed to futures contacts, close the downside risk while leaving open the upside potential for gains on favorable rate movements. This is one reason for the options markets' increasing role in hedging applications.

Another important determinant in an uncertain business environment is the fact that the decision maker often does not know if a future transaction will actually occur. To provide a committed offer the potential foreign exchange or interest rate risks should still be hedged. Under these circumstances options appear to be an ideal solution, because buyers of options can exercise the option at their choice, but are not committed to do so if the situation does not require doing so.

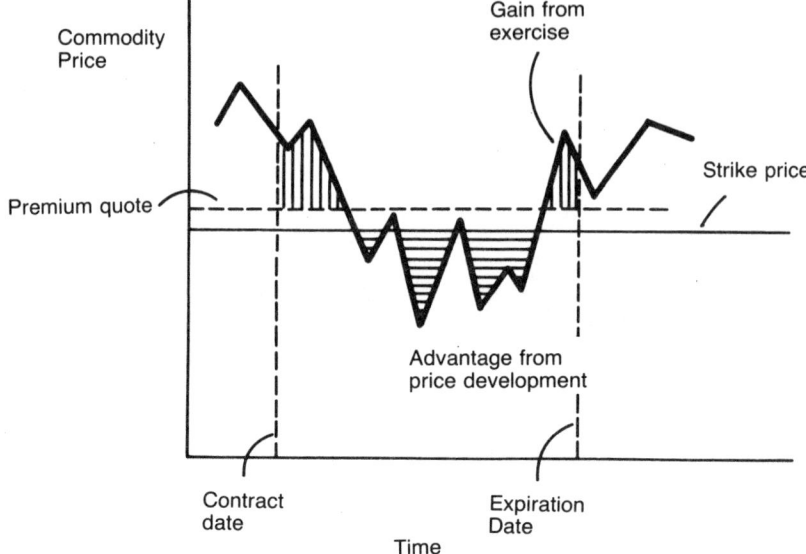

Figure 8-1. *Profitability Pattern of a Call Option.*

The profitability pattern of options is illustrated in Figure 8-1. A call option will be profitable for the holder if the market price of the underlying commodity increases above the strike price including the premium quote. If the market price drops below the strike price, the option holder will not exercise the option but will take full advantage of the favorable development in the commodity price.

A put option will be profitable if the market price of the underlying commodity falls below the strike price minus the premium quote (see Figure 8-2). If the market price increases above the strike price, the option holder will not exercise the option but will take full advantage of the favorable price development.

PROFIT AND LOSS PROFILES

A *call option* provides the holder with the right, but not the obligation, to purchase an asset at the strike (or exercise) price during a specified period. The buyer pays the premium up front

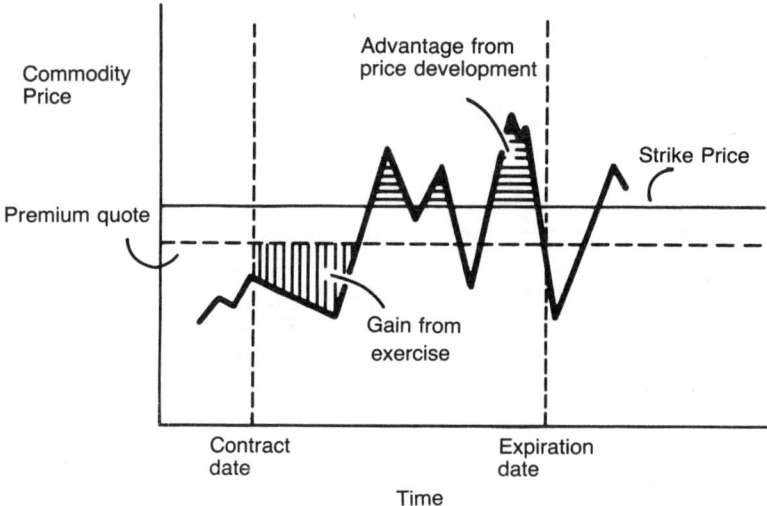

Figure 8-2. *Profitability Pattern of a Put Option.*

for that right. Conversely, the seller (or writer) of a call option is obliged to sell the asset to the holder against receipt of the up-front premium. Figure 8-3 provides a graphic presentation of the profit and loss profiles for the buyer's and seller's positions in a call option contract.

A *put option* provides the holder with the right, but not a obligation, to sell an asset at the exercise price during a specified

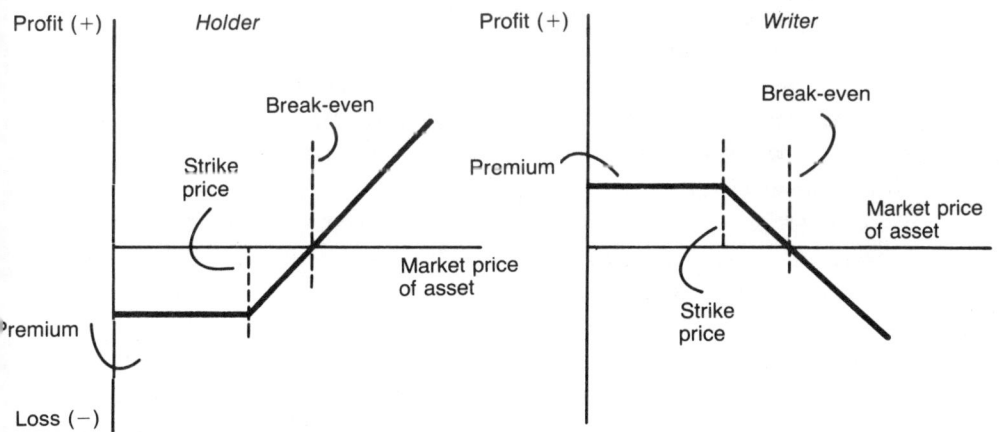

Figure 8-3. *Profit and Loss Profiles: Call.*

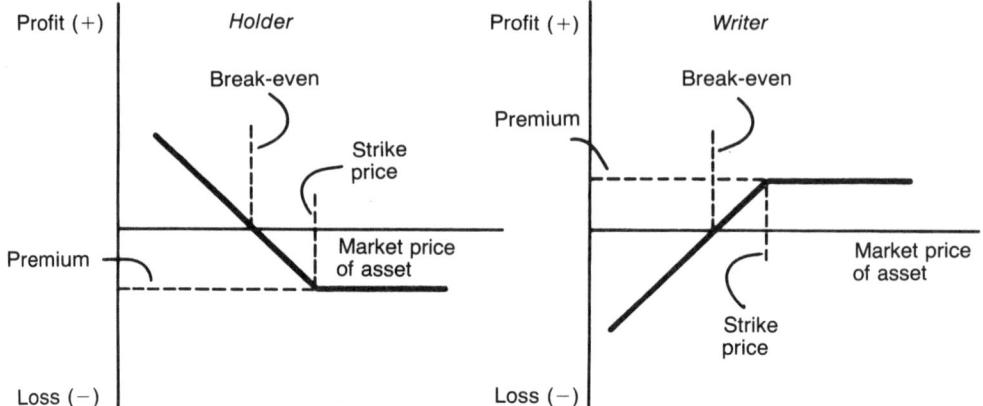

Figure 8-4. *Profit and Loss Profiles: Put.*

period. The option buyer pays the premium up front. Conversely, the put option writer is obliged to buy the asset from the holder against receipt of the premium up front (see Figure 8-4).

As shown in Chapter 6, the *intrinsic value* of the option is determined solely by the current market price of the underlying asset and the strike price of the option contract. The *time value* is a function of several factors, with time to maturity playing a major role: the shorter the time to maturity, the smaller the time value. At the expiration date the time value is zero and the option premium is equal only to the intrinsic value. The time value of the option is at its maximum value when the market price of the asset is close to the strike price.

An option may be "at," "out of," or "in" the money. An option is deemed *at the money* when the current market price of the asset equals the strike price of the contract. A call option whose strike price is above the current market price of the underlying asset is *out of the money*, as is a put option whose exercise price is below the current market price of the asset. There is no benefit for the option holder in exercising the option because the intrinsic value is zero. A call option whose strike price is below the current market price of the underlying asset is *in the money*, as is a put option whose strike price is above the going market price of the asset. Exercising the option is

Table 8-1

At the Money	Time value is at maximum. Strike price = Market price
Out of the Money	Intrinsic value is zero. Call: Strike price > Market price Put: Strike price < Market price
In the Money	Intrinsic value is positive. Call: Strike price < Market price Put: Strike price > Market price

beneficial to the holder since the intrinsic value is positive (see Table 8-1).

Whether an option is in, at, or out of the money at the time of purchase influences the profit and loss profile of an option. If the strike price of a call is lower than the current market price of the underlying asset, the contract is in the money, and the option premium will be high: It is beneficial to exercise the option right away. If the strike price is higher than the current market price, the call is out of the money, the intrinsic value is zero, and the option premium is relatively low. Variations in the size of the option premium will have a corresponding impact on the option holder's break-even points, as shown in Figure 8-5. The higher the call option premium is, the lower will be the market price before the option is beneficial to the holder.[1]

When writing a call option, one must determine which strike price to choose for a given market price of the underlying commodity. The choice of options with different strike prices is illustrated in Figure 8-6. When the strike price is higher than the current market price, the option premium will be low. And when the strike price is lower than the current market price, the option premium will increase in value as the option's intrinsic value increases.

As the graph makes apparent, the higher the strike price (S_3 > M), the higher will be the break-even point, while the option premium gets lower (P_3). Reducing the strike price (S_2

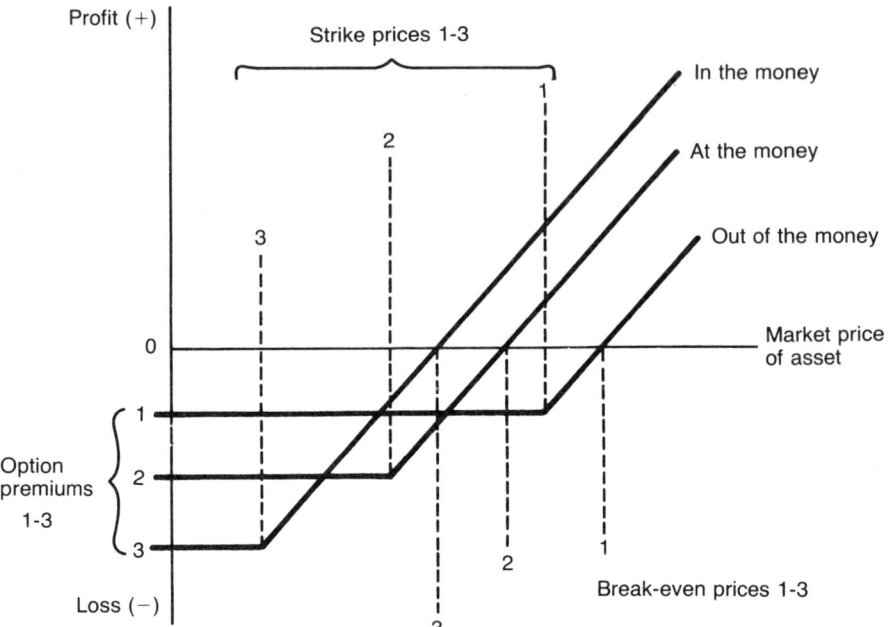

Figure 8-5. *Profit and Loss Profile of a Call Option.*

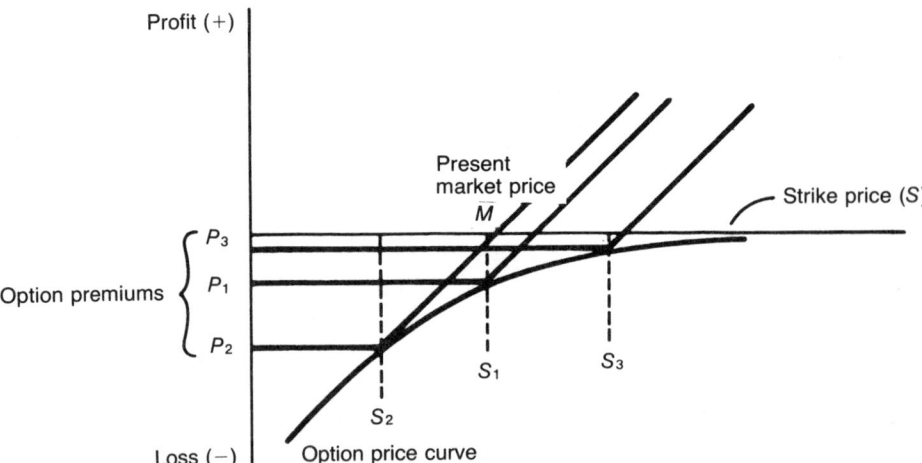

Figure 8-6. *Break-Even Points for a Call Option at Different Strike Prices.*

‹ *M*) reduces the break- even point, but it can never get lower than the actual market value of the commodity. At the same time the option premium increases (*P₂*). Hence for a given market price:

1. The maximum break-even point is infinitely high, for which an infinitely small premium is paid.
2. The minimum break-even point is the current market price, for which an infinitely large premium can be paid.

Assuming that the future market price moves at random, we can conclude from this that choosing too low a strike price will become far too expensive, and choosing too high a strike price hardly has any benefits if the premium is very low.

A similar set of circumstances applies to a put option, whose choice of a strike price is represented in Figure 8-7. If the strike price is lower than the current market price the option premium is low, and when the strike price exceeds the current market price the option premium increases corresponding to the increased intrinsic value of the put option.

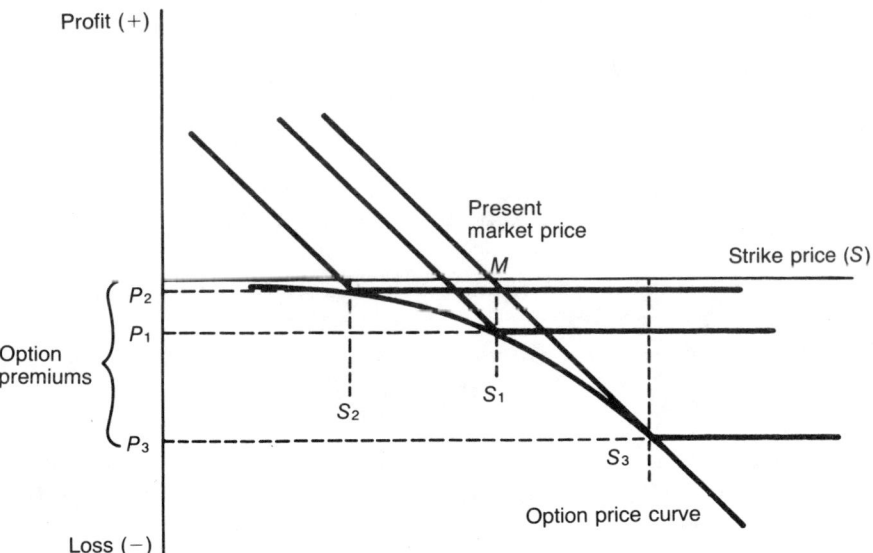

Figure 8-7. *Break-Even Points for a Put Option with Different Strike Prices.*

As is apparent, the lower the strike price is, the lower will be the break-even point, and the option premium will decrease at the same time. By increasing the strike price ($S_3 > M$), the break-even point is increased, but it can never exceed the current market price; however, the option premium increase (P_3). Hence for a given market price:

1. The minimum break-even point is infinitely low, for which an infinitely small premium is paid.
2. The maximum break-even point is the current market price, for which an infinitely large premium can be paid.

Therefore, assuming that the future market price moves at random, it would be optimal to choose a strike price slightly below the current market price.

As a general rule the optimum strike price to chose for an option buyer is a slightly out-of-the-money option, because the premium is relatively low and the upside potential for gain is high. If a highly in-the-money option is chosen, the premium will be relatively high, due to the high intrinsic value of the option and the relatively limited upside potential for a gain.

DELTA

The *delta* (or hedge-ratio) of an option indicates the amount by which the option premium changes when the market price of the underlying asset moves by one point.

The delta is not a constant but changes continuously as the market price of the asset changes. The graph showing the call option premium as a function of the market price of the underlying asset in Figure 8-8 illustrates that the delta factor is equivalent to the slope of the tangent to the option price curve. As shown in the figure, the delta factor is defined as the differential coefficient of the option price curve [$g\,(\cdot)$], with respect to the market price of the asset (P). The delta factor of an option at the money (2) is close to .5. The more the option gets in the money (3), the closer the delta factor gets to 1, showing that

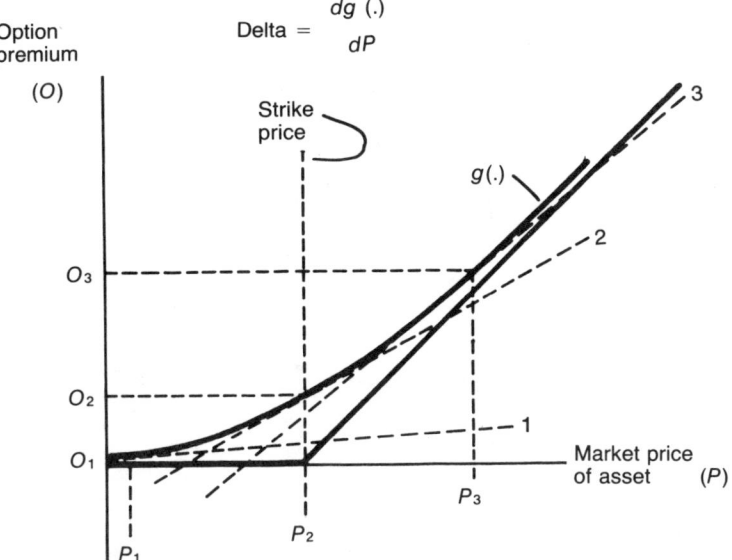

Figure 8-8. *Call Option Premium and Delta Factor.*

the option premium curve approximates the intrinsic value line. The further out of the money (1) the option is, the closer the delta factor gets to zero.

If we apply the previously discussed Black-Scholes call option pricing model (discussed in Chapter 6) to describe the option price curve [$g(\cdot)$], the delta factor is determined by one of the arguments of the formula:[2]

If, $\quad g(\cdot) \quad = \quad P \cdot N(x_1) - (e^{-f \cdot T}) \cdot E \cdot N(x_2)$ (Black-Scholes)

where, $x_1 \quad = \quad \ln(P/F) + (r_g + s^2/2) \cdot T)) / (s \cdot T)$

then, Delta $\quad = \quad N(x_1)$

This provides us with a formula to calculate the theoretical delta values.

The delta factor provides us with analytical information on the shape of the option premium curve, and it can prove useful when determining the optimal option choice.

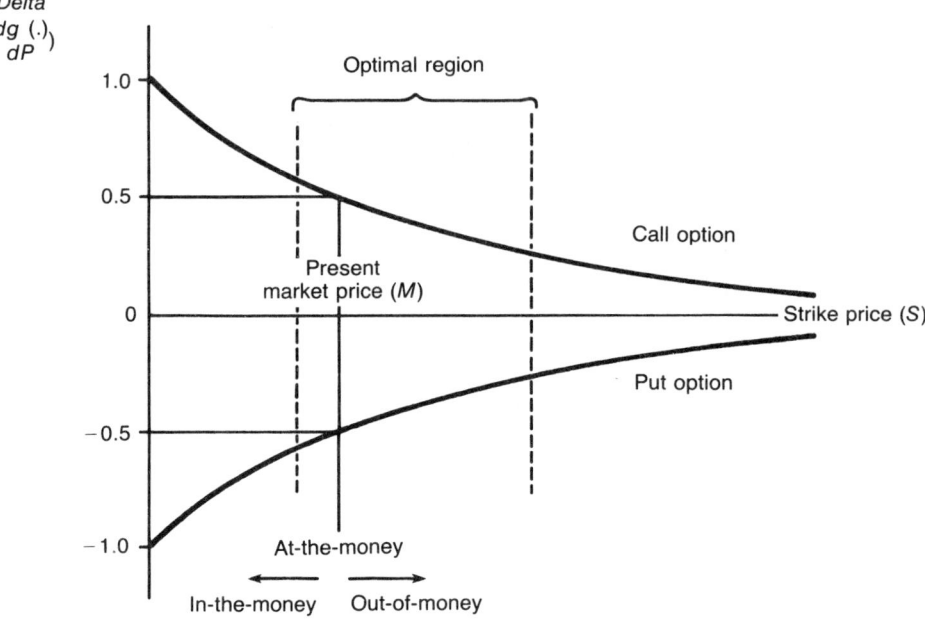

Figure 8-9. *Changing Delta Values for a Call and a Put Option at a Given Market Price.*

The changing delta values for a call and a put option at a given market price is illustrated graphically in Figure 8-9.

For a given market price, the delta of a *call option* would be close to 1 when the strike price is much lower than the market price (in the money) because the option price curve will be close to the intrinsic value of the call option. When the strike price is equal to the market price, then the delta will be close to 0.5 and will converge toward zero as the strike price increases over the market price (out of the money).

For a given market price, the delta of a put option would be close to –1 when the strike price is much higher than the market price (in the money) because the option price curve will be close to the intrinsic value of the put option. When the strike price is equal to the current market price (at the money), then the delta is close to –0.5 and will converge toward zero as the strike price falls below the market price (out of the money).

If the optimum option contract is the slightly out-of-the-money contract, then the delta value of the call option is slightly below 0.5 and the delta value of put option is slightly above –0.5 in the optimal region.

Chapter **9**

Hedging with Option Contracts

HEDGING A SHORT CURRENCY POSITION

Let's start with an example.

Example: A U.S.-based company is negotiating an important contract in May to be executed within two months and is therefore committed to give a firm pricing offer immediately. To meet the deadline on the offer, machinery worth 1,000,000 Swiss francs must be imported from a Swiss manufacturer to be on the spot in the U.S. during the month of October. The Swiss manufacturer has promised to ship the machinery in September against cash payment.

To hedge the potential payment of Sw. frc. 1,000,000 in September, the U.S. company can buy Swiss franc call options up to the contract amount of Sw. Frcs. 1,000,000. Assuming that the company approaches the Philadelphia Stock Exchange to buy the options, it would purchase 16 call option contracts of Sw. frcs. 62,500 each.

On this day in May, the Swiss franc foreign exchange rate is quoted at 2.0513 Sw. frc./US$ (0.4875 US$/Sw. frc.). In the present situation the company wants to hedge against a potential strengthening of the franc, which would cause them to pay more U.S. dollars for the import in September. The September call options are quoted as follows:

Strike Price ($/Sw. frc.)	Quote ($/Sw. frc.)	Call Premium
0.4800	0.0248	$1,550 (in the money)
*0.5000	0.0151	$ 943.50 (out of the money)

The company decides to buy the out-of-the-money call option because it is close to being at the money and the front-end call premium is considerably lower than that of the in-the-money contract. Hence for the purchase of 16 Swiss franc (50) call option contracts, the company will pay up front US$ 15,100 (16 × 943.75).[1]

The U.S. company wins the bid for the project and orders the machine from the Swiss manufacturer. In the coming period the expectation of a strengthening franc in general has proven correct, but there has been some exchange rate volatility. To assess the potential gain and loss position, calculations are made to get a feel for the sensitivity to the exchange rate movements:

Exchange Rate (US$/Sw. frc.)	Profit/(Loss)
0.4800	$(15,100)
0.4900	$(15,100)
0.5000	$(15,100)
0.5100	$(5,100)
0.5200	$ 4,900
0.5300	$ 14,000
0.5400	$ 24,900
0.5500	$ 34,900

In view of the fact that a change from the present exchange rate of .4875 US$/Sw. frc. to the break-even rate of 0.5150 constitutes only a 5% change in the foreign exchange rate, the premium of US$ 15,100 is considered reasonable by the company. The profit and loss profile is presented graphically in Figure 9-1.

The short Swiss franc position could also have been covered by the sale of 16 Swiss franc put options, which would incur a

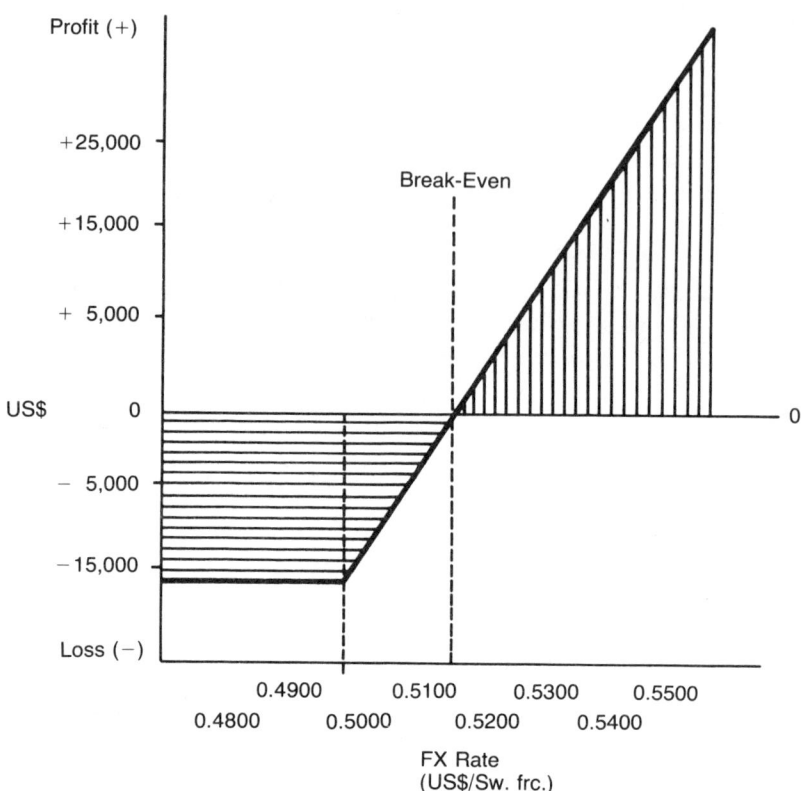

Figure 9-1. *Profit and Loss Profile of 16 Sw. Frc. (50) Call Options.*

front-end premium to the company as a writer. However, this does not constitute a perfect hedge, because the option to sell francs to the writer lies solely with the holder of the put option, and if the exchange rate moves against the put option writer the potential loss can be excessively high.

HEDGING A LONG CURRENCY POSITION

Example: During August a German company is bidding for delivery of equipment in December to a U.S.-based manufacturing company. The value of the equipment amounts to US$ 2,000,000 to be received upon delivery of the equipment. Because the exporting company will have receivables in U.S. dollars, the worry is that the dollar will weaken against the German mark, because such a development will reduce the export earnings measured in the domestic currency.

To hedge the potential receivables of US $ 2,000,000 in December, the German company can buy U.S. dollar put options against German marks up to the contract amount of US$ 2,000,000. This kind of put option provides the holder with the right to sell U.S. dollars against German marks at a predetermined exchange rate. This is equivalent to holding a mark call option against U.S. dollars, since it provides the holder with the right to buy DM against US$ at a predetermined foreign exchange rate.

> A **call** option of currency (x) against currency (y) is equivalent to a **(put)** option of currency (y) against currency (x).

So the German exporter approaches the Philadelphia Stock Exchange to buy the option contracts. On this exchange the mark option contracts have a denomination of DM 62,500 each. Given that the foreign exchange rate in August was around 3.2669 DM/US$ (0.3061 US$/DM), we see that the number of DM call options to purchase to hedge the full contract amount of US$ 2,000,000 is 104.5 [($2,000,000 / 0.3061) / 62,500]. Hence 105 DM call option contracts are bought on the exchange.

Suppose the December call options are quoted as follows:

Strike Price	Quote (¢/DM)	Call Premium	
0.3000	1.34	$837.50	(in the money)
0.3100	0.86	$537.50	(at the money)
*0.3200	0.46	$287.50	(out of the money)
0.3300	0.26	$162.50	(out of the money)
0.3400	0.13	$ 81.25	(out of the money)

The company decides to buy the out-of-the-money call option with strike price 32. Hence for the purchase of 105 DM (32) call option contracts, the company will pay up front US$ 30,187.50 (105 × 287.5) or DM 98,619.73 (30,187.50/.3061). To assess the option position the company carries out a profit and loss analysis reflecting the consequences of different developments in the foreign exchange rate:

Exchange Rate (US$/DM)	Profit/(Loss)
0.3200	DM (98,619.73)
0.3300	DM (90,774.27)
0.3400	DM 269,027.33
0.3500	DM 437,094.56
0.3600	DM 595,824.71

The exchange rate sensitivity analysis is presented graphically in the profit and loss profile in Figure 9-2. As shown there, the profit and loss profile of the call options this time does not follow a completely straight line. This relates to the fact that the dollar gain when converted into marks is impacted by the increasing US$/DM exchange rate. To get the profit and loss

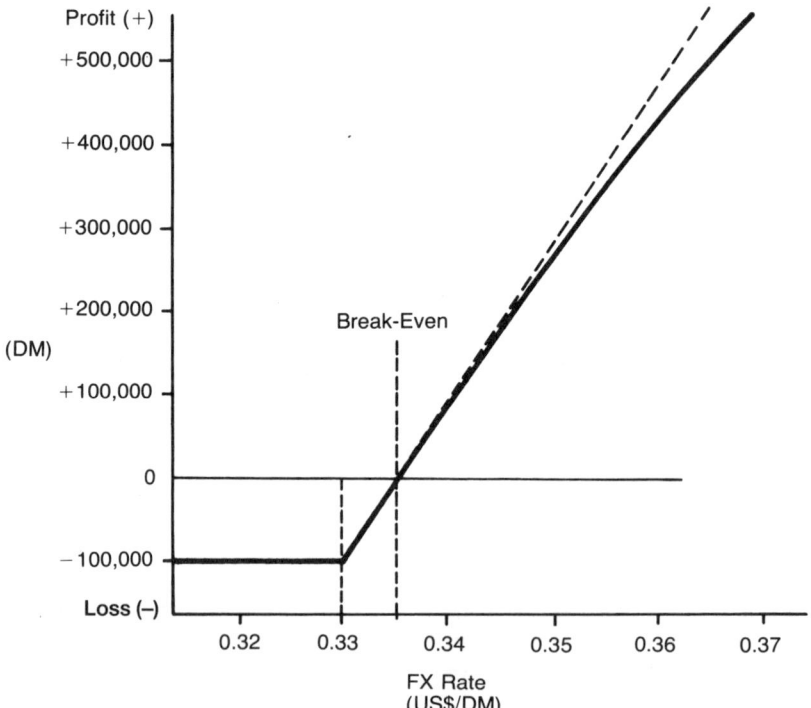

Figure 9-2. *Profit and Loss Profile of 105 DM (33) Call Options.*

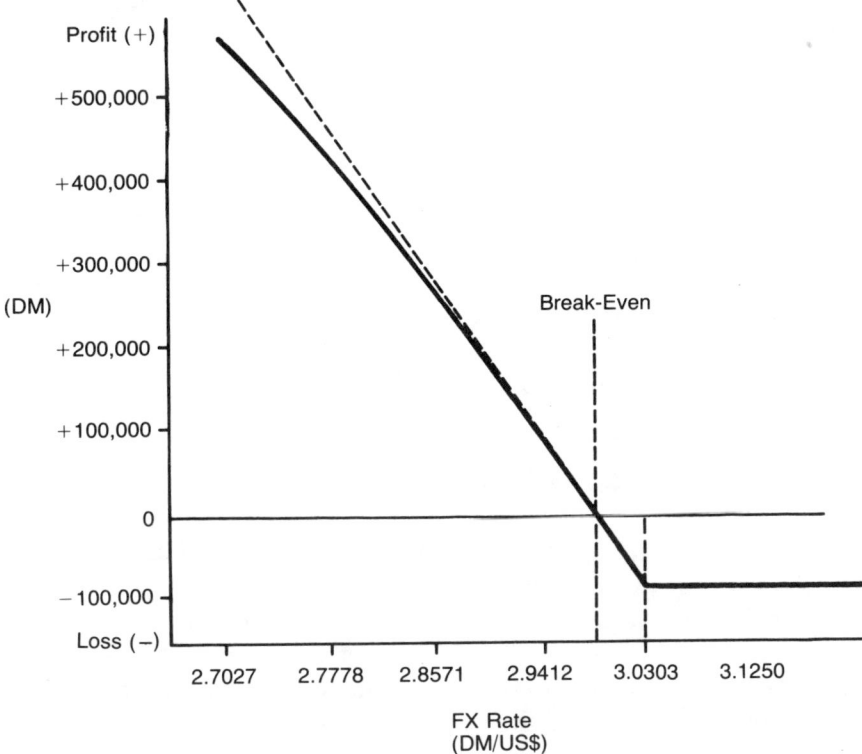

Figure 9-3. *Profit and Loss Profile of 105 DM (3.03) Put Options.*

profile of the put options, we simply revert the foreign exchange rate denomination from US$/DM to DM/US$ as marked along the horizontal axis in Figure 9-2. (See Figure 9-3.)

The long U.S. dollar position could also be covered by writing 105 dollar call options against receipt of a front-end option premium. Since the option to exercise lies solely with the holder of the call option, writing DM put options represents an imperfect hedge, whose analysis will not be pursued further here.

Another route to follow would be to approach the Montreal Exchange, which trades the Deutsche mark currency options in amounts of US$ 100,000 and which therefore follows the quotation of the interbank foreign exchange market. In this case the German exporter would buy 10 ($2,000,000/$100,000) U.S.

dollar put option contracts against DM. The following option quotes on the December contract were prevailing on the Montreal Exchange in August.

Strike Price	Quote (DM/$)	Put Premium	
3.225	.0922	DM 9,220	(at the money)
3.125	.0493	DM 4,930	(out of the money)
3.030	.0278	DM 2,780	(out of the money)

The German exporter would pay the put premium in German marks in an amount similar to that payable at the Philadelphia Stock Exchange (4,930 · .3061 · 20 = US$ 30,181.46) in order to obtain an equivalent hedge.

CROSS CURRENCY HEDGE

Example: A French company is exporting goods to a UK- based sales company. Receivables of £ Stg. 1,500,000 are expected in six months. To hedge the French franc value of the future pound sterling receivables, the French exporter would like to buy pound put options against French francs in an amount equivalent to the face value of the export order.

Because no option exchange market exists for pounds sterling against French francs, the French exporter must follow another route — namely, buying pound put options against U.S. dollars—for example,on the Philadelphia Stock Exchange—and at the same time buying franc call options against U.S. dollars. Thus the exporter (the option holder) has the right to sell pound sterling against U.S. dollars at a predetermined exchange rate, and concurrently maintains the right to buy French francs against U.S. dollars at a predetermined rate.

The six-month pound sterling put option is quoted as follows:

Strike Price (U.S.$/£ Stg.)	Quote (¢/£ Stg.)	Put Premium
*1.05	2.20	$ 275
1.10	4.30	$ 537.50
1.15	7.40	$ 925
1.20	12.00	$1,500

FX Rate: 1.0971 US$/£ Stg.

The six-month French franc call option is quoted as follows:

Strike Price (\$/Fr. frc.)	Quote (¢/Fr. Frc.)	Call Premium
*0.105	0.50	\$625

FX Rate: 0.1063 US\$/Fr. frc.

The French exporter decides to purchase *120* £ Stg. (105) put options (1,500,000 / 12,500) and to buy *120* French franc (0.105) call options [(1,500,000 × 1.05) / 0.105] /125,000). This should correspond to the purchase of 120 pound sterling put options against French francs with a strike price of 10.0 Fr. Frc./£ Stg. at a per-contract premium of U.S.\$ 900 (\$275 + \$625), that is, a total up-front premium of U.S.\$ 108,000 (Fr. Frc. 1,015,992.47).

A profit and loss analysis on the 120 £ Sterling put options was carried out:

Exchange Rate (Fr. Frc./£ Stg.)	Profit/(Loss) in Fr. Frcs.
8.00	1,984,007.53
8.50	1,234,007.53
9.00	484,007.53
9.50	(265,992.47)
10.00	(1,015,992.47)
10.50	(1,015,992.47)

FX Rate: 10.32 Fr. Frc./£ Stg. (1.0971/0.1063)

Due to the double front-end premium to be paid on the pound sterling put options and the French franc call options, this type of hedge is expensive. This expense is also reflected in the low break-even exchange rate, which corresponds to a change in the Fr. frc./£ Stg. exchange rate of around 10%.

Keep in mind, however, that the Fr. Frc./£ Stg. exchange rate can represent a whole scenario of foreign exchange rate movements of franc and pound against the U.S. dollar. Since there is no obligation to exercise both options simultaneously, various scenarios will provide a better profit and loss profile than presented. The calculations here assume that the \$/£ Stg. and the \$/Fr. Frc. change simultaneously in opposite directions and thus represent the "worst" exchange rate scenario. In actuality, the hedge is somewhat more complicated to analyze be-

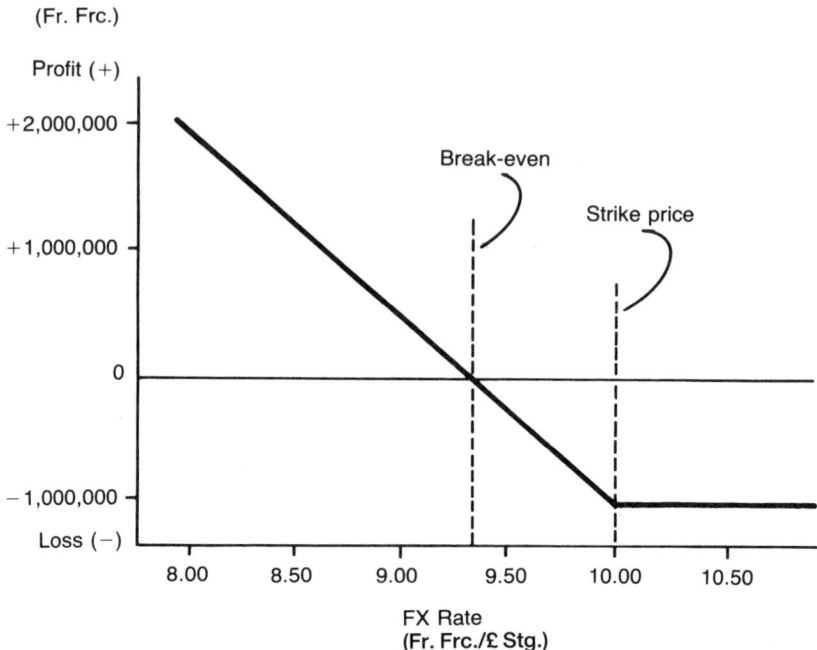

Figure 9-4. *Profit and Loss Profile of 120 Pound Stg. Put Options Against Fr. Frc.*

cause each of the two currency options should be looked upon independently and then analyzed vis-a-vis all the possible future cross currency foreign exchange rate scenarios.

    Looking first at the pound option, the purchase of 120 pound 12,500 put option contracts requires an initial premium of U.S. £ 33,000 (120 × $275). The corresponding profit and loss analysis for different foreign exchange rate developments is as follows.

Exchange Rate (U.S.dollar/£ Stg.)	Profit/Loss
1.05	(33,000)
1.00	42,000
.95	117,000
.90	192,000
.85	267,000

FX rate: 1.0971 U.S. $/£ Stg.

Turning to the French franc option, the purchase of 120 Fr. Franc 125,000 call options contracts results in an initial premium of U.S.$ 75,000 (120 × $625). The profit and loss analysis for different future foreign exchange rates is as follows.

Exchange Rate (U.S. dollar/Fr. Frc.)	*Profit/Loss*
.105	(75,000)
.110	0
.115	75,000
.120	150,000
.125	225,000

FX rate: 0.1063 U.S.$/Fr. Frc.

The two options' profit and loss profiles are illustrated in Figures 9-5 and 9-6. The combination of the two profiles are presented in Figure 9-7, with the cross currency exchange rate corresponding to 10.00 Fr. Frc./£ Stg.

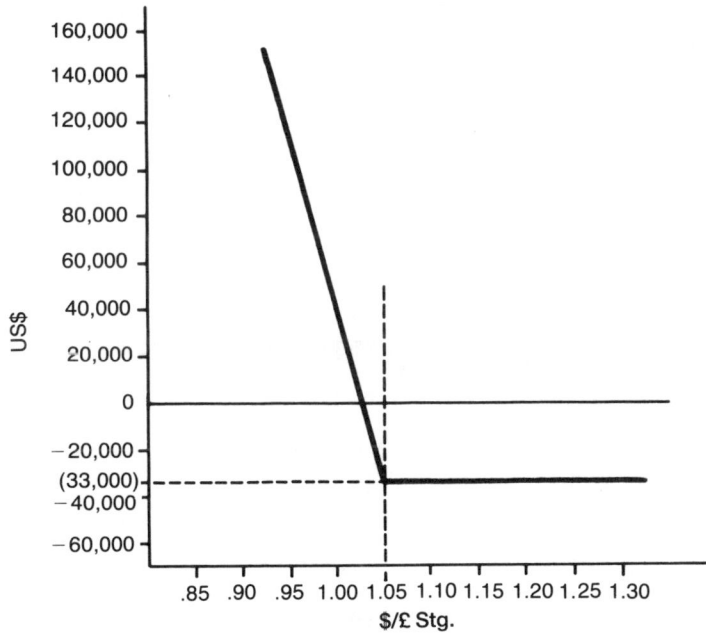

Figure 9-5. *Profit and Loss Profile of 120 Pound Stg. Put Options.*

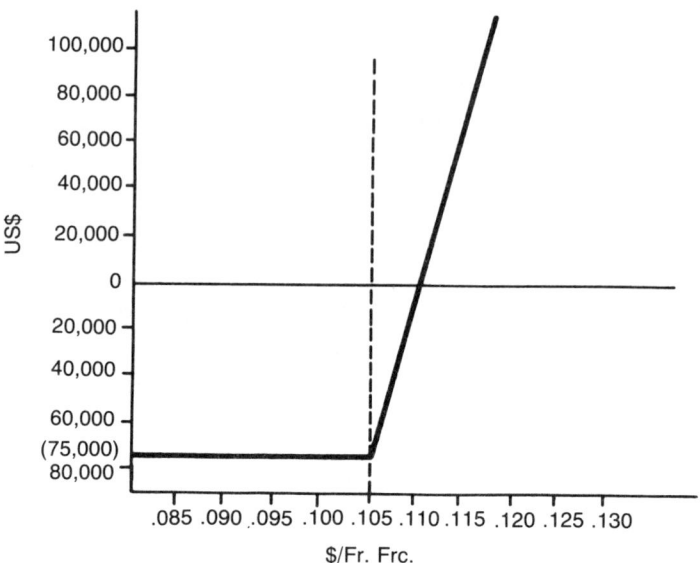

Figure 9-6. Profit and Loss Profile of 120 Fr. Franc Call Options.

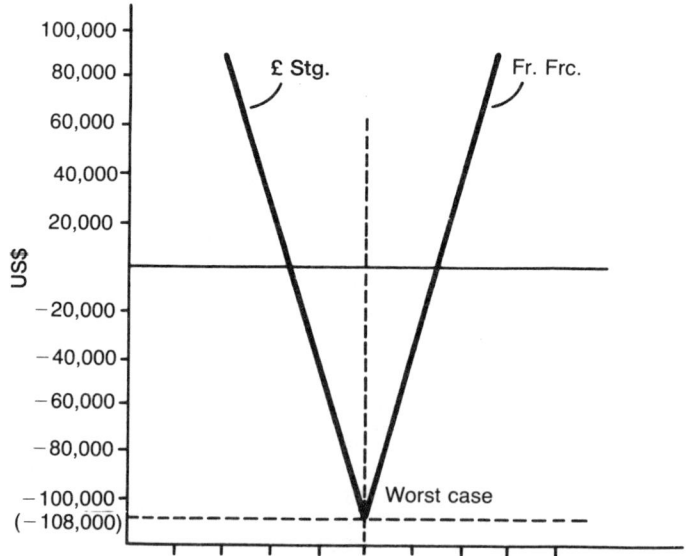

Figure 9-7. Combination of the Two Profiles—Cross Currency Exchange Rate 10.00 Fr. Frc./Pound Stg.

The next step would be to analyze the potential Fr. Frc./£ Stg. foreign exchange rate development. What is interesting is to look at the locked-in foreign exchange rate of 10.00 Fr. Frc./£ Stg. (made up of the combined strike prices of the pound put option and the franc call option) and potential deviations from this exchange rate, whether resulting in a higher or a lower rate.

To simplify further analysis, let x represent the US \$/£ Stg. exchange rate and y, the US \$/Fr. Frc. rate. At the combined strike price, the relationship could be expressed in as simple a manner as follows:

$x / y = 10$

or

$y = 1/10 \times x$

In a graphical form, this relationship appears as shown in Figure 9-8. All combinations of the US \$/£ Stg. and the US \$/Fr. Frc. rates that correspond to a cross currency rate of Fr. Frc./£ Stg. of 10.00 are contained on the straight line. Exchange rate combinations leading to a cross currency rate in excess of 10.00 Fr. Frc./£ Stg. are contained above the straight line, and exchange rate combinations leading to a cross currency rate below 10.00 Fr. Frc./£ Stg. are contained below the straight line.

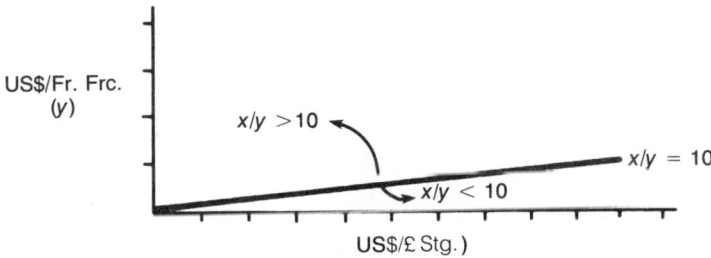

Figure 9-8

The various foreign exchange rate scenarios can then be listed as follows:

I. Fr. Frc/£ Stg. = 10.00	Profit and loss profile illustrated by the combined profit and loss profiles of the	

US$/£ Stg. put options and the US$/Fr. Frc.
call options. The "worst case" is the com
bined premium payout of US$ 108,000.

II. Fr. Frc./£ Stg. > 10.00

1. $/£ Stg. increases and $/Fr. Frc. decreases,
   flat cost line of US$ 108,000.

2. $/£ Stg. increases faster than $/Fr. Frc.
   profit curve will follow
   $/Fr. Frc. profit profile.

3. $/Fr. Frc. decreases faster than $/£ Stg. profit
   curve will follow the $/£ Stg. profile.

III. Fr. Frc./£ Stg. < 10.00

1. $/£ Stg. decreases and $/Fr. Frc. increases,
   combined gains of $/£ Stg. and $/Fr. Frc. profit
   profiles.

2. $/£ Stg. decreases faster than $/Fr. Frc., gain
   will follow $/£ Stg. profit profile.

3. $/Fr. Frc. increases faster than $/£ Stg., gain
   will follow $/Fr. Frc. profit profile.

This listing illustrates the complexity of cross currency hedging using traditional currency options against U.S. dollars. It also explains why it is an advantage to develop cross currency option contracts like the newly introduced £/Hfl. option contract on the European Options Exchange in Amsterdam, a development likely to be enforced for major cross currencies in the future.

Double Option Strategies

Before demonstrating the use of double option strategies for hedging, let us take a closer look at the "brokers' language" for various types of hedging strategies.

- A *bullish* option strategy is based on the expectation of an increase in the price of the underlying commodity.
- Conversely, a *bearish* option strategy assumes a decrease in the price of the underlying commodity.
- In a *vertical* option strategy, the option contracts have the same expiration dates but differing strike prices.

● Conversely, in a *horizontal* option strategy (often termed a *calendar spread*) the option contracts have the same strike price but differing expiration dates. Hereby the option trader can take advantage of the time development of the option premium and the price of the underlying commodity.

Vertical Bull Spread. This kind of spread can be established to hedge a *short* position in the underlying commodity. In the single option strategy, a short exposure is hedged by buying a call option. If an increase in the price of the underlying commodity is expected (a bullish market), the likelihood that a put with a lower strike price will be exercised is relatively low. So the hedger concurrently writes a put option against receipt of the option premium. The profit and loss profile of a vertical bull spread—that is, the combination of profiles of the put option and the call option—is illustrated in Figure 9-9.

A vertical bear spread can be established to hedge a *long* exposure of the underlying commodity. In the single option strategy, a long exposure is hedged by buying a put option. However, since expectations point to a decrease in the price of the underlying commodity (a bearish market), the likelihood that a put option with a higher strike price will be exercised is limited. So the hedger concurrently writes a call option against

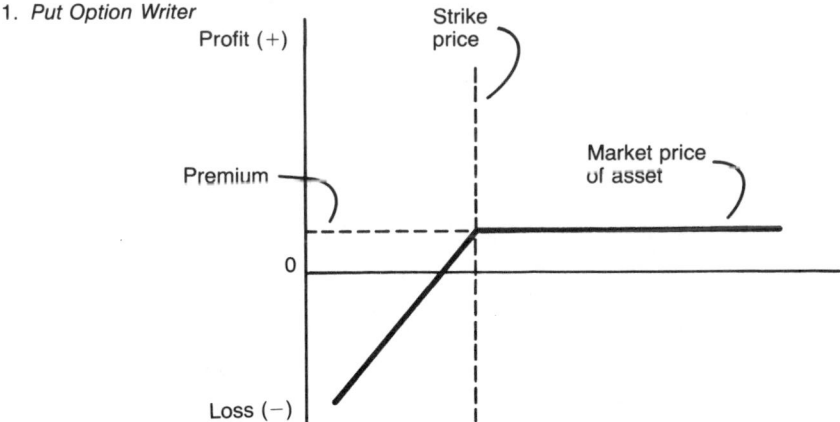

Figure 9-9. *The Profit and Loss Profile of a Vertical Bull Spread.*

2. *Holder of Call Option*

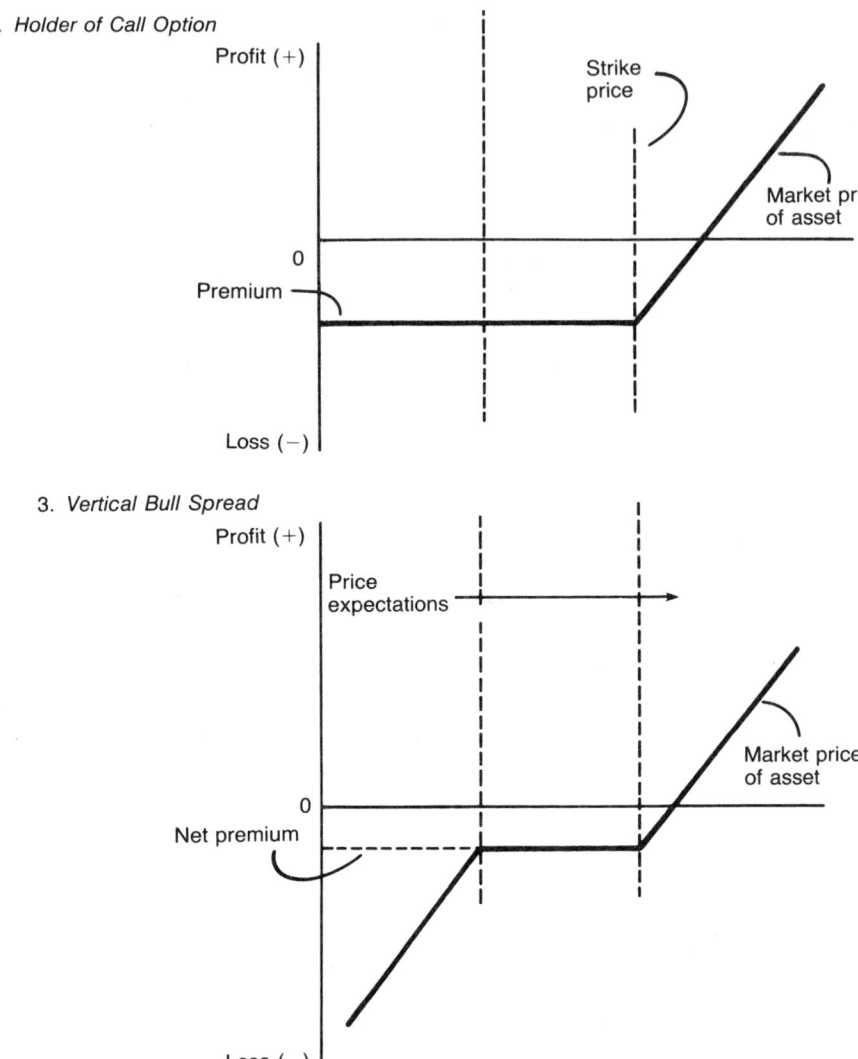

3. *Vertical Bull Spread*

Figure 9-9 *(cont.)*

receipt of the option premium. The profit and loss profile of a vertical bear spread can be illustrated graphically by combining the profit and loss profiles of the put and call options. (See Figure 9-10.)

1. *Holder of a Put Option*

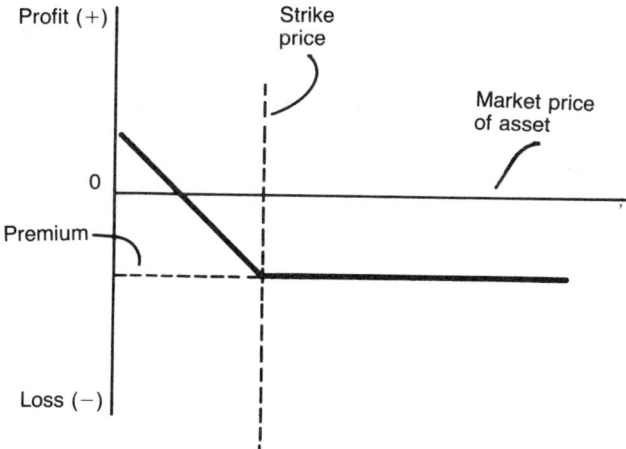

2. *Call Option Writer*

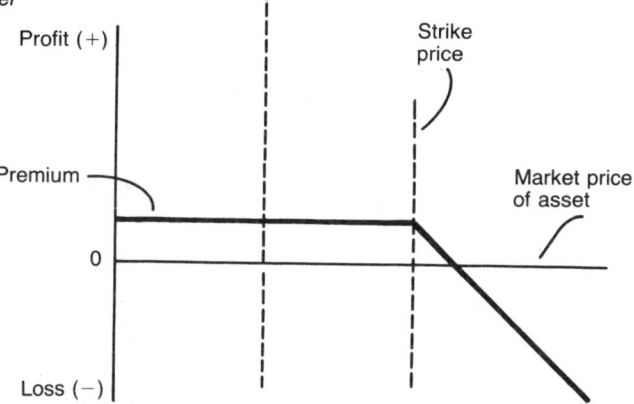

3. *Vertical Bear Spread*

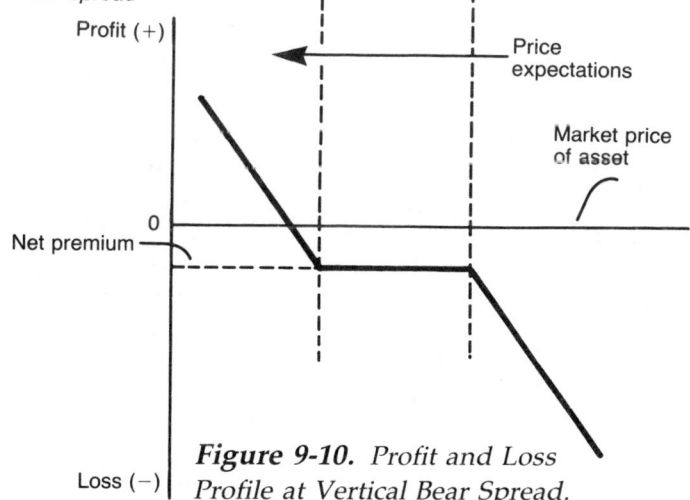

Figure 9-10. *Profit and Loss Profile at Vertical Bear Spread.*

173

Table 9-1 *Option Hedging Strategies.*

Single Option Strategies:

- Long Position   Buy put option, or sell
                                         call option.
- Short Position   Buy call option, or sell
                                         put option.

Double Option Strategies:

- Long Position   Buy put option and write
                                         a call (put strike price
                                         ‹ call strike price).

- Short Position   Buy call option and write
                                         a put (call strike price
                                         › put strike price).

The hedging strategies discussed so far are summarized in Table 9-1.

Straddle. A *straddle* position is established by buying a call option and a put option with the same strike prices. This option position gives the holder the right to buy the underlying commodity at a predetermined price, which is an advantage if the commodity's price escalates. Simultaneously the holder has the right to sell the commodity at a predetermined price, which is an advantage if the commodity's price collapses. Hence buying a straddle position will be advantageous when the price development is very volatile but with no distinct trend. The profit and loss profile of the straddle position, shown in Figure 9-11, is obtained by combining the profit and loss profiles of the call and put options.

Strangle. A *strangle* position is similar to the straddle position in that it entails the simultaneous purchase of a call and a put option, but the two options have *different* strike prices. The two option contracts would be bought at out-of-the-money strike prices to reduce the double premium cost, so that the strike price of the put option will be less than the strike price of the call option. The profit and loss profile of a strangle position is shown in Figure 9-12.

1. *Holder of a Call Option*

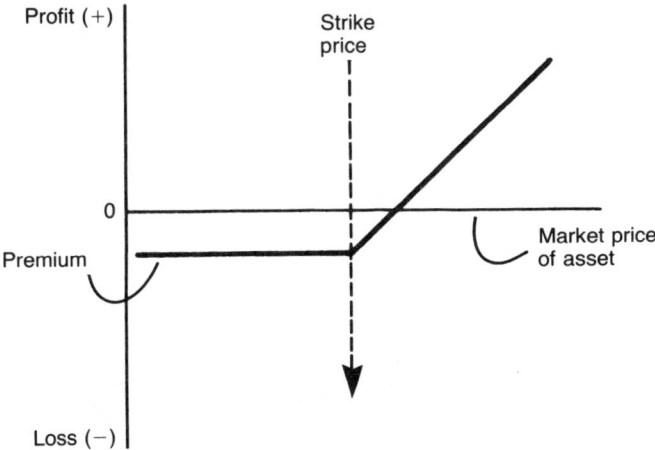

2. *Holder of Put Option*

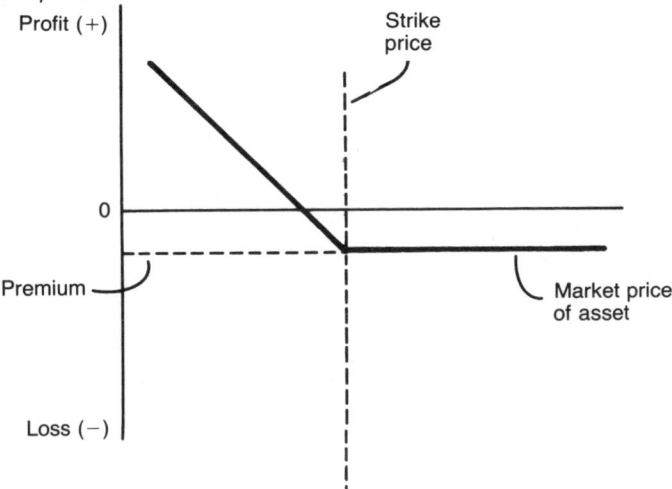

3. *Holder of Straddle*

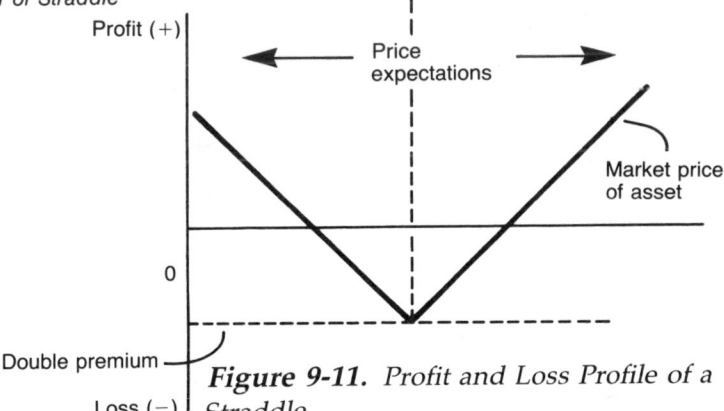

Figure 9-11. *Profit and Loss Profile of a Straddle.*

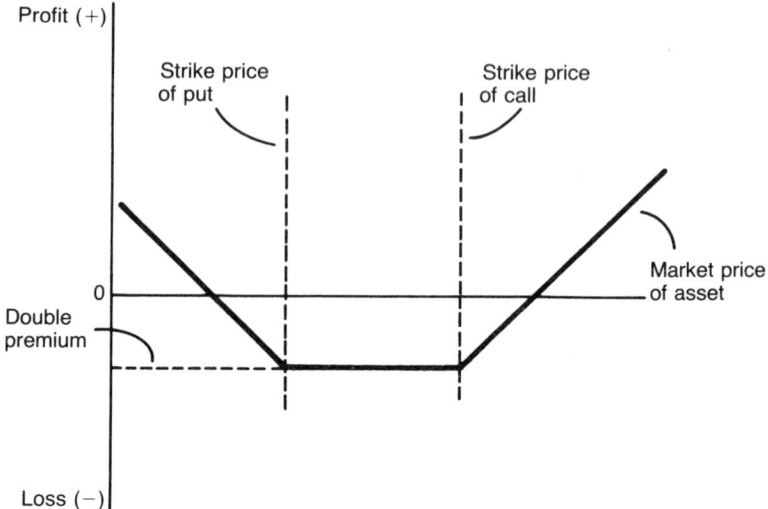

Figure 9-12. *Profit and Loss Profile of a Strangle.*

Butterfly. A *butterfly spread* position entails three strike prices. It is a combination of a bull spread and a bear spread, in which the bull spread utilizes the lower two strike prices and the bear spread utilizes the two higher strike prices. With the bull and the bear spreads created as discussed, Figure 9-13 presents the

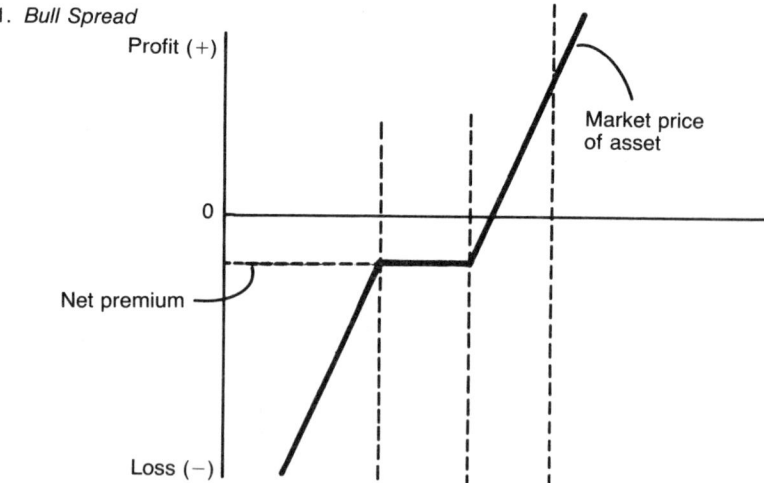

Figure 9-13. *Profit and Loss Profile of a Butterfly Spread.*

2. *Bear Spread*

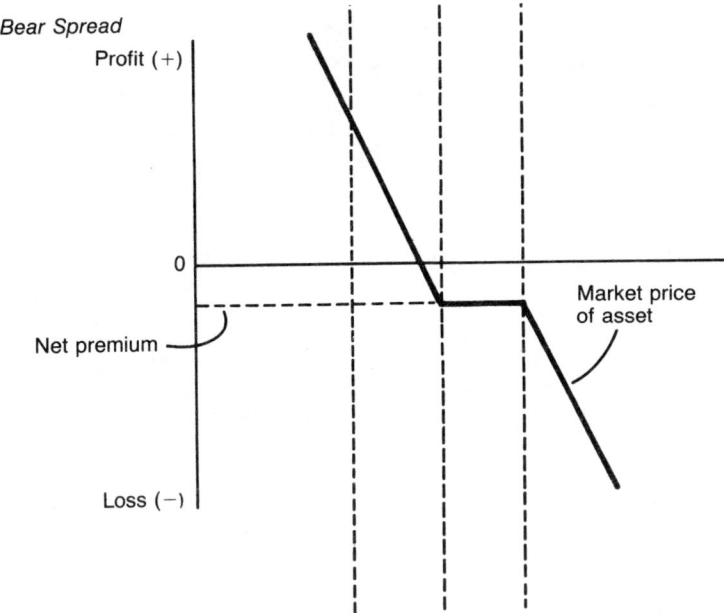

3. *Butterfly Spread*

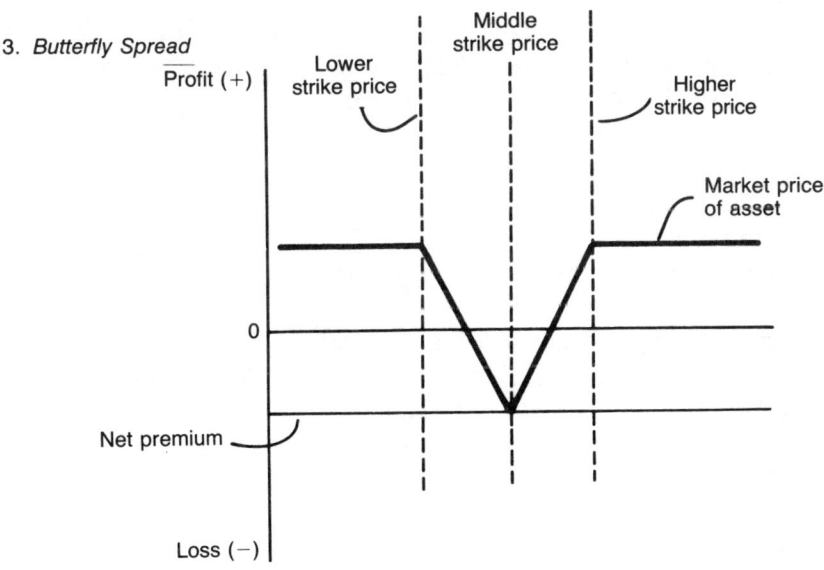

Figure 9-13. *(cont.)*

profit and loss profile of the butterfly spread. As shown in that graph, the butterfly spread takes the view of a volatile price development. Yet the position has both a limited risk and a limited profit potential as compared to the straddle position.

These option position strategies are summarized in Table 9- 2.

Table 9-2 *Option Position Strategies.*

- Straddle
  (one strike price):   Buy a call option and buy a put
                                               option at same strike price.

- Strangle
  (two strike prices):   Buy a call option and buy a put
                                               option at a lower strike price.

- Butterfly Spread*
  (three strike prices):   Write a put at lower strike price,
                                               buy a call and put at middle strike
                                               price, and write a call at
                                               a higher strike price.

* A butterfly spread can be established in several other ways: This formula corresponds to the examples discussed.

The straddle and butterfly positions represent hedged investment transactions rather than hedges of underlying cash transactions. These hedged option positions are pursued by professional brokers who use the futures and options markets for investment purposes.

Hedging a Short
Currency Position using Two Options

A Scandinavian institutional investor presently holds a securities portfolio in U.S. dollars, representing a total value of $10,000,000. The institution has taken the view that the German mark will strengthen against the U.S. dollar over the next year and therefore finds it opportune to switch the portfolio from dollar-denominated securities to mark-denominated securities. For various reasons the investor cannot switch the portfolio for three months. Applying a single option strategy to hedge the foreign exchange gap, the institution would buy DM call options in an amount equivalent to the total value of the portfolio. However, due to a very strong view that the mark will strengthen against the U.S. dollar, it simultaneously sells an equivalent number of DM put options at a lower strike price. The front-end premium income from the sale of the DM put options will count against the front-end premium to be paid for the purchase of the call options, thereby reducing the net premium for the hedge. At the same time, the likelihood that the put holder will exercise the options is considered very small, and so the downside risk is evaluated as being marginal.

Example: The three-month DM call and put options were quoted as follows on the Philadelphia Stock Exchange:

	Quotes (¢/DM)		Premium	
Strike Price ($/DM)	Calls	Puts	Calls	Puts
* 0.29	2.57	0.26	$1,606.25	$ 162.50
0.30	1.34	0.54	$ 837.50	$ 337.50
0.31	0.86	1.00	$ 537.50	$ 625.00
* 0.32	0.46	1.70	$ 287.50	$1,062.50
0.33	0.26	2.50	$ 162.50	$1,562.50
0 .34	0.13	3.30	$ 81.25	$2,062.50

FX rate: 0.3061 $/DM.

The institution chooses the DM (29) put option because it is so far out-of-the-money that the chance of exercise is reasonably small. The DM (32) call option is chosen because it gives a reasonable hedge in the bullish market. Hence the institution decides to buy 523 DM (32) call options [($10, 000,000/0.3061)/ 62,500] and to write 523 DM (29) put options. Thus the institution will pay an up-front premium for the call options of U.S. $ 150,362.50 (523 × $287.50) and will receive and up-front premium from writing the put options of U.S. $ 84,987.50 (523 × 162.50). The net premium payout of U.S. $ 65,375 is less than half the cost of the single option strategy.

To monitor the option position's sensitivity to changes in the foreign exchange rate, a calculation is carried out:

Exchange Rate ($/DM)	Calls	Puts	Bull Spread
0.28	(150,362.50)	(241,887.50)	$(392,250)
0.29	(150,362.50)	84.987.50	$(65,375)
0.30	(150.362.50)	84.987.50	$(65,375)
0.31	(150,362.50)	84,987.50	$(65,375)
0.32	(150,362.50)	84,987.50	$(65,375)
0.33	162,147.50	84,987.50	$ 247,135
0.34	472,517.50	84,987.50	$ 557,505
0.35	787,287.50	84,987.50	$ 872,275

With this data, constructing a graphical presentation of the profit and loss profile is easy (see Figure 9-14). As shown in the graph, the institution has obtained a hedge against a strengthening of the mark against the U.S. dollar for a limited fee. Yet there is a downside loss potential, however small the likelihood might be for it to materialize.[2]

Hedging a Long
Currency Position using Two Options

An international trading company is expecting Swiss franc receivables to hit its Euro Swiss franc account in three months. It plans to use these receivables for a U.S. $ 2,000,000 payment

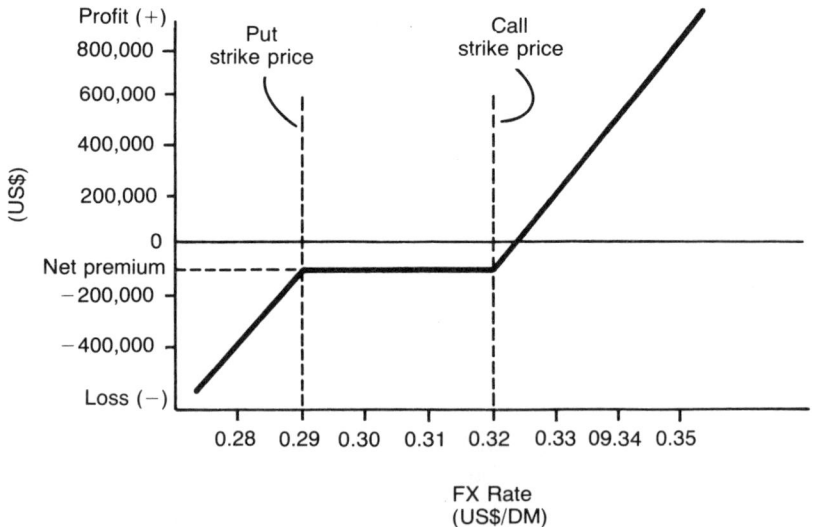

Figure 9-14. Profit and Loss Profile of 523 Long DM Calls and Short DM Puts.

also due at this time. The company has a strong belief that the franc will weaken against the U.S. dollar and conseuently would like to hedge this exposure. Applying the single option strategy. the company would buy a number of Swiss franc put options corresponding to the total amount of the dollar payment. Because their view is very strong that the franc will weaken against the U.S. dollar, the company also decides to write an equivalent number of Swiss franc call options.

Example: The three-month Sw. Frc. put and call options are quoted as follows on the Philadelphia Stock Exchange:

Strike Price (\$/Sw. Frc.)	Quotes (¢/Sw. Frc.) Puts	Calls	Premium Puts	Calls
* 0.36	0.31	1.17	$ 193.75	$731.25
0.37	0.54	0.72	$ 337.50	$450.00
0.38	0.88	0.48	$ 550.00	$300.00
* 0.39	1.55	0.19	$ 968.75	$118.75
0.40	2.26	1.12	$1,412.50	$ 75.00

FX Rate: 0.3594 $/Sw. Frc.

The company decides to buy the at-the-money Sw. Frc. (36) put option and to write the out-of-the-money Sw. Frc. (39) call option. Hence the company buys 89 puts [(2,000,000/ 0.3594) /62,500)] at a premium of $17,243.75 (89 × $193.75), and it writes 89 calls against receipt of a premium of $10,568.75 (89 × $118.75).

A sensitivity analysis on the foreign exchange fluctuation was carried out (see Figure 9-15):

Exchange Rate (\$/Sw. Frc.)	Puts	Profit/(Loss) Calls	Bear Spread
0.34	93,868.25	10,568.75	$104,437
0.35	38,266.25	10,568.75	$ 48,835
0.36	(17,243.75)	10,568.75	$(6,675)
0.37	(17,243.75)	10,568.75	$(6,675)
0.38	(17,243.75)	10,568.75	$(6,675)
0.39	(17,243.75)	10,568.75	$(6,675)
0.40	(17,243.75)	(45,056.25)	$(62,300)
0.41	(17,243.75)	(100,681.25)	$(117,925)

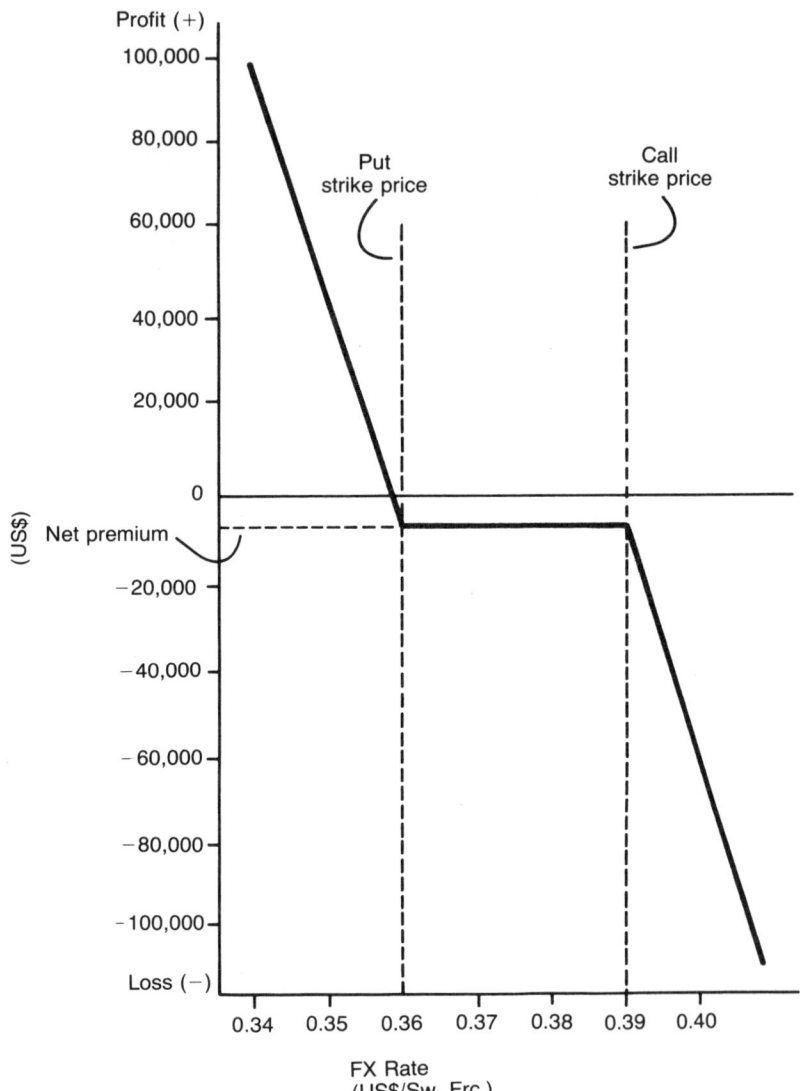

Figure 9-15. *Profit and Loss Profile of 89 Long Sw. Frc. Puts and 89 Short Sw. Frc. Calls.*

HEDGING A FUTURE SHORT INTEREST POSITION

A U.S.-based corporate entity is planning to raise funding in domestic U.S. dollars some time over the coming months. However, the cost of funding is not known in advance and consequently the corporation is interested in hedging against an increase in the general interest rate level. How can this be done by accessing the options market? The European three-month Eurodollar deposit option on the Philadelphia Board of Trade (PBOT), the Chicago Mercantile Exchange (CME), and the London International Financial Futures Exchange (LIFFE) provide access to U.S. dollar interest rate option contracts.

Alternatively, by turning to the Chicago Board of Trade Treasury bond options market, the corporation can obtain an option position that hedges against an increase in the Treasury bond yield. Suppose that the U.S. dollar loan is expected to materialize in December, that is, in four months. Then the potential borrower can buy a suitable number of December put options, which will give the holder the right to sell the Treasury bonds at a predetermined price. If the interest rate level increases—that is, if Treasury bond prices drop by more than the market expectation indicates—then the option holder will gain from exercising the Treasury bond put options, a gain which will compensate for the increased interest expense on the loan to be obtained.

The number of put option contracts to buy will depend on the correlation between the bond prices and the interest rate of the type of loan to be obtained. (See Chapter 5 on cross hedging.)

By applying double option strategies to this hedging situation, it is seen that a vertical bull spread can be established that will hedge the interest rate level within a certain band determined by the strike prices of the call write and put purchase involved in the hedge position.

Given that the borrowing is planned to take place over the Eurodollar market, the Eurodollar contracts obviously will represent a better hedging alternative than Treasury bond contracts.

Alternatively, let us look at an investor of net liquid entity who is expecting to hold U.S. dollar assets in the Euromarket within the foreseeable future.

Example: The following option quotes on the LIFFE U.S.$ 1,000,000 three-month Eurodollar deposit contract are prevailing for December delivery, four months hence:

Strike Price	*Implied Mkt. Rate*	*Quotes (pct. of 100%)* Calls	Puts	*Premium* Calls	Puts
91.00	9.00%	1.37	0.01	$13,700	$ 100
91.50	8.50%	0.91	0.05	$ 9,100	$ 500
*92.50	8.00%	0.50	0.14	$ 5,000	$1,400
*92.50	7.50%	0.22	0.36	$ 2,200	$3,600
93.00	7.00%	0.06	0.70	$ 600	$7,000

Current three-month Eurodollar deposit rate: 7.75% p.a.

The investor can hedge against a decrease in the interest rate by buying a suitable number of interest rate futures contracts. Similarly the position could be hedged by buying a suitable number of call option contracts, which will allow the holder to buy an equivalent number of interest rate futures contracts at a predetermined price at the expiry date. In this case a minimum interest rate will be guaranteed, whereas there is no upward limit on the potential gain from a possible increase in the interest rate level.

Say the investor is expecting to make a U.S.$ 1,000,000 three-month Eurodollar deposit maturing in December the return of which should be guaranteed. The hedger could then buy one call option contract at a strike price of, say, 92.50 which is slightly out of the money and hence carries a lower premium. The profit and loss calculation of this call option hedge would look as follows:

Futures Price	*Implied Market Rate*	*Option Premium*	*Exercise (Yes/No)*	*Gain*	*Net Gain*	*Effective Rate*
90.00	10.00%	$2.200	N	—	$(2,200)	9.12%
90.50	9.50%	$2.200	N	—	$(2,200)	8.62%
91.00	9.00%	$2.200	N	—	$(2,200)	8.12%
91.50	8.50%	$2.200	N	—	$(2,200)	7.62%

Futures Price	Implied Market Rate	Option Premium	Exercise (Yes/No)	Gain	Net Gain	Effective Rate
92.00	8.00%	$2.200	N	—	$(2,200)	7.12%
92.50	7.50%	$2.200	N	—	$(2,200)	6.62%
93.00	7.00%	$2.200	Y	$ 1,250	$(950)	6.62%
93.50	6.50%	$2.200	Y	$ 2,500	$ 300	6.62%
94.00	6.00%	$2.200	Y	$ 3,750	$1,550	6.62%
94.50	5.50%	$2.200	Y	$5,000	$2,800	6.62%

The gain from exercising the option when it is in the money is calculated as the number of ticks gained multiplied by the tick value of the underlying futures contract. If the futures price at expiration gets toward 93.00, the price gain from exercising the option will correspond to 50 ticks. When multiplied by the tick value of $25 for the three-month Eurodollar futures contract, the 50-tick amount gives $1,250 (50 × $25).

In pursuing this hedge, the investor has effectively secured a minimum rate of interest on the deposit of 6.62% p.a., whereas there is no limit on the upward potential for interest return.

Consider another situation, where a borrower is to obtain funding of U.S.$ 1,000,000 fixed to the three-month LIBID and would like to hedge the interest payment for the three-month period from December. This could be obtained by buying a put option contract at a strike price of, say, 92.00 which is slightly out of the money and hence carries a lower premium. The profit and loss calculation of this put option hedge is as follows:

Futures Price	Implied Market Rate	Option Premium	Exercise (Yes/No)	Gain	Net Gain	Effective Rate
90.00	10.00%	$1,400	Y	$5.000	$ 3.600	8.56%
90.50	9.50%	$1,400	Y	$3.750	$ 2.350	8.56%
91.00	9.00%	$1.400	Y	$2.500	$ 1.100	8.56%
91.50	8.50%	$1,400	Y	$1.250	$(150)	8.56%
92.00	8.00%	$1,400	N	—	$(1.400)	8.56%
92.50	7.50%	$1,400	N	—	$(1.400)	8.06%
93.00	7.00%	$1,400	N	—	$(1.400)	7.56%
93.50	6.50%	$1,400	N	—	$(1.400)	7.06%
94.00	6.00%	$1,400	N	—	$(1.400)	6.56%
94.50	5.50%	$1,400	N	—	$(1.400)	6.06%

By engaging in this hedge, the borrower has guaranteed a maximum funding rate of 8.56% p.a. whereas there is no down-ward limit on gains from a decreasing interest rate level.

Let us turn back to the investor and take the view that the interest rate level is very likely to fall and that the likelihood of an increase above 8% p.a. is marginal. In this situation the hedger could buy the call option with strike price 92.50 to guarantee a minimum return and simultaneously write a put option at a strike price of 92.00, corresponding to the 8.00% limit. In this case the premium income from the put write will reduce the net premium payout on the position. The investor has established a vertical bull spread in the interest rate option contracts, which covers for an increase in the interest futures price but which concurrently takes a position on the downside movement of the futures price. So it does not represent a complete hedge.

The profit and loss calculation of the vertical bull spread is obtained by combining the profit and loss profiles of the preceding call and put options (see Figure 9-16).

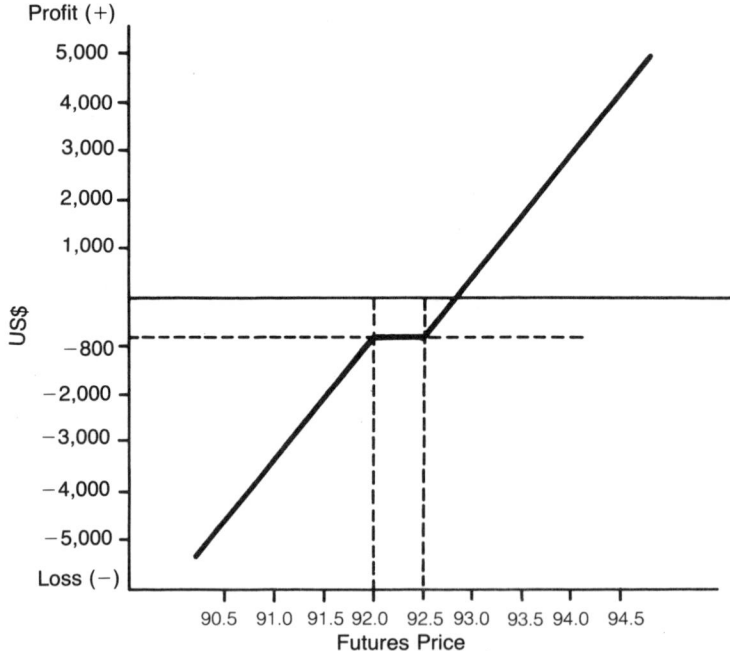

Figure 9-16. *Profit and Loss Profile of a Vertical Bull Spread.*

Futures Price	Implied Market Rate	Net Premium	Call Buy	Net Gain Put Write	Spread
90.00	10.00%	$800	($2,200)	($3,600)	($5,800)
90.50	9.50%	$800	($2,200)	($2,350)	($4,550)
91.00	9.00%	$800	($2,200)	($1,100)	($3,300)
91.50	8.50%	$800	($2,200)	$ 150	($2,050)
92.00	8.00%	$800	($2,200)	$1,400	($ 800)
92.50	7.50%	$800	($2,200)	$1,400	($ 800)
93.00	7.00%	$800	($ 950)	$1,400	$ 450
93.50	6.50%	$800	$ 300	$1,400	$1,700
94.00	6.00%	$800	$1,550	$1,400	$2,950
94.50	5.50%	$800	$2,800	$1,400	$4,200

This is to say that if the three-month Eurodollar deposit rate increases above 8.00% p.a., the position holder will lose money because he will have to honor the put option. If the interest rate falls below 7.5% p.a., however, he will gain from exercising the call options. (See Figure 9-17.)

A borrower could establish a vertical bear spread. First, he would buy a put option, which would require payouts by the option writer in case the interest rate falls below the level indicated by the call option.

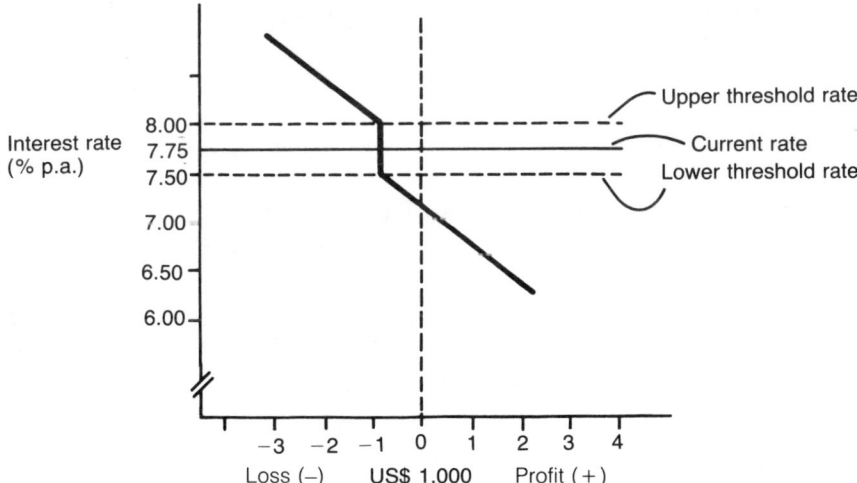

Figure 9-17. *Profit and Loss Profile of a Vertical Bear Spread.*

HEDGING A SHORT STOCK POSITION

Example: A portfolio manager is expecting funds of U.S.$ 10,000,000 in three months. The funds are scheduled to be invested in a well diversified portfolio of corporate stocks. However, the fear is that stock prices in general will rise in the near future. This can be hedged by buying a suitable number of stock index call options, such as the S&P 500 index option contract on the Chicago Mercantile Exchange.

The three-month call options are quoted as follows:

Strike Price	Quote	Call Premium	Stock Index	Profit/(Loss)
170	15.00	$7,500	175	$(299,700)
175	11.20	$5,600	180	$(299,700)
180	8.00	$4,000	185	$(299,700)
*185	5.55	$2,775	190	$(29,700)
190	3.65	$1,825	195	$ 240,300
195	2.35	$1,175	200	$ 510,300
			205	$ 780,300

The portfolio manager decides to purchase the out-of-the-money contract with a strike price of 185. The number of contracts purchased amounts to 108 [10,000,000 / (185 × 500)], and the premium to pay up front equals $299,700 (108 × $2,775). (See Figure 9-18.)

CONCLUSION

As in the case of financial futures, the development of each option hedge must be closely monitored. One reason for such diligence is that it provides a full overview of the institution's collective hedging activities vis-a-vis the risk profile endorsed by the management board. Another is that it establishes a tracking mechanism that enables the financial management to learn from previous experience. Again it is extremely important to know the exact trading practices of the option exchanges involved. Transaction costs, such as brokerage fees and margin requirements, can turn out to be very important factors and must be fully understood.

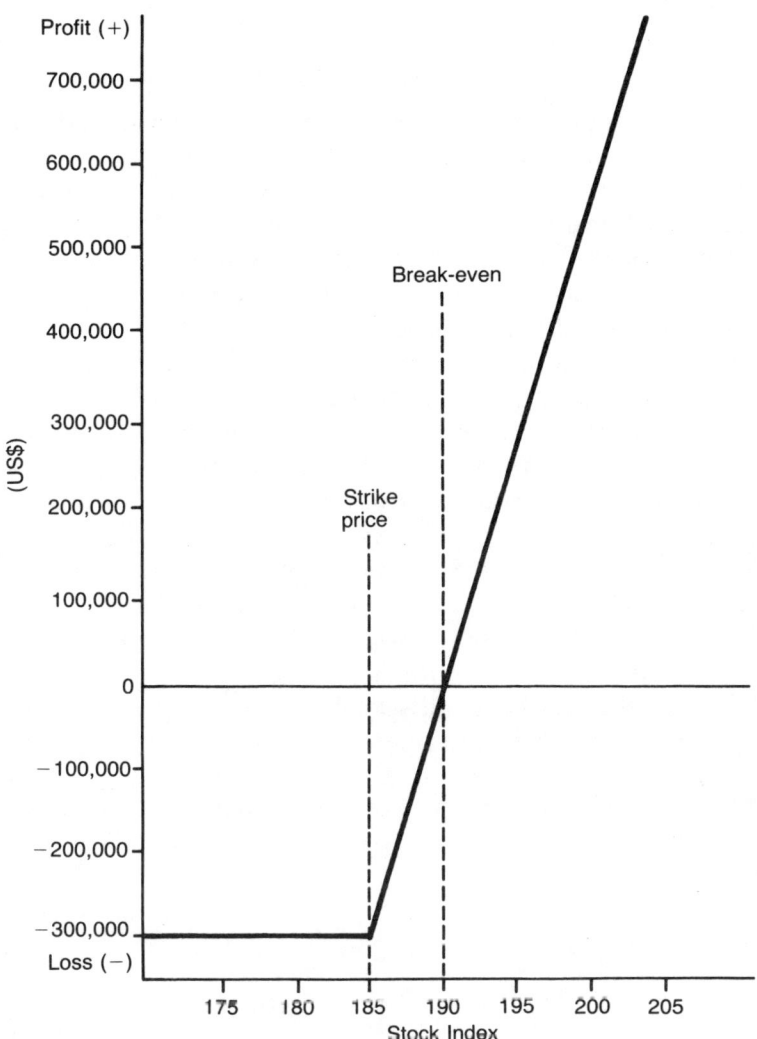

Figure 9-18. *Profit and Loss Profile of 108 S&P Stock Index Call Options.*

Unlike financial futures, option contracts are interesting for hedging purposes because they offset or minimize the downside risk, while leaving open the upside potential for gains. Double option strategies all take a view on price movements and therefore carry an element of downside risk, which should be carefully scrutinized. Single option strategies, however, provide holders with complete hedges.

For most institutions the taxation and reporting aspects are essential. In general the net premium on an uncovered option position is considered an investment, which will lead to capital gains or losses at maturity. If the option position is linked to an asset for hedging purposes, the cost of the hedge is considered part of the cost of trading the asset. However, tax laws change, as do reporting requirements, so consultation with local auditors is always recommended.

The option exchanges provide the financial world with liquid and efficient markets for a wide variety of option positions, which have a whole range of hedging applications. A disadvantage of exchange-traded options is that they are traded in standard sizes which will not always completely match the requirements of the hedger's position. Also, the limited duration of option contracts sometimes restricts their usage. Nevertheless, the vast number of participants on the options exchange are investors who, through relatively small initial capital investments, can position themselves at an overall profit and thereby they become indispensable counterparts to the hedgers approaching the same markets.

PART IV

FINANCIAL HEDGING
OVER-THE-COUNTER

In response to the continued expansion of the futures and options exchanges, the major international commercial banks and investment banks have developed a wide spectrum of financial services delivered directly to the client over-the-counter (OTC), as opposed to dealings on the exchanges. Usually the OTC services are tailor-made to the specific situations of the client and thereby break free of the restrictions imposed by standardized exchange-traded contracts. However, the financial institutions offering the OTC services themselves hedge their net positions on the futures and options exchanges, and therefore the emergence of exchange-traded futures and options contracts have been an encouragement and, to some extent a prerequisite, for the development of OTC services.

Forward Agreements

An international currency forward market has existed for many years. Today it represents a major trading arena, together with spot dealings in the treasury departments of banks around the world. However, interest rate forwards have developed in the wake of the expanded trading in interest rate contracts on the futures exchanges over the recent years.

CURRENCY FORWARDS

Example: If an institution needed to create a forward cover for the purchase of, say, US $ 1,000,000 against Swiss francs in six months, it would buy U.S. dollar 1,000,000 spot against Swiss francs. The franc amount used for the dollar purchae would be borrowed at the six-month money market rate, and the dollar amount would be deposited at the going six-month U.S. dollar money market rate. The dollar interest received on the deposit will, at the end of the six-month period, be converted into francs, and the receipts will be included in the Swiss francs payable against the loan plus interest (see Figure 10-1).

The following market rates are prevailing:

Spot foreign exchange rate	2.0000 Sw. Frc./US $
Six-month Euro dollar rate	12.00% p.a.
Six-month Euro Swiss franc rate	7.00% p.a.

In general the following rule of thumb applies:[2]

*The currency of the **higher** interest rate is always traded forward at a **discount**.*

The banking system as a whole will manage its net open forward position by engaging in cover transactions in the Euromarket. So the swap calculation in the forward market generally will follow the interest rate differential approach that was just described and that is in accordance with the interest rate parity theory discussed in Chapter 4.

The preceding example was slightly simplified because it did not take into consideration that foreign exchange and interbank interest rates are quoted with two-way *bid* and *offer* prices.

Example:

	Bid	*Offer*
Spot foreign exchange rate (Sw.Frc./$)	1.9990	2.0010
Six-month Euro U.S. dollar rate (% p.a.)	11⅞	12⅛
Six-month Euro Swiss franc rate (% p.a.)	.6⅞	7⅛

In the case of a forward purchase (bid) of U.S. dollars against Swiss francs, the dollars are bought spot at the offered rate of 2.0010 Sw. Frc./US$. Francs are borrowed at the interbank offered rate of 12⅛%, and the equivalent dollar amount is deposited at the interbank bid rate of 6⅞%. The swap bid is calculated as follows:

$$\text{Swap (bid)} = \frac{2.0010 \times (.06875 - .12125) \times 180}{360} = -0.0525$$

Conversely, in the case of a forward sale (offer) of U.S. dollars against Swiss francs, dollars are sold spot at the bid rate of 1.9990 Sw. Frc. US$. Francs are deposited at the interbank bid rate of 11⅞%, and the equivalent dollar amount is borrowed at the interbank offered rate of 7⅛%. The swap offered is calculated as follows:

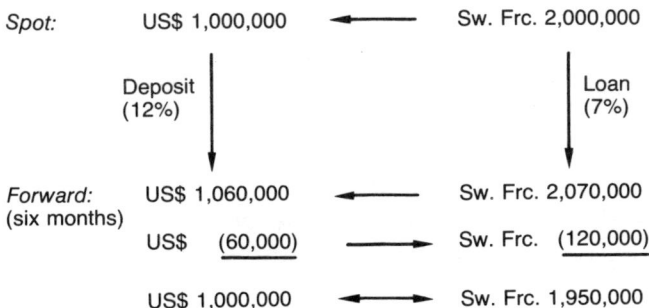

Figure 10-1. *Diagram of a Forward Currency Arrangement.*

The forward foreign exchange rate, also called the *outright rate*, is equal to 1,9500 Sw. Frc./US. $[1] The difference between the spot and forward rate is 0.0500, which is often termed the *swap*. The swap value is a function of the interest rate differential between the U.S. dollar and the Swiss franc, as shown in the following formula:

$$\text{Swap} = \frac{\overset{\text{Spot}}{\underset{\text{rate}}{\text{exchange}}} \times \overset{\text{Interest}}{\underset{\text{differential}}{\text{rate}}} \times \overset{\text{Number}}{\underset{\text{days}}{\text{of}}}}{360}$$

The calculation of the interest rate differential depends on the denomination of the foreign exchange rate. Here the foreign exchange rate is denominated as Sw. Frc./US $, so that the interest rate differential is calculated as the Swiss franc interest rate minus the U.S. dollar interest rate, that is:

$$\text{Swap} = \frac{2,000 \times (.07 - .12) \times 180}{360} = -0.500$$

The minus indicates that the dollar is bought forward at a discount.

Spot rate	2.0000 Sw.Frc./$
Swap	− 0.0500 Sw.Frc./$
Outright rate	1.9500 Sw.Frc./$

$$\text{Swap (offer)} = \frac{1.9990 \times (0.07125 - .11875) \times 180}{360} = -0.0475$$

Consequently, the two-way forward foreign exchange quote is 0.0525/0.0475 (Sw. Frc./US$).

By convention the negative sign is omitted, but we can see that it is at a discount because the bid swap quote is higher than the offer swap quote. Hence the outright rate is found as follows:

	Bid	Offer
Spot rate (Sw. Frc./US$)	1.9990	2.0010
Swap (Sw. Frc./US$)	0.0525	0.0475
Outright rate (Sw. Frc./US$)	1.9465	1.9555

When an institutional client asks for a forward quote with a commercial bank, usually a spread will be subtracted from the bid quote and added to the offer quote. The spread compensates the bank for the transaction costs and the counterparty risk engaged in when closing the forward agreement.

Like financial futures in currencies, the forward agreement locks in the future exchange rate, but it also eliminates the basis risk inherent in any financial futures position. And, since markets in currency forwards exist in a wide variety of cross currencies, they have wider applications than do currency futures contracts.

INTEREST RATE FORWARDS

Several commercial banks now offer forward rate agreements (FRA) in U.S. dollars, pounds sterling, and other currencies on request. An institutional borrower or lender can fix the future interest rate on loans and deposits for periods of up to several years, with the maximum maturity depending on the currency in question. As discussed in Chapter 5, the institution offering the forward rate agreement can cover the transaction through an opposite position in the cash market.

Example: We want to create a forward rate for a $1,000,000 three-month loan in three months' time. So we would borrow

$1,000,000 for six months and deposit the amount for three months.

The following interbank rates prevail on the money market:

	Bid	Offer
Three months (% p.a.)	10⅜	10⅝
Six months (% p.a.)	11⅞	12⅛

We would borrow enough six-month dollars at 12⅛% so as to leave us with $1,000,000 after three months at a three-month deposit rate of 10⅜% (see Figure 10-2). The break-even interest rate for the three-month loan in three months is found to be 13.52 % p.a. [400/$1,000,000 ($1,033,810.54 – $1,000,000)].

Conversely, if we want to create a forward rate for a $1,000,000 three-month deposit in three months, we would borrow a dollar amount at 10⅝%, which after three months is to be repaid by $1,000,000. The dollar amount would be deposited for six months at 11⅞% (see Figure 10-3). The break-even rate on the three-month deposit in three months is calculated as 12.78% [400/$1,000,000 · ($1,031,963.47 – $1,000,000)].

Another avenue for the intermediary offering forward interest rates is to cover the position directly in the financial fu-

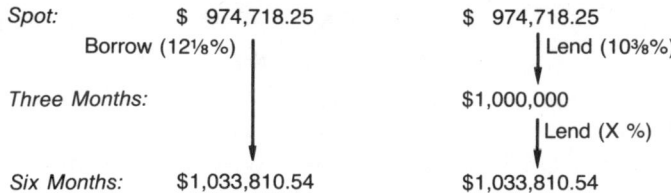

Figure 10-2. *Interest Rate Forward Arrangement (Asset hedge).*

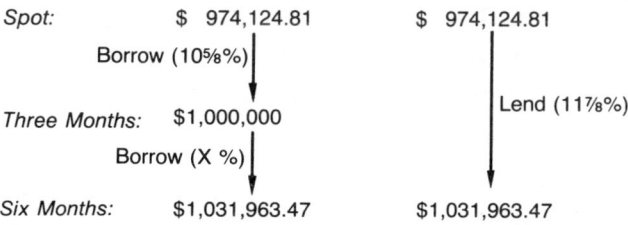

Figure 10-3. *Interest Rate Forward Agreement (Liability Hedge).*

tures market. In this case the institution offering the forward rate assumes the basis risk of the futures position prevailing over the course of the forward period.

Banks offering forward rate agreements will charge a front-end fee or a per-annum spread, payable throughout the forward period. This commission charge will cover not only the bank's transaction costs, but also the increased capital requirements caused by the implied cash market position. In case the transaction is covered on the financial futures market, the commission compensates for the bank's increased basis risk imposed by the futures position.

The institution buying the forward rate agreement can fix the forward interest rate on any loan or deposit without going through the administrative procedures involved in managing a financial futures hedge and without incurring any risk. The amount and maturity of a forward rate agreement are usually flexible, as opposed to the financial futures hedge where the hedge is tied into the fixed maturity dates of the futures contracts, and usually the hedger has the choice between taking delivery or not at the date of drawdown. If the institution decides not to take delivery, the only exchange is the difference in interest payments on the contractual amount at maturity.

Example 1: A construction company needs capital of $1,000,000 for a six-month period in four months to carry out a project. To lock in the future cost of capital required to complete the project, the company buys a forward rate agreement guaranteeing that the $1,000,000 can be borrowed for six months within four months time at a rate of, say, 12⅜% p.a. The company pays a fixed fee of perhaps ¼% p.a. during the ten months of the forward rate agreement to obtain the forward obligation from the bank. Hereby the risk associated with the future financing cost is eliminated, and the company can carry out a feasibility study with full certainty, at least as far as funding costs are concerned.

Example 2: An international trading company periodically raises funds through issuance of bankers' acceptances (BAs). Traditionally there has been an interest rate advantage of ⅝%

Table 10-1. *Comparing Exchange Futures Contracts with OTC Forward Agreements.*

Futures Exchange	OTC Forwards
• Trading is done on a trading floor consisting of buyers and sellers of contracts and contract prices are determined by open outcry.	• Banks give two-sided quotes and deals are closed over the phone.
• Brokers who are members of the exchanges trade for their own accounts and on behalf of third parties.	• Transactions are done directly between banks and institutional clients.
• Market participants are unknown to each other, and settlement is done through the exchange clearing house.	• Participants are known to each other, and the deal implies acceptance of counterparty risks among the participants.
• All participants pay initial margin, and cash settlement is done by marking-to-market on a daily basis. The exchange brokers charge third parties a brokerage fee to cover handling costs	• No margin is required, but counterparty risk is carried by changing a spread around the two-sided forward price.
• Actual delivery of the underlying goods is possible, but only rarely takes place.	• Most trades result in delivery.
• Contracts have standard amount and standard maturities.	• Contract amounts and maturity dates are flexible, but at times requirements are made for the minimum size of contract amount. Maturities often exceed those of the futures exchanges.
• Most currency futures are quoted against U.S. dollars and only for major currencies. Interest rate futures exist only in U.S. dollars and pounds sterling	• In principle, quotes can be given for any cross currency exchange rate and foreign currency interest rate.
• A futures position imposes a "basis risk" on the position holder.	• There is no basis risk to the buyer of a forward agreement, which is assumed by the institution offering the forward agreement.

on bankers' acceptance financing as compared to direct bank financing. In one month the company will have a financing requirement of $3,000,000 for two months, but management is worried that interest rates will increase. The company then buys from the bank a forward rate agreement which secures the borrowing of $3,000,000 in the Euro interbank market for two months in one month's time at a cost of, say, 12½% p.a

At the time of drawdown the ⅝% advantage remains. The company therefore decides not to draw the funds from the bank, but rather to fund itself through the issuance of banker's acceptances. The forward rate agreement is cancelled and a cancellation fee is calculated by marking-to-market. Let's say that the interbank offer rate has increased to 13½% p.a. The rate has then increased by 1% as compared to the forward rate fixed at 12½% p.a. The cancellation fee is calculated as the p.a. interest differential between the forward rate and the new spot rate prevailing at the date of drawdown.

In this case the cancellation fee is in favor of the company, which will be credited the interest amount of 1% p.a. (that is, $5,000) on $3,000,000 for the two-month loan period. The company will issue banker's acceptances and raise funds at the new market rate of 12⅞% p.a. (13½% − ⅝%). The company pays the bank a commission of ¼% p.a. during the three-month period of the forward rate agreement. Hence by engaging in the forward rate agreement, the company has secured a future funding cost at an all-in rate of 12⅛% p.a., which is 1⅜% p.a. below the going interbank offered rate.

Example 3: An institutional investor periodically places idle dollar liquidity in short-term commercial paper because this type of investment carries a lower price risk than do, say, U.S. Treasury bonds. An investor expects to have idle liquidity of US$ 5,000,000 during a two-month period in one month's time, but fears that the interest rate level might drop in the meantime. To fix the future investment rate, the investor buys a forward rate agreement from a bank, which locks in the future investment rate in the Euro interbank market at 11½% p.a. for the two-month period. At the date of drawdown, the interbank bid rate has dropped to 10½% p.a. and the commercial paper rate is at the same level. The investor decides to invest in the commercial paper and therefore cancels the forward rate agreement by marking-to-market.

The cancellation fee is the difference between the forward rate of 11½% p.a. and the spot rate of 10½% p.a. The bank therefore pays the interest amount of 1% p.a. on $5,000,000 for the two-month period to the investor. The investor pays a commission of perhaps ¼% p.a. to the bank during the three-month period of the forward agreement. So the investment in commercial paper is done at an all-in rate of 11⅛% p.a. In case the commercial paper rate had dropped more than the interbank bid rate, the investor could choose to deliver the funds directly to the bank to secure the fixed return of 11⅛% p.a.

The forward rate agreement locks in the future interest rate, that is, it provides a complete hedge against the downside risk. Yet it does not leave open the upside potential for gains from a favorable development in interest rates.

Case: Interest Rate Forward Contract:
Project Finance, Delay Start/Stepped Structure,
Interest Rate Gapping

A construction company, the St. Louis Constructers, Inc., had just been awarded a US $ 15,000,000 contract in December 1985 for a major real estate development project in a St. Louis suburban area, as part of the municipal urban development plan to commence in May 1986. The project was to be a forerunner for several other development projects, to be commenced upon the initial project's completion. To be awarded the first contract meant a "foot in the door" when future bids were to be solicited.

The initial construction project was scheduled for completion over an eighteen-month period thus requiring a stepped-up financing scheme throughout the construction period. The municipality would make gradual and partial downpayment as construction work was satisfactorily completed. Hence a 10% advance payment would be paid as the construction work commenced in May, around 20% of the total contract price would be paid after six months in November, and another 20% would be due for payment after twelve months in May 1987. The remaining 50% would be paid upon satisfactory completion of the work after eighteen months, scheduled for November 1987.

According to William Sorensen, the Financial Controller of the St. Louis Constructers, Inc.:

> We had been awarded the contract in very hard competition, and partially in a situation where we wanted to utilize some excess capacity built up in similar works which we had just completed. Obviously we made our bid on very competitive terms with a view to the future construction works which could flow to us if we were awarded the first construction project.

Because St. Louis Constructers had to invest money in the initial mobilization of equipment and construction workers, they foresaw some heavy drawdowns on the variable rate overdraft facilities made available by their major banks. The interest rate volatility made the future interest expense an unknown factor in the company's calculations. As William Sorensen put it:

> The interest rate uncertainty provided us with a bit of a headache when making our cash projections. You see, we were willing to consider the new project at a "breakeven" price or a slight profit but obviously wouldn't like to lose money on it if we could avoid it. Fortunately, in discussing this issue with one of our banks, they suggested that we engage in interest rate contracts in order to fix the future interest rate.

In mid-December 1985 the short-term interbank offered rate (one to three months) had moved down to around 8% p.a. from a level well beyond 10% earlier in the year. This meant that the St. Louis Contractors could fund themselves presently at a rate of 8.50 – 8.75% p.a. Looking at the cash flow analysis a funding rate of 8.75% would result in an overall profit to St. Louis Constructers of around $110,000 on the total construction project. However, assuming instead a funding rate of 12% throughout the period April 1986–November 1987, this profit figure would turn into a loss of around $122,600. See Table 10-2.

Table 10-2 *Liquidity Forecast.*

Date	Incremental Investment Need ($1,000)	Current Working Capital Need ($1,000)	Down-payments ($1,000)	Expected Cumulative Overdraft ($3,000)	Interest Expense (US$ at) 8% p.a.	Interest Expense (US$ at) 12% p.a.
Apr. 86	1,000	100	1,100	1,100	7333	11000
May 86	1,000	425	1,500	1,025	6833	10250
Jun. 86	1,000	425		2,450	16333	24500
Jul. 86	1,000	400		3,850	25667	38500
Aug. 86		300		4,150	27667	41500
Sep. 86		325		4,475	29833	44750
Oct. 86	1,500	325		6,300	42000	63000
Nov. 86	500	335	3,000	4,135	27567	41350
Dec. 86		355		4,490	29933	44900
Jan. 87		355		4,845	32300	48450
Feb. 87		360		5,205	34700	52050
Mar. 87		360		5,565	37100	55650
Apr. 87	1,000	400		7,215	48100	72150
May 87		345	3,000	4,560	30400	45600
Jun. 87		345		4,905	32700	49050
Jul. 87		345		5,250	35000	52500
Aug. 87		355		5,605	37367	56050
Sep. 87		400		6,005	40033	60050
Oct. 87		380		6,385	42567	63850
Nov. 87		350	7,500	– 765	– 5100	– 7650
Dec. 87		275		– 490	– 3267	– 4900
Total	7,000	7,260	15,000		575060	862600

Now it just so happened that the market was bullish in December 1985 and future interest rates in general were expected to drop. So St. Louis Constructers could lock in the future rates at rather favorable terms against a 0.25% p.a. fee, payable to the bank throughout the period of the forward contracts.

By engaging in these interest rate forward contracts (Table 10-3), the average all-in funding cost could be locked in at a rate below 9.25% p.a. and thus guarantee a profit of around $80,000 on the project, everything else being equal. William Sorensen commented on it this way:

We considered it worthwhile to fix a maximum interest rate under the given circumstances. Despite a general expectation of dropping interest rates, we found the chance

Table 10-3. Forward Rate Contracts.

Period	Locked-In Rate	Amount
2nd quarter 1986	8.50% p.a.	$2,500,000
3rd quarter 1986	8.60% p.a.	$4,500,000
4th quarter 1986	8.75% p.a.	$4,500,000
1st quarter 1987	9.00% p.a.	$5,500,000
2nd quarter 1987	9.00% p.a.	$5,000,000
3rd quarter 1987	9.25% p.a.	$6,000,000

that the interest rate would increase again to be so significant that we decided to eliminate the risk of an increase in the rate and instead concentrate our efforts on our real business, namely to manage and monitor the construction development and avoid any potential cost overruns during the construction period.

CHAPTER **11**

Option Agreements

In the foreign exchange forward market, a "pseudo-option" has existed for years. This traditional "option" in the forward market gives the buyer of a forward agreement the right to choose the time of exercise of the forward agreement before the maturity date. However, because the "option" *must* be exercised before or on the maturity date, it does not constitute a true option. A *true option* provides the holder with the right but *not* the obligation to exercise before maturity. In principle it is similar to a forward agreement, but it does not oblige the option holder to exercise the forward transaction.

Parallel to the development of exchange-traded option contracts, an over-the-counter (OTC) market has been created by the major international banks, merchant banks, and brokerage houses, providing tailor-made currency and interest rate options to institutional clients. As of the mid-1980s, only limited trading has been done among the financial institutions themselves.

CURRENCY OPTIONS

True options in the OTC market take many shapes, in accordance with specific hedging requirements of institutional clients. Option quotes can be obtained for all major currencies against dollars, and most international currencies can be quoted. In addition, cross currencies will be quoted on request, which is a clear advantage compared to hedging with option exchange contracts.

Expiration Dates

OTC options normally have maturities of up to one year, but maturities are often longer. The final maturity date is flexible and can be fixed or broken (or irregular) dates, as opposed to exchange-traded options.

The expiration date of an option agreement is the last day on which it can be exercised and usually corresponds to the spot date of the underlying currency. In spot foreign exchange deals, settlement takes place two days after the spot transactions, except transactions in U.S. dollars against Canadian dollars and Mexican pesos, which settle the following day.

Example: A Swiss franc call option, written for value on May 17, has an expiration date of May 15. Most banks require to be informed by the option holder before a certain deadline on the expiration date in order to execute the option.

Contract Size

Usually the size of the option agreement entails a minimum requirement, often about US $ 1,000,000. For smaller transactions, the costs are too high to make it worthwhile. Above the minimum requirement, the amount is flexible. It can be set at broken amounts at the buyer's choice to match a specific position.

Strike Price

The strike price is chosen by the option buyer and quotes are given to match the request of the client. (Exchange-traded option terminology also pertains to the OTC market.) Although the holder of a European option can exercise only at the expiration date, he can lock in profits prior to expiration by engaging in an offsetting forward agreement. Hence it can be argued that the strike price of a European option should be based on the outright rate. The holder of an American option can exercise the option at any time up to the expiration date, and profit can be locked in prior to expiration either by engaging in an offsetting forward agreement or by accessing the foreign exhange spot market. So it can be argued that the strike price of an American option should be based on the foreign exchange spot rate. Whether one or the other principle is used does not matter, as long as the market participants among themselves agree on the practice and terminology of the deal.

This is especially true of an at-the-money strike price. Whether it is defined as the current spot price or as the forward rate, be sure to obtain agreement on the definition of the at-the-money strike price, when requesting option quotes, in order to avoid confusion and misinterpretation of competitive bids.

Premium

Quotes are usually given for American-type options as well as for European-type options. Since the American option is slightly more expensive than the European, it usually pays to clarify whether the flexibility of the American option brings additional benefits to the option buyer in a given hedging situation.

Usually the option premium is paid up front and is quoted as a percentage of the currency amount of the option agreement, with the calculation of the currency amount based on the current spot exchange rate.

However, under special circumstances the premium can be paid in arrears. For example, the premium for the *limited option* is not paid until the contract's expiration date. In this case the option holder *must* act on the option on the expiration date. If the option is profitable, the option holder will exercise the option and pay the premium as the percentage calculated on the currency amount. The currency amount is determined by using the strike price of the option agreement. If the option is unprofitable, the option holder will not exercise the option but will pay the premium on the currency amount calculated from the current spot price prevailing at the expiration date.

Table 11-1. *Types of Options.*

- *True Option*

  —A right to buy or sell a currency before a future date at a predetermined price.
  —No obligation to exercise
  —Amount in excess of $1,000,000 is flexible.
  —Maturity date is flexible.
  —Strike price at buyer's choice.
  —Premium payable up front.

- *Limited Option*:

  —Same as true option, but premium payable on maturity date.

- *Option-on-an-Option:*

  —A right to buy an option before a future date at a predetermined premium.
  —Buyer selects terms of future option.
  —Bank quotes premium payable up front.

The feature of the delayed payment of premium has cash implications for the option buyer, who will pay the premium at the time that, for example, a foreign currency receivable will materialize.

Often financial managers have an aversion against paying a front-end fee for something whose outcome is unknown. For this reason traditional forward contracts are often adhered to because they provide the contract buyer with full certainty about the future foreign exchange rate, even though this might not be an optimal hedging solution for the specific situation. Most users of forward contracts do not make comparative calculations between the forward contract and the comparable option contract at the maturity date to analyze whether the hedging decision was optimal. Although previous decisions represent "sunk cost," which cannot be reversed, such analysis might bring about more knowledge so as to determine the optimal hedging technique to pursue in similar future situations.

Paying the option premium at the option's expiration date makes it easier for the option buyer to see the advantage of the option purchase. The profitability of the option is then a straightforward calculation.

Example: An American company is expecting a receivable of DM 2,500,000 in three months and has bought a German mark limited put option against US$ with an at-the-money strike price of 2.5000 DM/US$ at a premium of 3%. After the three-month period, the spot rate has gone to 2.3500 DM/US$ and so the option is not exercised. If nevertheless the put option is exercised at the strike price, the German marks receivables would bring the company $1,000,000. Conversely, if the marks receivables were sold on the spot market at the current foreign exchange rate, they would bring the company $1,063,829.79.

Because the option puts no limitation on the upside potential for price gains, the company earns $63,829.78 more than if it had engaged in a forward agreement at a forward rate of 2.5000 DM/U.S.$. On expiration date, the company pays a 3% premium of $31,914.89 (.03 × $1,063,829.79). The net gain from the favorable exchange rate development amounts to $31,914.89 ($63,829.78 – $31,914.89), when compared to the situation where the future German mark receivables had been covered by a forward contract at the same future foreign exchange rate.

Option-on-an-Option Agreement

A more recent development on the OTC option market is the creation of the *option-on-an-option agreement*. The holder of an option-on-an-option has the right to purchase an option at or before a certain future date at a predetermined premium. The buyer determines the characteristics of the option to purchase in the future, and the bank will quote a premium to be paid up front or in arrears. The option-on-an-option can be advantageous, for example, to a construction company negotiating a future contract that might require hedging of foreign currency flows.

Option Writer's Risks

When writing options, financial institutions have to hedge considerable option position day by day. The option writer has two inherent risks to cover: an unfavorable development in the *forward rate* and an unfavorable development in the *spot rate*.

Example: Refer to the first example on the Swiss franc forward rate in Chapter 10 (page 195). Assume that a three-month Swiss franc European call option has been written at a strike price of 1.9500 Sw. Frc./US$ (0.5128 US$/Sw. Frc.). If the U.S. dollar interest rate increases by 1% and the Swiss franc interest rate decreases by 1%, then the swap is calculated as – 0.0700 and the new outright rate amounts to 1.9300 Sw. Frc./US$ (0.5181 US$/Sw. Frc.). In this situation a holder of a European option could sell francs forward at 0.5181 US$/Sw. Frc. and exercise the call option at 0.5128 US$/Sw. Frc., thereby realizing a gain of 53 points. The chance of exercise would also increase in the case of a continued strengthening of the Swiss franc spot exchange rate toward the expiration date. The option position could be closed by the option writer by buying francs *forward* and selling them spot against the dollar.

A three-month Swiss franc American call option has been written at a strike price of 2.0000 Sw. Frc./US$ (0.500 US$/Sw. Frc.). If the franc's spot foreign exchange rate starts to strengthen against the U.S. dollar, the chance that the option holder will exercise increases. This open position can be closed by the option writer by buying francs *spot* against the dollar.

The decisions on *when* to close the call option gap, *how* to close it (either through the spot purchase of the currency or through the purchase of the currency forward), and the timing of the transactions is very much based on subjective evaluations of the future foreign exchange rate as a part of the overall foreign exchange position management of the financial institution. Similar exposure management applies to the put options written by the institution. Consider that hedged options that are out of the money also represent a position to the option writer. Hence the option position must be hedged and unhedged in response to the current change in the foreign exchange rate.

Applying Black-Scholes

From the preceding discussion, we deduce that the call option premium on an in-the-money American option must exceed the difference between the spot rate and the exercise price.

Table 11-2.

Call Option Premium >	(Spot foreign exchange rate > 0 − exercise price)
Call Option Premium >	(Forward foreign exchange rate > 0 −exercise price)*

* Discounted to present value at current money market rate.

Otherwise the option holder can exercise the option at a profit right after purchase.

Similarly, the call option premium on a European or an American option must exceed the difference between the forward exchange rate and the exercise price. If not, the option holder can lock in a future profit right after purchase by selling the currency forward and exercising the option at expiration date. See Table 11-2.

So, as also discussed in Chapter 6, the option price depends on (1) the current spot foreign exchange rate, (2) the forward foreign exchange rate, (3) the strike price, (4) the maturity date of the option agreement, and (5) the volatility of the foreign exchange rate. These relationships are formalized in the Black-Scholes formula, which can be applied to approximate the "efficient" call option premium.

Buying a call option and writing a put option on a currency at the same strike price (*conversion*) corresponds to buying a forward agreement for the purchase of the currency in question. In an efficient market the cost of acquiring an amount of the future currency either way must be equal in size. Otherwise arbitrage transactions would generate profits.

The cost of the currency acquired through the option position (or through a forward agreement) is calculated as follows:

$$\text{Forward rate} = \text{Exercise price} + \text{Call premium} - \text{Put premium} + \text{Interest on net premium}$$

that is,

$$\text{Call premium} - \text{Put premium} = \text{Forward rate} - \text{Exercise price}$$

(The "Forward rate" and "Exercise price" are discounted to present value at current money market rate.)

From the equation we can establish a relationship between the call option premium and the put option premium that enables us to utilize the Black-Scholes formula also to calculate the put option premium.[1]

The Role of Volatility

In view of the inherent risk associated with the management of an option position, another approach has been to look at the option agreement as an "insurance policy" which protects the option holder against adverse and volatile changes in the foreign exchange rate. Seen in this perspective, the option premium becomes an "insurance premium," covering the cost of a likely loss on the option position in the future. To analyze the future loss structure and to assess the potential risk associated with a given option agreement, statistical simulation analysis can be applied.

In this analysis the foreign exchange rate volatility plays an important role. The volatility calculation is based on the change in the foreign exchange rate within regular intervals during a given period. There is no general agreement on which time intervals to use or on which periods to analyze. The matter of the fact is that all statistical analysis is carried out on historical data. However updated these might be, what really matters is the expected exchange rate volatility over the future period of the option agreement.

So judgement is again called for when determining the appropriate exchange rate volatility figure for a given option agreement.

Example: Let's calculate the foreign exchange rate volatility of the Deutsche mark exchange rate against the U.S. dollar in monthly intervals over the past twelve months.

Notice an increase in the exchange rate volatility over the latter half of the year. If the expectation is that this pattern will remain over the coming months, we will use the annualized monthly change of 15.76% for our calculations.

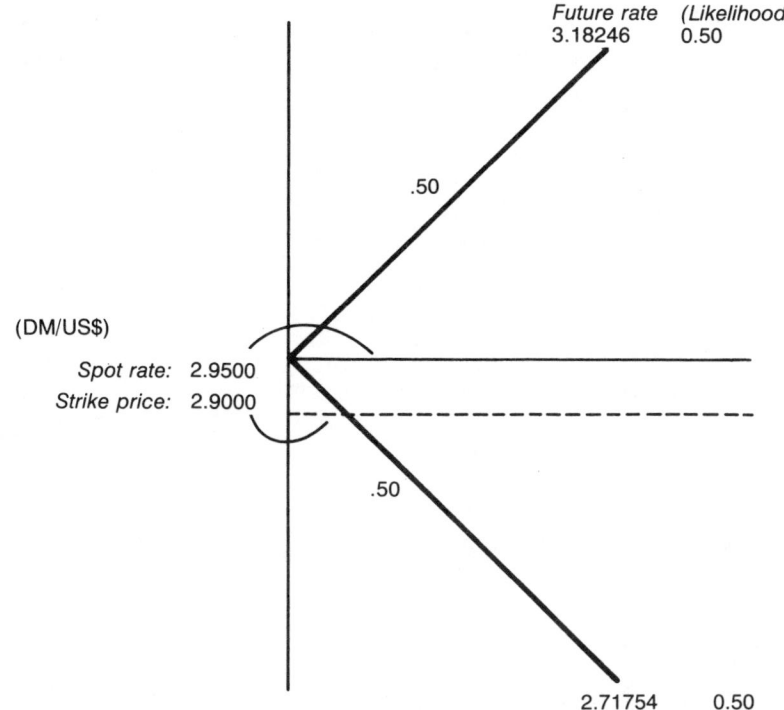

Figure 11-1. *Graph to Determine Foreign Exchange Rate Volatility.*

Example: The spot foreign exchange rate is 2.9500 DM/US$ and we are about to quote for a three-month European call option with strike price of 2.9000 DM/US$. Assuming a future annual change of 15.76% in the exchange rate, we expect that the exchange rate might increase or decrease by 7.88% ($15.76\%/\sqrt{4}$) over the coming three-month period. If the foreign exchange rate develops at random, we assign a 50% likelihood that the foreign exchange rate will increase and a 50% likelihood that it will drop. (See Figure 11-1.)

The option holder will exercise the call option only if the foreign exchange rate drops below the exercise price. The option writer's potential payout on this call option can be calculated as .50 (0.0000) + .50 (2.900 − 2.71754) = 0.09123. Given that the three-month interest rate presently is 12% p.a., the present

Table 11-3. Calculating Foreign Exchange Rate Volatility (Example).

Date	Rate (DM/US$)	Pct. Change	Pct. Change	Squared
Sept. 28	2.7500			
Oct. 31	2.6300	− 4.36%	19.01	
Nov. 30	2.5875	− 1.62%	2.62	
Dec. 31	2.7300	+ 0.55%	0.30	
Jan. 31	2.7005	− 1.08%	1.17	
Feb. 28	2.6400	− 2.24%	5.02	
Mar. 29	2.5908	− 1.86%	3.46	
Apr. 30	2.6705	+ 3.08%	9.49	9.49
May 31	2.7900	+ 4.47%	19.98	19.98
Jun. 28	2.9803	+ 6.82%	46.51	46.51
Jul. 31	3.1515	+ 5.74%	32.95	32.95
Aug. 30	3.1008	− 1.61%	2.59	2.59
Sept. 30	2.9900	− 3.57%	12.74	12.74

Sum total			155.84	124.26
Monthly average (Pct. variance)			12.99	20.71
Square root (Pct. Standard deviation)			3.60	4.55
Annualized pct. change	12 × 3.60 =		12.47%	
Annualized pct. change	12 × 4.55 =			15.76%

value of the potential payout is 0.0886 (0.09125/1.03)´, which as a percentage of the spot price amounts to 3.0% (0.0886/0.0295).

This then corresponds to the up-front premium required to cover the future potential payouts of the call option.

Figure 11-2 presents the up-front premium required for shorter sequences, such as months.

Example: The monthly change in the foreign exchange rate is 4.55% $(15.76/\sqrt{12})$. In the first month there is a 50% likelihood that the foreign exchange rate increases to 3.0842 and a 50% likelihood that the foreign exchange rate decreases to 2.8158. And so on.

If the spot foreign exchange rate ends up above 2.9000 DM/US$, the option will not be exercised. This will happen only if the foreign exchange rate falls below the strike price. Hence the potential payout on the call option is calculated as:

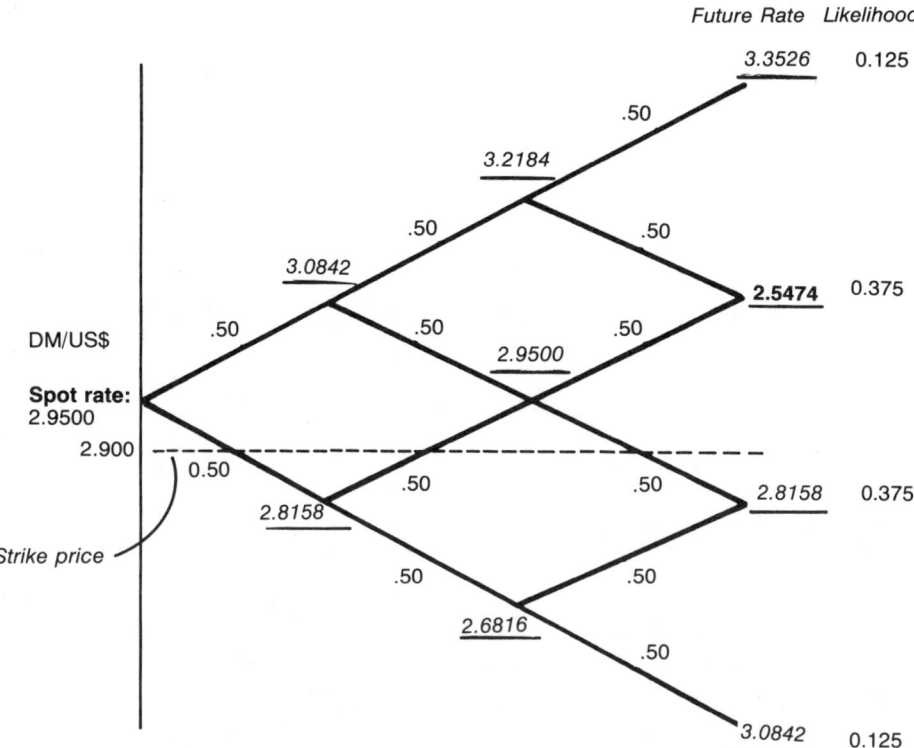

Figure 11-2. *Up-Front Premiums for Monthly Periods.*

$$
\begin{array}{l}
+\ \ .125\,(0.000) \\
+\ \ .375\,(0.000) \\
+3.75\ \ (2.9000-2.8158) \\
+\ \ .125\,(2.9000-2.5474) \\
\hline
+\ 0.07565
\end{array}
$$

The present value amounts to 0.0734 (0.07565/1.03) which as a percentage of the spot price makes up 2.5%.

The smaller we make the time intervals, the more interactions will be performed and the closer we will get to determining the option premium—which adequately reflects the risk attached to writing the option. The more interactions we perform, the more the statistical distribution of the resulting future foreign exchange rate will approach the normal distribution. See Figure 11-3. The mean value will then be equal to the initial

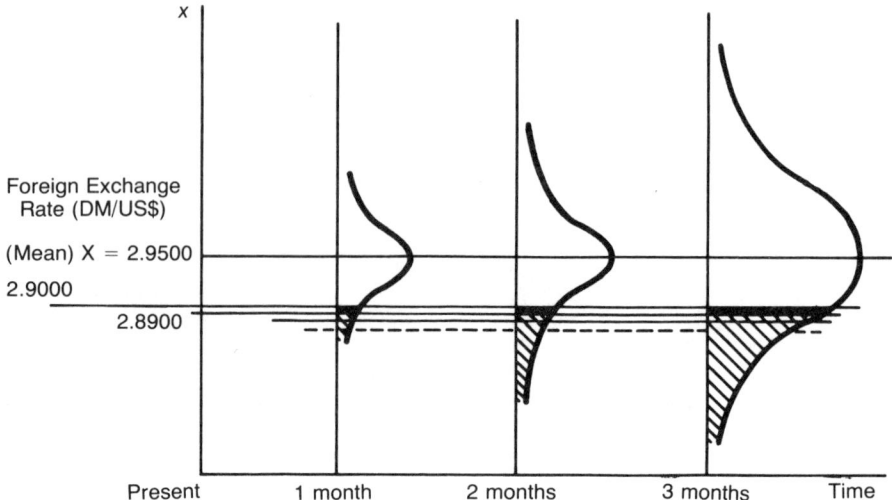

Figure 11-3. *Graph of Normally Distributed Foreign Exchange Rate Development.*

spot exchange rate and a standard deviation equal to the one previously determined to reflect the future volatility of the exchange rate.

This value can be used in a further analysis of the call option. The likelihood that the foreign exchange rate will fall within a certain interval, such as between 2.8900 and 2.9000 DM/US$, can be found by applying a tabularized cumulative normal distribution. This likelihood is then multiplied by the cost of exercise, to find the expected cost of the exchange rate falling inside this interval. This is performed for all similar intervals below the strike price. The costs of falling within each interval are then added together to give the total expected cost of the call option with a strike price of 2.9000 DM/US$.

Cost of call option = Sum P [(($Y - 0.01 \times n$) < x < ($y - 0.01$ ($n - 1$))) $\times$ ($0.01 \times n$)] for all n

where:

P = Likelihood of event.

x = Variable foreign exchange rate (DM/US$).

y = Strike price of 2.9000 DM/US$
n = 1, 2, 3, 4, 5, ..., sufficiently large number.
0.01 = Determined to be the appropriate interval size.
$(0.01 \cdot n)$ = Cost of exercise in that specific interval.

To analyze an American option we have to monitor the development of the current spot exchange rate through each iteration. By calculating the intrinsic value of the call option at each iteration, we can determine the value of the option if it is exercised before final maturity. This value is compared to the calculation of the option value if exercised at expiration. Whichever is the higher of these two values will represent the cost of the option, which then becomes the option premium to charge the option writer.

Several option pricing models, based on this line of thought, have been developed over the years. Although most of these require a very high level of mathematical sophistication, none of them presents a perfect solution to the option pricing dilemma. They all make assumptions about the future price volatility that might not hold true.

INTEREST RATE OPTIONS

The over-the-counter market on interest rate options is being continuously developed by the major international banks, and many financial institutions now offer both call and put options on interest rates. So far OTC interest rate options are quoted only in U.S. dollars but other major currencies may follow as the market develops.

Parallel exchange markets for interest rate options are the U.S. Treasury bond options of the Chicago exchanges, the LIFFE pound sterling long gilt option, and the three-month Eurodollar deposit options of the Philadelphia Board of Trade and the LIFFE, which provide an opportunity to hedge U.S. dollar interest rates for maturities of up to nine months. By combining the U.S. dollar interest rate options with foreign exchange options, interests rate option hedges can be created in other major currencies. However, the up-front premium payable on the option contracts involved will make this solution unattractive to pursue for most institutions.

The OTC interest rate call option agreement gives the holder the right but not the obligation to obtain funds of a certain maturity over a given period at a predetermined rate.

Example: A call option might provide the holder with the right to exercise a $5,000,000 four-year loan at a fixed rate of 12% p.a. if the option is exercised within the next three months.

Conversely an interest rate put option agreement gives the holder the right but not the obligation to deposit liquidity of a certain maturity over a given period at a predetermined interest rate.

Table 11-4. *Comparing Exchange-Traded Options with OTC Option Agreements.*

Exchange Options	OTC Options
• Trading is done on the exchange trading floor and prices are determined by "open outcry."	• Banks quote the option premium for the specific option agreement over the phone.
• Market participants are unknown to each other, and settlement is done through the exchange clearing entity.	• Participants are known to each other and a transaction implies an acceptance of counterparty risk.
• Buyers of options pay a premium up front. Option writers pay initial margin and are marked-to-market on a current basis.	• Option buyers can pay premium up front or in arrears. So far only limited possibility for writing options.
• Option contracts have standard amounts and fixed maturity dates of up to nine months' duration.	• Contract size is flexible over a minimum requirement of US$ 1,000,000. Maturity dates are flexible and exceed that of exchange-traded options.
• All currency options contracts are quoted against U.S. dollars and only for major currencies. Interest rate options only exist on U.S. Treasuries and three-month Eurodollar deposits (European type).	• Quotes are given on all international currencies against U.S. dollars and on cross rates. Interest rate options are quoted in U.S. dollars.

Example: A put option could provide the holder with the option to exercise a $10,000,000 one-year deposit at a fixed rate of 11½% p.a., if the option is exercised within the next three months.

CONCLUSION

OTC options in many ways provide the option buyer with a flexibility that cannot be met by engaging in exchange-traded options, notably with regard to maturities and quotes on cross currencies. On the other hand, OTC contracts are not as easily bought and sold as the highly liquid option exchange options. Although a number of financial institutions offer clients the opportunity to write options over-the-counter, the market is a developing one. So far, the market serves to provide the holder of exchange-traded options with the extra flexibility to close option positions and thereby take advantage of favorable market developments. In the end, the question of which market to approach depends on two things: (1) the organizational resources available to the hedger to monitor current developments on the option exchanges, and (2) how well each market can accommodate true hedges to close specific foreign exchange and interest rate gaps.

Interest Rate Agreements

With the appearance of actively traded financial futures markets in U.S. Treasuries, Eurodollar deposits, and pound sterling gilts, the financial intermediaries have been able to develop different types of hedging services to guarantee the future interest rate level to the buyer. The financial institutions will hedge their exposure by taking up corresponding positions in financial futures contracts or by the increasing number of option contracts on interest rate futures now being offered.

Thus the financial intermediary assumes the basis risk associated with the financial futures and/or options hedge. As experienced exchange dealers, they in effect carry out the handling of the financial futures and/or options hedge, which to most institutions constitutes a resource-intensive function. The institutional client is therefore offered a risk-free interest rate hedging product.

The interest rate hedging services offered by the financial institutions guarantee a maximum future interest rate for borrowers or a minimum future interest rate for investors. As opposed to the hedges that can be arranged by accessing the option exchanges, the OTC services extend the interest rate guarantee for periods exceeding the normal maturities available on the exchanges.

The compensation for a longer-term interest rate guarantee

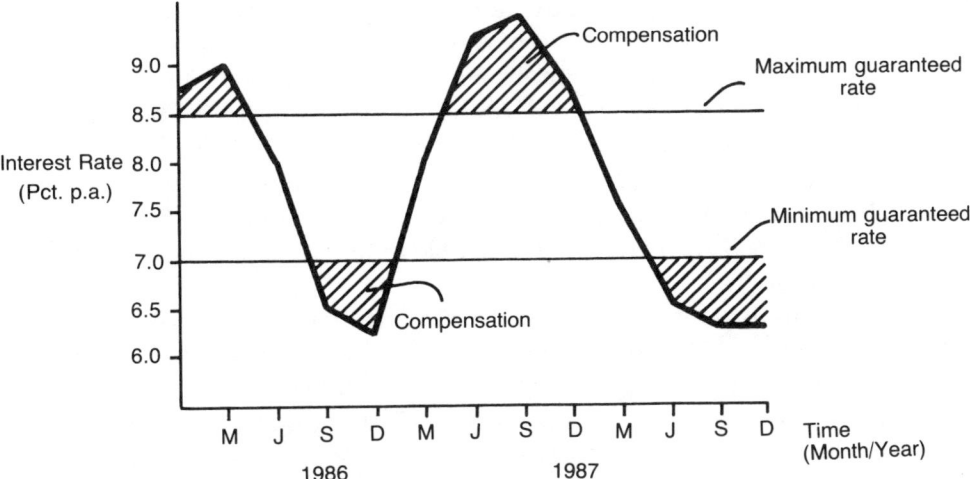

Figure 12-1. *Graph of Compensation on Guaranteed Rates.*

is settled periodically (usually quarterly corresponding to the exchange maturities) on a cash basis until the maturity of the agreement. Compensation therefore corresponds to the cash settlement principle prevalent on the financial futures and options exchanges.

In principle, the client who has been guaranteed a maximum interest rate level will obtain cash settlement compensation whenever the interest rate exceeds the guaranteed rate. Conversely, the client who has been guaranteed a minimum interest rate level will obtain cash settlement compensation whenever the interest rate falls below the guaranteed rate. (See Figure 12-1.)

The OTC market also offers services corresponding to the vertical bull and bear spreads, which can be established by trading options contracts on the exchanges. (See Chapter 8.)

CEILING RATE AGREEMENT

This type of interest rate agreement provides the holder with a hedge against an increase in the interest rate level without actual delivery of funds taking place. This type of agreement will guarantee a maximum borrowing rate for a period of up to ten years. For this type of hedge the institutional client will pay an up-front fee (sometimes payable quarterly in arrears), quoted as a percentage p.a. on the contract amount. The agreement is often settled quarterly; that is, if at the end of each quarter the actual borrowing rate has exceeded the agreed rate, the bank will pay the client the difference in the interest amount. If the actual borrowing rate is below the agreed rate, nothing will happen.

This type of hedging service is interesting not only to the institution that is planning to raise funds and looking to put a maximum limit on the future interest expense. It is also interesting to an institution that fears the effect of an expected increase in interest rates on its already existing floating rate debt.

Example: A public company has floating rate debt of US $ 10,000,000 raised three years ago with a final bullet repayment maturing five years after drawdown. The loan was obtained at a rate of LIBOR + 1¼%, payable quarterly in arrears throughout the loan period. Now management is fearing that a recent increase in the interest rate level will turn into a permanent trend over the last two years of the loan.

So the company buys a 10,000,000 ceiling rate agreement that guarantees that LIBOR will not exceed a certain level over the next eight quarters. In this case, the LIBOR serves as a rate basis for the quarterly settlement. Assume that rates have been quoted and that the actual interest rate develops as follows:

Period	Maximum Rate	Fee	Fee Payable	Actual LIBOR	Bank Compensation
3 months in 3 months	9.00% p.a.	½% p.a.	$ 12,500	8.75% p.a.	—
3 months in 6 months	9.10% p.a.	½% p.a.	$ 12,500	9.00% p.a.	—
3 months in 9 months	9.20% p.a.	⅝% p.a.	$ 15,625	9.50% p.a.	$ 7,500
3 months in 12 months	9.30% p.a.	⅝% p.a.	$ 15,625	10.05% p.a.	$ 18,750
3 months in 15 months	9.40% p.a.	¾% p.a.	$ 18,750	10.65% p.a.	$ 32,250
3 months in 18 months	9.50% p.a.	¾% p.a.	$ 18,750	11.25% p.a.	$ 43,750
3 months in 21 months	9.60% p.a.	1% p.a.	$ 25,000	11.85% p.a.	$ 56,250
3 months in 24 months	9.70% p.a.	1% p.a.	$ 25,000	11.50% p.a.	$ 45,000
Total fees			$143,750		
Total bank compensation					$203,500

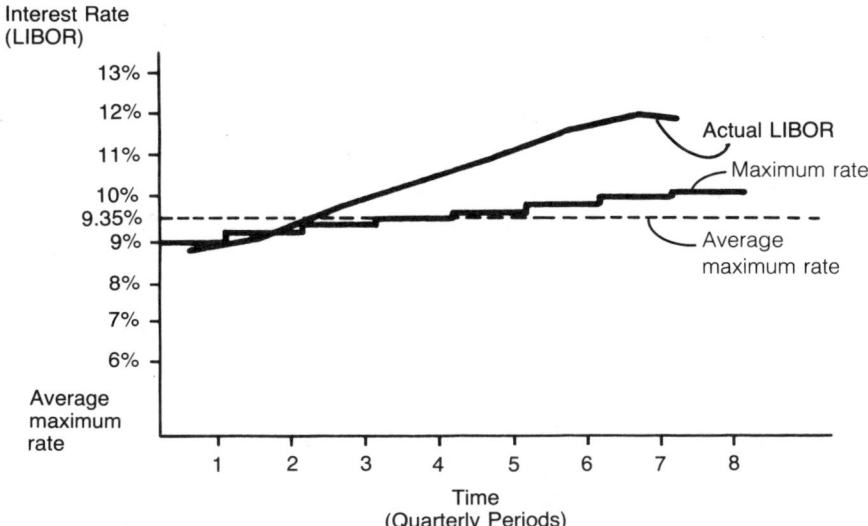

Figure 12-2. *Guaranteed Borrowing Rate.*

In the first six months, the actual LIBOR was lower than the maximum rate and hence nothing happens. In the third quarter the actual LIBOR exceeded the maximum rate by 30 basis points and hence the bank paid the company the difference in the interest amount, namely $7,500 ($10,000,000 × .30/400), and so forth.

The corporation has thus guaranteed a maximum LIBOR on average over the last two years of the loan of 9.35% p.a., that is, a total guaranteed loan rate of 10.60% (9.35 + 1.25). However, the corporation still takes full advantage of the interest rate being lower than the maximum rate. This saved the company $6,250 in the first quarter and $2,500 in the second quarter.

FLOOR RATE AGREEMENT

This interest rate agreement provides the holder with a hedge against a decrease in the investment rate. That is, the holder can be guaranteed a minimum return on a certain investment portfolio in a period of up to ten years. The agreement is settled quarterly. If at the end of the quarter the actual investment rate is below the agreed rate, the bank will pay the difference in interest amount. If the actual investment rate is above the agreed rate, nothing happens. For this type of interest rate hedge, the holder will pay an up-front fee potentially arranged for payment quarterly in arrears. The fee is usually quoted as a percentage p.a. calculated on the contract amount. The agreement is of interest to any institution that has to periodically place excess liquidity or that maintains a fixed maturity floating rate investment and would like to secure a minimum return on the investment in a falling interest rate environment.

Example: A commercial bank is about to extend a two- year floating rate loan of US$ 15,000,000 at LIBOR + 1½% with interest payable quarterly in arrears, and the management board takes the view that the dollar interest rate will continue its recent declining trend. The bank then buys a floor rate agreement of US$ 15,000,000, which guarantees the institution a minimum interest rate on the future loan. Assume that the rates have been quoted and that the actual interest rate developed as follows:

Period		Minimum Rate	Fee	Fee Payable	Actual LIBOR	Bank Compensation
3 months in	3 months	8.90% p.a.	½% p.a.	$ 18,750	8.55% p.a.	$ 13,125
3 months in	6 months	9.05% p.a.	½% p.a.	$ 18,750	8.45% p.a.	$ 22,500
3 months in	9 months	9.20% p.a.	½% p.a.	$ 18,750	9.10% p.a.	$ 3,750
3 months in	12 months	9.35% p.a.	½% p.a.	$ 18,750	9.50% p.a.	—
3 months in	15 months	9.50% p.a.	⅝% p.a.	$ 23,437	9.00% p.a.	$ 18,175
3 months in	18 months	9.60% p.a.	⅝% p.a.	$ 23,437	8.75% p.a.	$ 31,875
3 months in	21 months	9.65% p.a.	⅞% p.a.	$ 32,812	8.50% p.a.	$ 43,125
3 months in	24 months	9.70% p.a.	1% p.a.	$ 37,500	8.00% p.a.	$ 63,750
Total fee				$192,186		
Total bank compensation						$196,300

In this case the bank has a guaranteed LIBOR in average over the two-year period of 9.37% p.a., which guarantees a return on the loan of minimum 10.87% p.a. (9.37% + 1.50). However, in case the interest rate exceeds the minimum rate, the holder of the agreement takes full advantage of the excess interest over the guaranteed rate.

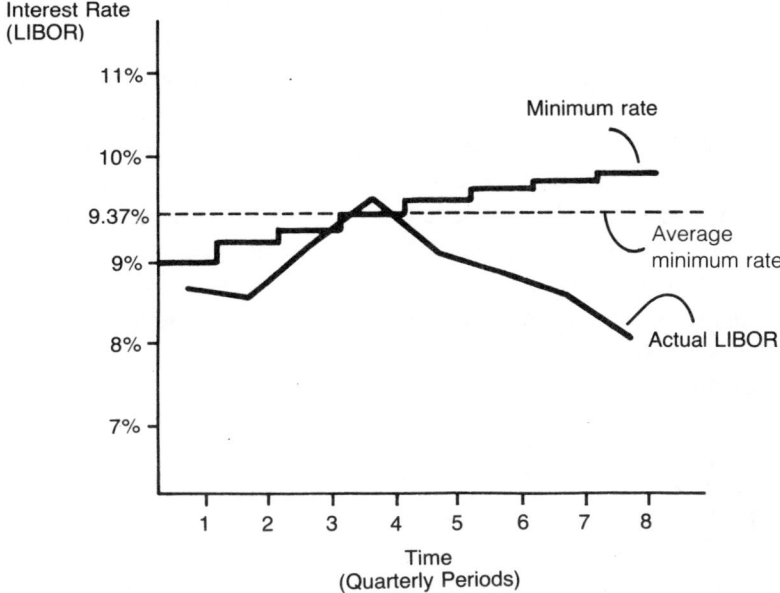

Figure 12-3. *Guaranteed Investment Rate.*

As a rule the front-end fee represents the threshhold value with which to compare the expected volatility of the interest rate level. If a company buys a two-year ceiling rate agreement at an average fee of .72% p.a., then it has taken the view that on average the interest rate will increase by more than .72% over the two-year period. Conversely, if a bank buys a floor rate agreement at an average fee of .64% p.a., then it fears that on average the interest rate might drop by more than .64% over the next two years.

The interest rate agreements can be arranged in different ways by incorporating other interest rate bases for the quarterly settlement or by applying a fixed interest rate for the whole contract period.

The preceding examples illustrate situations where the advantage to the buyer of the interest rate agreements is significant as calculated on an ex post basis. Obviously such is not always the case. On average the system must be in balance so that gains and losses even out over the long run and at the same time leave a reasonable net gain to cover the transaction and development costs of the market intermediaries. The hedger, however, is willing to pay such a premium to avoid the administrative burden of doing the hedge directly on an exchange and to effectively eliminate the uncertainty of the future interest rate. Whether to engage in an interest rate agreement is an ex ante decision to be analyzed by the financial management given the uncertainty of the future; it involves an evaluation of the potential risks of maintaining an interest rate gapping position. Hence the premium paid for an interest rate agreement will also contain a compensation element for the privilege of obtaining full knowledge or a guarantee on the future interest rate development.

COMBINED CEILING RATE AND FLOOR RATE AGREEMENTS

A *ceiling rate agreement* guarantees a maximum borrowing rate and gives the holder the full benefit of a drop in the interest rate below the maximum rate. However, the borrower might take the view that the likelihood of a drop in the interest rate is negligible. So he might want to buy a combined ceiling rate and floor rate agreement. That is, if the rate exceeds the maximum guaranteed level, such as 10% p.a. for a five-year period, the bank will compensate the holder quarterly for the difference in the interest amount. However, if the interest rate drops below, say, 8% p.a. over the same five-year period, the company will compensate the bank quarterly by the difference in the interest amount. Hence the buyer is guaranteed a maximum borrowing rate of 10%. If the interest rate is between 8 and 10% p.a., the buyer will take full advantage of the lower interest rate, but if it drops below 8% p.a., he will incur a loss. (Compare this type of hedge to the vertical bull spread, described in Chapter 8.)

Conversely, a *floor rate agreement* guarantees a minimum investment rate. giving the holder the full benefit of an increase in the interest rate above the minimum rate. Again, if the investor takes the view that an increase in the interest rate is very unlikely, he may want to buy a combination of a floor rate agreement and a ceiling rate agreement. That is, if the interest rate is below the minimum rate of, say, 9% p.a. then the bank will compensate the holder quarterly by paying the difference in the interest amount. If the interest rate is between 9 and 11% p.a., the holder will take full advantage of the higher interest rate. If the interest rate exceeds 11% p.a., the holder will compensate the bank quarterly for the difference in the interest amount. (Compare this type of hedge to the vertical bear spread described in Chapter 8.)

The combined ceiling rate and floor rate agreement is often termed a *dollar rate agreement*. Its advantage is that the front-end fee is lower than the fees on the corresponding ceiling rate agreement or floor rate aqreement. Keep in mind, however, that the collar rate agreement does *not* provide a full hedge to the holder.

Case: Interest Rate Agreement: Ceiling Rate (Mortage Association, Maturity Mismatch Interest Rate Gapping)

In November 1985 the Lauderdale Building Society held a US$ 14,000,000 portfolio of 15-year mortgage loans on its books. The mortgage loans were signed to cover commercial building contracts completed at year-end 1984, and so the final maturity of the loans was determined to be December 1, 1999. Repayment of principal and interest on this specific mortgage portfolio was arranged as 30 equal semiannual annuities with a locked-in rate of 11.50% p.a. Repayment dates were set at June 1 and December 1 each year until maturity. (See Table 12-1.)

In compliance with normal business practice, Lauderdale Building Society funded most of its long-term commitments through issuance of medium-term savings bonds. However, due to the incremental nature of this commercial transaction and a continued fall in interest rates, the US $ 14,000,000 mortgage loan was being funded through short-term interbank loans at an interest rate determined at the going money market rate plus ¼–½% spread.

The Treasurer of the Lauderdale Building Society, Mr. Fitzgerald, was well aware of the ups and downs in the inter-

Table 12-1. Repayment Schedule of U.S. 14.000,000,
15-year Mortgage Portfolio.

Date	Outstanding	Annuity	Principal	Interest
Dec 84	14,000,000.00	—	—	—
Jun 85	13,814,972.66	990,027.34	185,027.34	805,000.00
Dec 85	13,619,306.25	990,027.34	195,666.41	794,360.93
Jun 86	13,412,389.02	990,027.34	206,917.23	783,110.11
Dec 86	13,193,574.05	990,027.34	218,814.97	771,212.37
Jun 87	12,962,177.22	990,027.34	231,396.83	758,630.51
Dec 87	12,717,475.07	990,027.34	244,702.15	745,325.19
Jun 88	12,458,702.55	990,027.34	258,772.52	731,254.82
Dec 88	12,185,050.61	990,027.34	273,651.94	716,375.40
Jun 89	11,895,663.68	990,027.34	289,386.93	700,640.41
Dec 89	11,589,637.00	990,027.34	306,026.68	684,000.66
Jun 90	11,266,013.79	990,027.34	323,623.21	666,404.13
Dec 90	10,923,782.24	990,027.34	342,231.55	647,795.79
Jun 91	10,561,872.38	990,027.34	361,909.86	628,117.48
Dec 91	10,179,152.70	990,027.34	382,719.68	607,307.66
Jun 92	9,774,426.64	990,027.34	404,726.06	585,301.28
Dec 92	9,346,428.83	990,027.34	427,997.81	562,029.53
Jun 93	8,893,821.15	990,027.34	452,697.68	537,419.66
Dec 93	8,415,188.53	990,027.34	478,632.62	511,394.72
Jun 94	7,909,034.53	990,027.34	506,154.00	483,873.34
Dec 94	7,373,776.68	990,027.34	535,257.85	454,769.49
Jun 95	6,807,741.50	990,027.34	566,035.18	423,992.16
Dec 95	6,209,159.30	990,027.34	598,582.20	391,445.14
Jun 96	5,576,158.62	990,027.34	633,000.68	357,026.66
Dec 96	4,906,760.40	990,027.34	669,398.22	320,629.12
Jun 97	4,198,871.78	990,027.34	707,888.62	282,138.72
Dec 97	3,450,279.57	990,027.34	748,592.21	241,435.13
Jun 98	2,658,643.31	990,027.34	791,636.26	198,391.08
Dec 98	1,821,487.96	990,027.34	837,155.35	152,871.99
Jun 99	936,196.18	990,027.34	936,196.18	53,831.28
Total		29,700,820.20	14,000,000.00	

bank money market rates, which from year to year—and even from month to month by historical experience—could fluctuate widely. Fitzgerald analyzed the short term interest rate structure and usually based his intermediate funding strategy on a short-term view of the interest rate movement. Given presently declining interest rates, he had funded the portfolio by rolling over three-month money market loans in the view that the interest rate level at least in the short to medium term would continue to drop. See Table 12-2 and Figure 12-4.

The money market funding strategy would obviously provide flexibility to "play" the market by switching short-term

Table 12-2. Last Twenty Months' Mid-Month Closing Rates (Three-Month Money Market Rate + ¼% Spread).

Mar. 15,	84	$10^{13}/_{16}$%
Apr. 16,	84	$10^{1}/_{4}$%
May 15,	84	$9^{11}/_{16}$%
Jun. 15,	84	$9^{3}/_{8}$%
Jul. 16,	84	$8^{15}/_{15}$%
Aug. 15,	84	$8^{3}/_{4}$%
Sep. 14,	84	$8^{5}/_{8}$%
Oct. 15,	84	$8^{1}/_{2}$%
Nov. 15,	84	$8^{11}/_{16}$%
Dec. 14,	84	$9^{1}/_{8}$%
Jan. 15,	85	$9^{1}/_{4}$%
Feb. 15,	85	$9^{3}/_{8}$%
Mar. 15,	85	$9^{1}/_{4}$%
Apr. 15,	85	$9^{7}/_{16}$%
May 15,	85	$9^{1}/_{2}$%
Jun. 14,	85	$9^{1}/_{8}$%
Jul. 15,	85	$8^{3}/_{4}$%
Aug. 15,	85	$8^{11}/_{16}$%
Sep. 16,	85	$8^{7}/_{8}$%
Oct. 15,	85	$8^{1}/_{2}$%

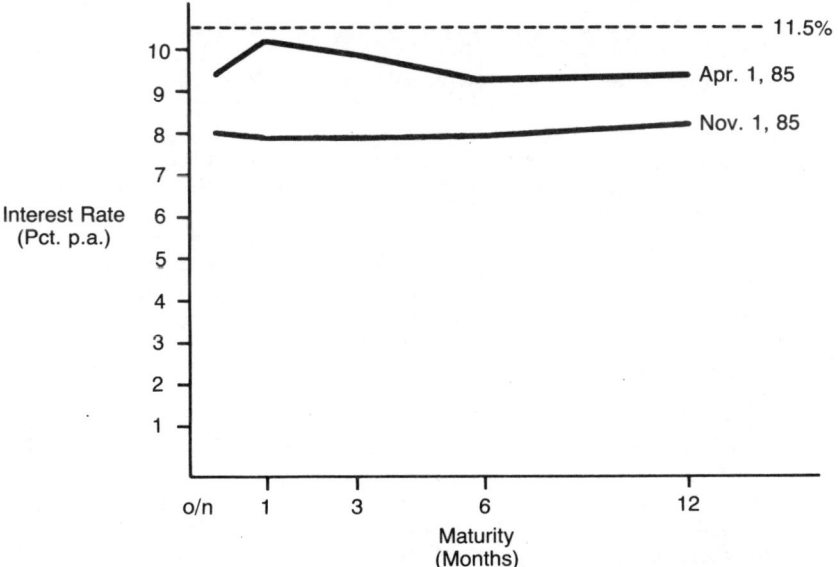

Figure 12-4. Interest Rate Structure, Money Market Rates.

funding maturities according to changes in the interest rate structure. It had led to an overall lower-than-average funding cost over the past year in the falling interest rate environment. However, Mr. Fitzgerald was also aware that a fifteen-year fixed rate commitment represents considerable interest rate risk in case the short-term interbank money market rate increased above the fixed return of 11.50% p.a. on the mortgage portfolio.

As Mr. Fitzgerald expressed it:

> The interest rate gapping concerned us and senior management, and the whole issue had been discussed at several board meetings since the fall of 1984.

In early November 1985 the all-in six-month funding rate was around 8½% p.a., thus securing a reasonable interest rate differential to the Lauderdale Building Society in the short to medium term. The prevailing interest rate outlook favored a continued drop in the interest rate level, but with some uncertainties (Table 12-3). Hence the board, meeting on Mr.

Table 12-3. Money Markets (Financial Times).

"Volcker Causes Some Confusion"

In New York the Federal funds rate was high, at around 8 percent, as payment was made for bills and bonds bought at Treasury auctions. withdrawing money from the banking system. This caused a distortion to the general interest rate picture, leaving no clues about monetary policy following the Federal Open Market Committee meeting at the beginning of the week.

An unexpected fall of $2.2 bn in the U.S. M1 money supply measure has been running well above target, but Mr. Paul Volcker, chairman of the Federal Reserve Board, indicated the target will be ignored, and the Fed will not move to aggressively tighten monetary policy.

This caused some confusion in financial markets, because in the light of the policy aimed at weakening the dollar it was not expected that rates would be increased. Signs of a sluggish economy has led to speculation the Fed may well cut its discount rate before year end but Mr. Volcker's comments were interpreted as suggesting a slight tightening by the FOMC.

Mr. Karl Otto Poehl, president of the German Bundesbank, said during the week there was no intention of following Japan in raising interest rates. The central bank drained a little liquidity in Frankfurt, by not fully replacing a maturing securities repurchase agreement, keeping interest rates around 4.5 percent. But as expected the Bundesbank council left monetary policy unchanged.

Fitzgerald's recommendation, decided to fund short term for an interim period of two years and to lock in the interest rate differential for the remaining 12½ years to maturity from June 1987 onward.

To guarantee a maximum funding rate, Mr. Fitzgerald contacted a few money center banks to obtain quotes on ceiling rate agreements which would approximately match the funding need of the building contract until maturity. Take into consideration the periodic annuity payments coming in and the interest payments on the short-term funding going out. See Table 12-4.

Table 12-4. Cash Flow Analysis.

Date	Short-Term Funding need	Annuity Payment	Interest on Funding*
Dec 84	14,000,000	990,027	595,000
Jun 85	13,604,973	990,027	578,210
Dec 85	13,193,156	990,027	560,709
Jun 86	12,763,838	990,027	542,463
Dec 86	12,316,274	990,027	523,442
Jun 87	11,849,689	990,027	503,612
Dec 87	11,632,274	990,027	482,939
Jun 88	11,125,186	990,027	472,820
Dec 88	10,607,979	990,027	450,839
Jun 89	10,068,791	990,027	427,924
Dec 89	9,506,688	990,027	404,034
Jun 90	8,920,695	990,027	379,130
Dec 90	8,309,798	990,027	353,166
Jun 91	7,672,937	990,027	326,100
Dec 91	7,009,000	990,027	297,882
Jun 92	6,316,855	990,027	268,466
Dec 92	5,595,294	990,027	237,800
Jun 93	4,843,067	990,027	205,830
Dec 93	4,058,870	990,027	172,502
Jun 94	3,241,345	990,027	137,757
Dec 94	2,389,075	990,027	101,535
Jun 95	1,500,584	990,027	63,775
Dec 95	574,332	990,027	24,409
Jun 96	− 391,286	990,027	− 16,630
Dec 96	−1,364,683	990,027	− 57,999
Jun 97	−2,412,709	990.027	−102,540
Dec 97	−3,505,276	990,027	−148,974
Jun 98	−4,644,277	990,027	−197,382
Dec 98	−5,831,686	990,027	−247,847
Jun 99	−7,069,560	990,027	−300,456
Dec 99	−8.360,043	990,027	−355,302

*Assuming an 8.5% short-term funding rate until Dec. 1987.

By assuming an average funding rate of 8½% p.a., Mr. Fitzgerald obtained an approximate estimate of the current funding need of the building contracts. Liquidity flows would balance around year 10 and so he obtained ceiling rate quotes up to June 1995 (Table 12-5).

Table 12-5. *Ceiling Rate Quotes.*

Date	Contract Size ($1.000,000)	Contract Periods (Months in Years.)	Guaranteed Rate	Fee
Dec. 87	11.1	6 mos. in 2.5 yrs.	8.90%	0.60%
Jun. 88	10.6	6 mos. in 3.0 yrs.	8.90%	0.60%
Dec. 88	10.0	6 mos. in 3.5 yrs.	8.90%	0.60%
Jun. 89	9.5	6 mos. in 4.0 yrs.	9.10%	0.75%
Dec. 89	8.9	6 mos. in 4.5 yrs.	9.10%	0.75%
Jun. 90	8.3	6 mos. in 5.0 yrs.	9.25%	1.20%
Dec. 90	7.6	6 mos. in 5.5 yrs.	9.25%	12.2%
Jun. 91	7.0	6 mos. in 6.0 yrs.	9.25%	1.20%
Dec. 91	6.3	6 mos. in 6.5 yrs.	9.50%	1.50%
Jun. 92	5.6	6 mos. in 7.0 yrs.	9.50%	1.50%
Dec. 92	4.8	6 mos. in 7.5 yrs.	9.75%	1.80%
Jun. 93	4.0	6 mos. in 8.0 yrs.	9.75%	1.95%
Dec. 93	3.2	6 mos. in 8.5 yrs.	10.00%	2.25%
Jun. 94	2.4	6 mos. in 9.0 yrs.	10.20%	2.55%
Dec. 94	1.5	6 mos. in 9.5 yrs.	10.25%	2.70%
Jun. 95	0.6	6 mos. in 10.0 yrs.	10.50%	2.85%

The Lauderdale Building Society signed the ceiling rate agreements and was henceforth guaranteed a maximum future funding cost at the quoted rates. Assuming a short-term funding rate in the money market until December 1987 of 8½% p.a., the ceiling rate agreements secured Lauderdale Building Society an average maximum funding rate of around 8.65% p.a. In addition, the Lauderdale Building Society paid a contract fee that was calculated on the total funding need over the life of the building contracts; this amounted on average to around 0.90% p.a. Hence the Lauderdale Building Society effectively guaranteed a maximum funding rate of less than 10% p.a. on the fifteen-year building contracts, given that the short-term interest rate gapping would hold. The guaranteed future funding rate based on funding over the interbank market appeared to be relatively favorable as compared to other alternative sources of funding.

The break-even rate on the money market funding over the coming two-year period until December 1987 was around 14.5% p.a. which under the general interest rate outlook at the time comforted management of the Lauderdale Building Society. Due to the interest rate uncertainties over the longer term until the maturity of the mortgage loans in December 1999, however, the management of the Lauderdale Building Society preferred to lock in or guarantee a maximum future long-term funding rate.

INTEREST RATE AND CURRENCY SWAPS

In the early 1980s investment bankers and brokerage houses developed techniques that enabled institutions to switch assets and liabilities from one type of interest rate basis into another or from one currency denomination to another. At first, the market developed as pure counterparty transactions where two, three, or more institutions with different asset and liability profiles were matched to provide each institution with a better exposure.[1] This type of arrangement could involve, for example, a Japanese airline, an American shipping company, and an Asian sovereign borrower—to mention just one possible constellation. In general the greater the contact with a diversified world-wide customer base, the higher the potential is for a successful match of interests. This obviously favored the large international financial institutions in the early development of the swaps market. However as transaction volume has increased and the concept has become more familiar to potential benefactors, an active interbank market has developed for the most common types of swap transactions.

Interest Rate Swap Agreements

By entering into an interest rate swap agreement, an institution can switch an asset or liability from a fixed rate basis to a floating rate basis in the same currency or vice versa. By finding two institutions with opposite interests, an intermediary can arrange a swap transaction.

Example: A construction company has raised US $ 40,000,000 five-year floating rate debt to fund a future project and would like to lock in the future interest expense related to the project. Conversely, a commercial bank has launched a five-year fixed coupon Eurodollar issue of US $ 40,000,000 to fund its portfolio of floating rate loans. These two counterparties can enter an interest rate swap through an intermediary and obtain the type of liability that each is looking for.

This is done simply by having each of the two institutions service the other's interest payments throughout the life of the loans. Since the two liabilities are in the same currency, there is no exchange of principal in the swap. The construction company pays fixed rate interest to the intermediary, and the intermediary pays the floating rate interest to the company to service its floating rate liability. The commercial bank pays floating rate interest to the intermediary, and the intermediary pays fixed interest to the commercial bank to service its fixed rate liability. The outcome is that the construction company has obtained a fixed rate liability, and the commercial bank has obtained a floating rate liability resulting in a better match of the interest rate basis of their assets and liabilities.

The two counterparties, who usually are unknown to each other, deal solely with the intermediary, and their contractual obligations with regard to the swap transaction are solely made against the intermediary. Conversely, the intermediary assumes the counterparty risk of the two counterparties. The intermediary will charge a front-end fee, usually fixed as a percentage of the transaction amount, for performing the brokerage function and for managing the counterparty risk in the transaction.

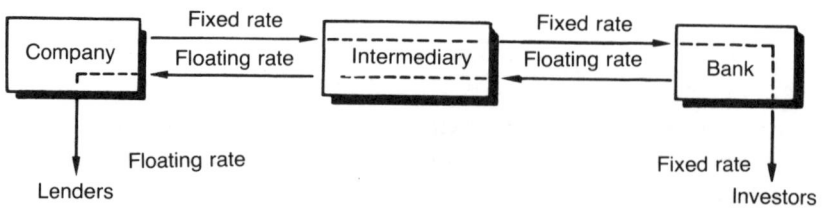

Figure 12-5. *Interest Rate Swaps.*

Very often two exactly matching counterparties cannot be found, and several institutions have to be matched together to cover the transaction. As the transaction volume has increased, however, it has become common practice for the intermediaries to run short-term open positions, which to some extent can be hedged in the financial futures market. Today two-sided bid and offer quotes are given by the major swap intermediaries in all the major international currencies. The basis for the quotes is usually a common fixed rate indicator of the currency in question. An interest rate swap in U.S. dollars is typically quoted around the going U.S. Treasury bill rate, whereas pound sterling quotes relate to the gilt rate, Deutsche mark quotes to the Schuldschein rate, and so on.

Example: A U.S. dollar interest rate swap quoting 50-70 indicates: (1) The intermediary bids for a dollar floating rate interest at LIBOR by providing fixed rate interest at the going U.S. Treasury bill rate plus 50 basis points. (2) It offers a dollar floating rate interest at LIBOR against receipt of fixed rate interest at the U.S. Treasury bill rate plus 70 basis points.

An institutional investor holds a three-year floating rate dollar portfolio at LIBOR + ¼% and would like to fix the return on the investment over the three-year period. By reacting to this quote for a U.S. dollar interest rate swap, the investor would provide the intermediary with interest at LIBOR + ¼%. In return he would receive a fixed interest payment equal to the going U.S. Treasury bill rate at the time of signing the swap agreement plus 50 basis points and plus the 25 basis points spread over LIBOR. If the U.S. Treasury bill rate at the time of signing is 9.25%, the return on the investment has been effectively locked in at a rate of 10% p.a. (9.25 + .50 plus .25) over the three-year period.

Currency Swap Agreements

By entering a currency swap agreement an institution can switch an asset or a liability from one currency to another. The swap transaction can be done from a fixed interest basis into a floating rate basis in the other currency, or from a floating rate basis into a fixed rate basis in the other currency.

The currencies are swapped initially through a normal spot foreign exchange transaction so that each of the counterparties have full availability of the currencies they are seeking. Throughout the life of the two obligations, each of the counterparties pay the other's interest obligations in accordance with the swap agreement. At maturity the currencies are swapped back to the original currencies through a forward foreign exchange transaction, usually effectuated at the initial spot exchange rate.

Example: A public entity has acquired a seven-year fixed coupon US$ 35,000,000 loan. It would like to switch it into floating rate Swiss francs to diversify the loan portfolio among different currencies and to take advantage of an expected de-

Table 12-6. *Summary of Interest Rate and Currency Swaps.*

Interest Rate Swaps

- Fixed interest payments into floating interest payments in the same currency,
  or
- Floating interest payments into fixed interest payments in the same currency
  or
- Interest payments on an interest rate basis into another interest rate basis in the same currency.

Currency Swaps

- One currency into another currency,
and
- Fixed interest payments into fixed interest payments in the other currency,
  or
- Floating interest payments into floating interest payments in the other currency,
  or
- Fixed interest payments into floating interest payments in the other currency,
  or
- Floating interest payments into fixed interest payments in the other currency.
  or
- Interest payments on one interest rate basis into another interest rate basis in the other currency.

crease in the interest rate level. Concurrently a corporate entity has just issued a seven-year Sw. Frc. 100,000,000 floating rate note. It seeks to switch it into a fixed rate U.S. dollar liability to lock in the funding cost and to match the company's dollar receivables.

In this situation the currencies will be swapped initially at the current spot exchange rate of 2.8571 Sw. Frc./US$ (0.3500 US$/Sw. Frc.). The public entity will pay US $ 35,000,000 to the intermediary against receipt of Sw. Frc. 100,000,000. Conversely, the corporation will pay Sw. Frc. 100,000,000 to the intermediary against receipt of US $ 35,000,000. At this point the two counterparties have the currencies they want. See Figure 12-6(1).

1. Receiving proceeds from initial loan:

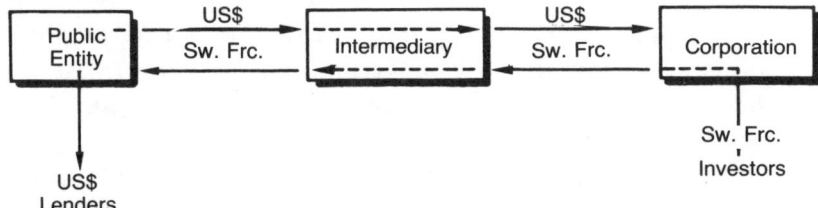

2. Paying interest throughout the life of the loan:

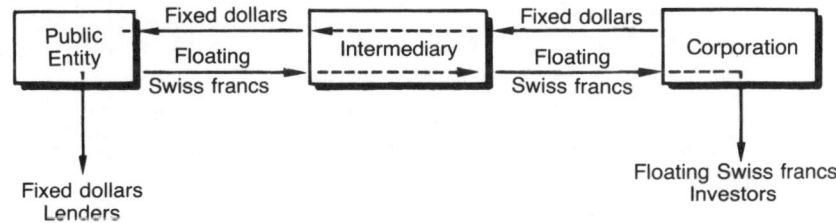

3. Paying back principal at maturity:

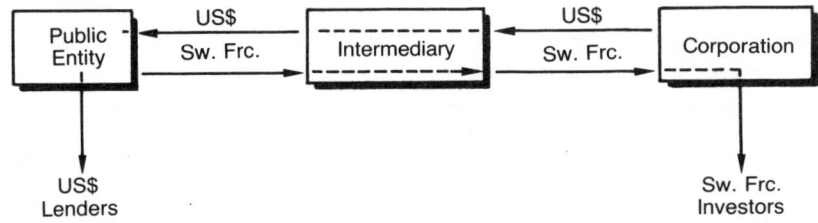

Figure 12-6. Currency Swap.

Throughout the seven years of the two loans, the public entity will pay floating rate Swiss franc interest to the intermediary against receipt of fixed rate U.S. dollar interest from the intermediary to service the fixed rate dollar loan. The corporation will pay fixed rate dollar interest to the intermediary against receipt of floating rate Swiss franc interest payments from the intermediary to service the floating rate franc loan. See Figure 12-6(2).

At maturity of both loans, the two principal currency amounts are again swapped back at the initial spot exchange rate of 0.3500 US $/Sw. Frc. The public entity pays Sw. Frc. 100,000,000 to the intermediary against receipt of US $ 35,000,000 for repayment of the dollar loan. The corporation pays US$35,000,000 to the intermediary against receipt of Sw. Frc. 100,000,000 for repayment of the franc note. See Figure 12-6(3).

Through this swap, the public entity has performed a debt service as if it had on its books a floating rate Swiss franc liability, and the corporation has acted as if it had a fixed rate dollar liability. However, the public entity—and only the public entity—is fully liable for the dollar loan against the lenders, and only the corporation is liable for the Swiss franc note against the investors. Because each of the two counterparties in all likelihood is unknown to the other, the intermediary assumes the counterparty risk. The swap arrangement is solely negotiated with the intermediary and each of the counterparts have no obligations to each other. The intermediary will charge an up-front fee for performing the broker role and for assuming the counterparty risk of the transaction.

The currency swap is an especially flexible hedging arrangement when an asset or a liability represents a combined interest rate and currency exposure. The cash flow statement providing the institution's liquidity forecast would reveal such exposures. For example, a German institution has a net outflow in U.S. dollars emanating from a floating rate loan agreement. If it is in the interest of the German institution to lock in the future cash outflow in German marks, then it could engage in a currency swap agreement bringing the floating rate U.S. dollar commitment into a fixed rate mark commitment. As is obvious by now, currency swap agreements have their particular strength when hedging international financial commitments. Although they can be useful for other hedging purposes, the vast majority of swap agreements are closed to hedge existing financial commitments or to optimize new financial arrangements for borrowers and investors.

The swap markets have other advantages and uses. Swap arrangements very often can furnish cheaper financing to an institution raising new funds because it can approach the cheapest financial market to raise its debt and then swap it into the type of liability wanted initially. The swap technique can also be used to take advantage of expected changes in foreign exchange rates and the interest rates. If the institution's expectation favors an increase in the interest rate level, investors could swap fixed rate assets into floating rate assets and borrowers could swap floating rate liabilities into fixed rate liabilities in order to take advantage of expected future interest rate movements. Conversely, if the interest rate level is expected to drop, the investors could swap floating rate assets into fixed rate assets, and borrowers could switch fixed rate liabilities into floating rate liabilities. Also, if the market believes that the interest rate will go up, it might indicate a favorable time for a floating rate investor to lock in the higher future rate. Conversely, if the general market outlook favors an interest rate drop, it could signal an opportune moment for the floating rate borrower to lock in a lower future rate. Hence the swap technique can be used to take advantage of expected rate movements or to lock in future rates when the market appears to be favorable. It goes without saying that the currency swaps can be similarly applied to take advantage of favorable foreign exchange rate expectations.

Some critics have voiced concern that the arbitrage process of the swap technique diminishes the monetary policy measures in the currency areas involved and that the swap process undermines the credit checking in connection with lending transactions. However, the arbitrage element in swap transactions merely takes advantage of discriminatory features of the international financial markets. The legal obligations of borrowers do *not* change hands in these transactions. Therefore swap transactions appear to be beneficial in the sense that they diminish the effects of inefficient discrimination on the international financial markets which usually induces an unwarranted increase in interest rates. The counterparty risk is managed by the swap intermediaries. Provided that a thorough credit checking is performed among the international financial institutions engaged as intermediaries, the inherent counterparty risk should not become an obstacle for engaging in swap agreements

Swap agreements have proven to be a useful tool for hedging long-term assets and liabilities in institutions with international engagements. The potential for such swaps appears to be a function of a number of circumstances:

- *Market inefficiencies*: Different capital markets often have different appetites for different types of borrowers. One type of institutional borrowers may have tapped one a capital market extensively, leading to weakening demand for such financing among the investors providing the funds. In this case another type of borrower might get better borrowing terms in that market. Hence it might be an advantage for the initial borrower to approach another capital market and swap the proceeds with the new borrower in the initial market.

- *Availability of a certain type of financing*: When market access is restricted by queuing arrangements, a potential borrower, which ranks high on the queuing list, might swap loan proceeds with a newcomer to the market, which otherwise might have to wait very long to get the wanted financing.

- *Subsidized lending:* Many national export credit institutions lend the domestic currency at favorable rates. The beneficiary might not need this currency, but would rather obtain a liability in another currency.

- *Differences between the domestic interest rate level and the rates on the Euromarkets.*

These are some of the possible causes leading to the development of a currency swap market.

Case: Currency-Interest Rate Swap:
Manufacturing Company, Currency-Interest Rate Gapping

The Atlanta-based moulding company. A&T Manufacturing, Inc., had just signed a contract with a major German supplier in August 1985 for the delivery of tools and equipment at a total value of DM 13,900,000 — close to US $ 5,000,000 at the going exchange rate. The German exporter had guaranteed a favorable three-year mark loan on the total amount of the purchase price to commence upon delivery. However, if A&T Manufacturing accepted this financing option, the loan would have to be repaid in DM and hence the loan repayment would represent a currency exposure on the part of the borrower. In Auqust 1985 the foreign exchange rate was around 2.7800 DM/US$, but there was considerable uncertainty as to the future movement of the US$ exchange rate. As the Chief Financial Officer of A&T Manufacturing, Sam Bariolli, expressed it:

> We received a very attractive medium-term loan offer from our German supplier. The loan was to be repaid semiannually at an interest rate equivalent to the DM interbank offered rate, which at that time was around 5% p.a. and hence considerably lower than the equivalent U.S. interest rate. However, the DM loan at the same time presented us with a dilemma because the foreign exchange exposure from this loan was extremely difficult to evaluate. The dollar continued to be relatively strong despite recent drops, but there seemed to be increasing political pressure to deflate the strength of the dollar exchange rate further. We feared that the dollar might weaken considerably over the coming years which would make a DM loan unattractive to us despite the favorable interest terms.
>
> We really wanted to know the exact cost of the equipment in order to refine our cost-benefit evaluation of the plant and to create certainty at least as far as our financial charges were concerned.

In this situation A&T Manufacturing contacted their major bank to get a comparative offer for a three-year fixed rate loan

Table 12-7. Loan Structure—DM Loan (2.78 DM/US$ Constant Exchange Rate.)

Date	Outstanding (DM)	Assumed Repayment (DM)	Interest Six-month DM Rate	Payments (DM)	Total DM Payment
Jan. 86	13,900,000	—	5.00%	—	—
Jul. 86	11,583,334	2,316,666	4.90%	347,500	2,664,166
Jan. 87	9,266,667	2,316,667	4.80%	283,792	2,600,459
Jul. 87	6,950,000	2,316,667	4.80%	222,400	2,539,067
Jan. 88	4,633,334	2,316,666	4.75%	166,800	2,483,466
Jul. 88	2,316,667	2,316,667	4.75%	110,042	2,426,709
Jan. 89	0	2,316,667		55,021	2,371,688
		DM 13,900,000		DM 1,185,555	DM 15,085,555
	(In US$ Equivalent)				
Jan. 86	5,000,000	—		—	—
Jul. 86	4,166,667	833,333		125,000	958,333
Jan. 87	3,333,334	833,333		102,084	935,417
Jul. 87	2,500,000	833,334		79,999	913,333
Jan. 88	1,666,667	833,333		60,000	893,333
Jul. 88	883,334	883,333		39,584	872,917
Jan. 89	0	883,334		19,791	853,125
		$5,000,000		$426,458	$5.426,458

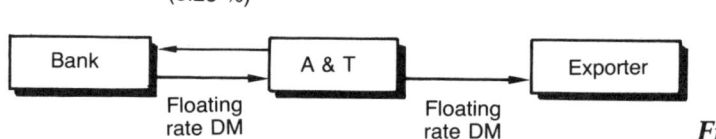

Figure 12-7

Table 12-8. Comparative Analysis (Loan Repayment).

Date	Unchanged $ Rate (2.78)	5% drop in $ Rate (2.64)	10% drop in $ Rate (2.50)	Direct Fixed (9.75%)	Swap Payment (8.25%)
Jan. 86	—	—	—	—	—
Jul. 86	958,333	1,009,154	1,065,666	1,077,083	1,039,583
Jan. 87	935,417	985,022	1,040,184	1,031,266	1,005,208
Jul. 87	913,333	961,768	1,015,627	991,698	970,834
Jan. 88	893,333	940,707	993,386	952,130	936,458
Jul. 88	872,917	919,208	970,684	912,563	902,083
Jan. 89	853,125	898,367	948,675	872,995	867,709
	5,426,458	5,714,226	6,034,222	5,837,735	5,721,875

in U.S. dollars to fund the import purchase. It turned out that a fixed rate dollar offer would cost around 9.75% p.a. based on the same repayment structure as proposed by the German exporter. At the same time an equivalent dollar variable rate offer could be done at a rate of around 8.50% p.a. for the first six-month period, considerably higher than the DM alternative.

As Sam Bariolli engaged in further discussions with the bank on the matter, it appeared to the bank representative that they could take advantage of the favorable DM offer from the German exporter by swapping the variable payments in DM into a more favorable fixed rate payment structure in U.S. dollars. By engaging in a US$/DM fixed/floating rate swap, it turned out that A&T Manufacturing could get away with paying a fixed dollar rate of 8.25% p.a.—considerably lower than the alternative fixed rate proposal and even lower than the variable rate offer at 8.50% p.a. Under this scheme A&T Manufacturing Inc. exchanged the DM principal into dollars at the current exchange rate. Throughout the life of the loan, the company paid fixed rate dollar interest to the bank which in turn passed variable rate DM payments to A&T Manufacturing, which was used for loan repayments to the German exporter. Principal amounts would be exchanged at the initial foreign exchange rate at which the loan amount was exchanged on due dates. (See Figure 12-7.)

By engaging in a fixed rate dollar/floating rate German mark swap, A&T Manufacturing obtained the best of two worlds. It eliminated the uncertainty of the DM/US$ exchange rate, and it managed to lock in and convert the favorable DM interest rate into an equivalently favorable U.S. dollar fixed interest rate. (See Table 12-8.)

Case: Currency-Interest Rate Swap:
Financial Institution, Pass-Through Structure,
Currency-Interest Rate Gapping

Algemene Bank Institut, an expanding European financial intermediary, for the first time could establish an international bond issue for a major international borrower. The bank offered a unique ten-year fixed rate issue totalling DM 300,000,000 at an all-in rate of 6.70% p.a. Since this was the first time this major and well reputed borrower was introduced in the bond market,

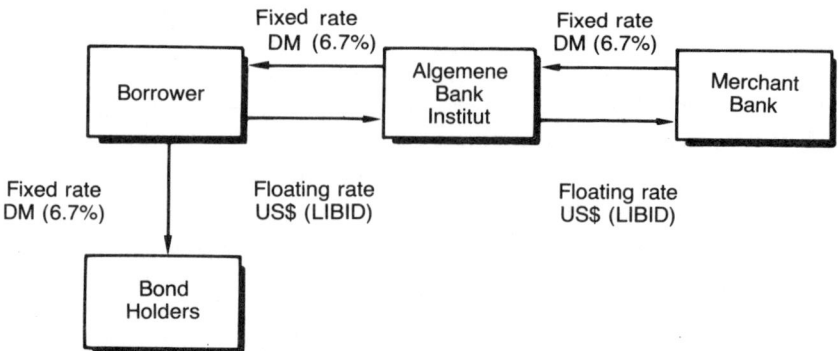

Figure 12-8. *Interest Rate Structure.*

the funding rate obtained was very favorable compared to the going market rate at the time of issue. Also, the Algemene Bank Institut was able to attract new investors to this issue through its domestic bank associates, and it could therefore offer even better terms than normally was the case for this type of issue.

However, the borrower maintained the major part of its cash flows in U.S. dollars and hence would prefer to obtain the funding in U.S. dollars to eliminate the currency exposure at loan repayment. The view of the borrower at that time was that the U.S. interest rate would decline further over the coming 12–24 months and would therefore favor a floating rate funding proposal. (See Figure 12-9.)

As the head of the international bond department expressed it:

> We were in a situation where we could arrange fixed rate long-term funding in DM to a major international borrower on very favorable terms with the fixed funding rate being something like ⅛–¼ percentage points below the current market rate for a similar issue. As the borrower was likely to give preference to a floating rate dollar proposal, we proceeded to arrange a currency/interest rate swap converting the fixed rate DM funding into a floating rate dollar proposal.

Algemene Bank Institut approached several major international financial institutions to obtain quotes for a DM/US $ fixed/

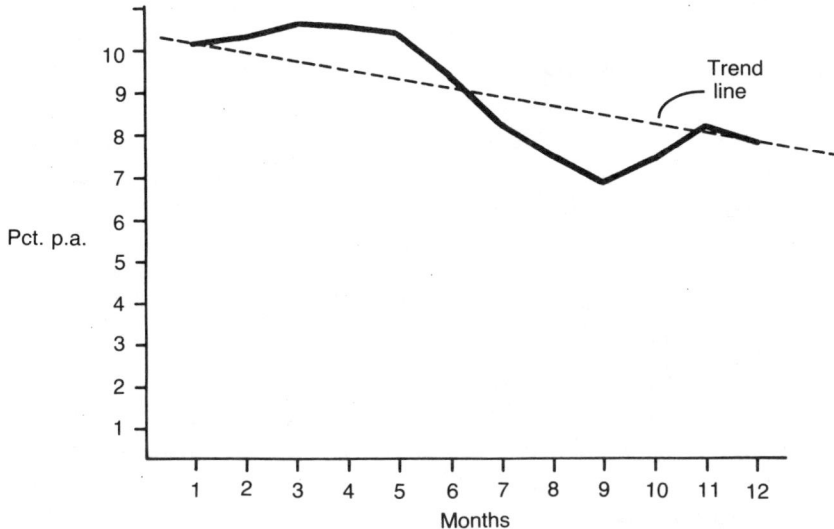

Figure 12-9. *Interest Rate Development over Past 12 Months. (End of Month, 3 months U.S. $ LIBID).*

floating rate swap. The most competitive offer was obtained from a well-known London-based merchant banking group proposing to provide DM payments at the Bundesbank bond yield against receipt of U.S. dollar payments at three months LIBOR – 0.60% p.a. This meant that the 6.70% fixed rate DM paments could be converted into LIBOR – 0.10% = LIBID, which represented a very favorable variable funding rate in dollars.

Thus Algemene Bank Institut was able to offer a ten-year US $ 100,000,000 (approximate dollar value at current DM/US$ foreign exchange rate) funding proposal at a rate of three-month LIBID. The borrower considered this a very interesting proposal and accepted the offer.

Table 12-9. *Interest Rate Structure.*

Bundesbank Bond Yield:		6.2 % p.a.
Eurodollar Interbank BID Rate:	1 month	8.05% p.a.
	3 months	7.96% p.a.
	6 months	7.92% p.a.
	1 year	7.98% p.a.
	2 years	8.50% p.a.
	5 years	8.85% p.a.

Case: Interest Rate Swap: Financial Institution,
Asset and Liability Mismatch,
Interest Basis Gapping

Since Mid State Bank Corp. acquired a 25% stake in a bank conglomerate in the London market in 1981, the bank increasingly looked to the Eurocurrency market as a potential source of funding—although being a conservative bank, it had not engaged heavily in this type of cross currency funding. The majority of the short-term loans booked carried a variable interest rate which would vary in accordance with movements in the domestic short-term interest rates. For longer-term commitments, the bank usually based the interest rate on the bank's prime rate. The prime rate was a variable rate but not as volatile as the short-term money market rates which could periodically move whimsically.

This was the problem. The management of Mid State Bank was aware that the prime rate—which, to a large extent, is determined by domestic competitive forces—is by nature very difficult to adapt to immediate changes in the short-term market rates. To the extent that the bank funded longer-term loans by obtaining short-term money market placements, the interest rate margin could get squeezed in periods when the interbank market was experiencing an upward move in interest rates. This factor would only be reflected in the prime rate after a

Table 12-10.

Mid State Bank Corp.
Balance Sheet
(US$ 1,000,000)

Assets:		Liabilities	
Cash	214.5	Deposits	3,349.6
Interbank Placements	259.7	Interbank placements	
		– Foreign banks	442.5
Securities	466.0	– Domestic banks	189.9
Loans & advances	3,529.8	Other liabilities	219.9
Other assets	150.3	Total liabilities	4,001.9
		Net Worth	418.4
Total assets	4.620.3	Total liabilities & NW	4,420.3

considerable time lag and then only if the upward move in interest rates was longer-term and persistent in character.

In November of 1985 the Mid State Bank Corp. had booked a four-year committed loan structure to a major corporate client totalling US$ 25,000,000 with annual repayments of principal and interest on November 10. The interest calculation on the loan was based on the going Mid State Bank prime rate plus 7/8%. The incremental funding for this loan was obtained from the London affiliate at LIBOR. Since the loan was booked, the London interbank rate had seen both upward and downward moves and in March 1986 the market carried a bullish sentiment with continued expectations of an interest rate drop. With the prime rate largely fixed with a view to domestic competition, management had envisaged the risk of a squeeze on the interest rate margin as LIBOR increased from 8 to 9% from November 1985 to January 1986. They also thought that the present drop in the interest rate in March 1986 to 7⅝% could represent a good time to close the interest rate gap.

Charles Hoover, CEO of the Mid State Bank Corp., voiced his concern for a potentially unfavorable interest rate development:

> Even if there is a natural interlinkage between the domestic interest rate level and the rate prevalent in the Eurocurrency markets, our prime rate is influenced by other factors than simply the movement in the short-term interbank rate on the international money markets. Therefore, as we increasingly obtain funding on LIBOR basis to expand our portfolio of domestic loans based on the prime rate, the interest differential will be vulnerable to different movements in the two interest rates.

Table 12-11. Interest Rate Development.

	Nov. 1985	Jan. 1986	Mar. 1986
The U.S. prime rate	9½	9½	9½
Three-months Eurodollar Offered Rate	8 1/16	8 15/16	7⅝

The Mid State Bank Corp. found that the solution to the basis risk issue was to engage in an interest rate basis swap with one of the major money center banks. Mid State Bank obtained quotes from several money center banks on interest rate swaps converting the prime rate into a LIBOR-based rate. In this specific case Mid State Bank Corp. accepted to exchange LIBOR for prime—1.25%. The swap arrangement was adapted specifically to the repayment structure of the four-year $25,000,000 loan. Under the swap arrangement Mid State Bank Corp. at each maturity date would pay the interest amount on the principal outstanding, based on prime—1.25%. In turn it would receive from the money center bank the equivalent interest amount based on LIBOR.

By engaging in this interest basis swap, Mid State Bank Corp. effectively locked in an interest rate spread of 2⅛% on the $25 million loan, thus securing lifetime earnings on the loan during the four years to maturity in November 1989 of $1.3 million.

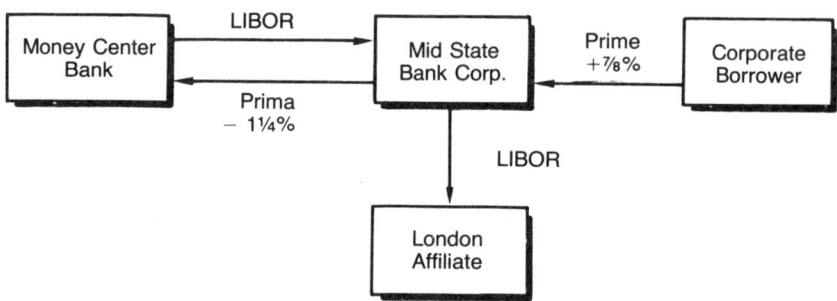

Figure 12-10

Table 12-12. *US $ 25,000,000 Loan Repayment Schedule.*

Date	Outstanding	Net Interest Revenue (Spread 2⅛%)
Nov. 10, 1985	$25,000,000	—
Nov. 10, 1986	$18,750,000	$ 531,250.00
Nov. 10, 1987	$12,500,000	$ 398,437.50
Nov. 10, 1988	$ 6,250,000	$ 265,625.00
Nov. 10, 1989	0	$ 132,812.50
Locked-in net interest revenue		$ 1,328,125.00

LONG DATED FORWARD AGREEMENTS

In principle long-dated forward agreements function in the same way as standard forward agreements. The difference, as the name indicates, is that long-dated forwards exceed the normal length of interbank forward agreements with contracts maturing up to twenty years hence. The main transaction volume, however, is concentrated in maturities from three to seven years. The financial service is used by international institutions to hedge long-term assets and liabilities in foreign currencies and thus represents a close substitute to currency swap agreements.

The problem for the financial institutions offering long-dated forwards is that interbank money markets with maturities over three years are practically nonexistent. Consequently the transactions cannot be hedged in the traditional way by accessing the two currencies' money markets, as with currency forwards. So the long-dated forward market, like the currency swap market, has developed as counterparty transactions where the financial institution offering long-dated forward agreements tries to match the transactions among a group of counterparties. However, financial institutions increasingly take open positions in long-dated forwards in the expectation of future transaction volume which will eventually close the gaps. The periodic open positions can be partly hedged in the financial futures market. For the same reason there is no developed interbank market for long-dated forward agreements.

A long dated forward is quoted as a premium or discount on the going spot foreign exchange rate as discussed earlier in Chapter 10.

Example: A non-American international trading company is expecting periodic cash inflows of US$ 10,000,000 every year over the next seven years. The company will get a long-dated forward quote for each of the seven periods, which effectively lock in the future cash inflow in the domestic currency.

Conversely, a non-Swiss sovereign borrower has obtained a 15-year 9% fixed coupon bullet loan of Sw. Frc. 100,000,000 with annual interest payments. The sovereign entity can request 15 long-dated forward quotes for the Sw. Frc. 9,000,000 coupon payments and one quote for the principal repayment of the Sw. Frc. 100,000,000 due in 15 years. Hereby the sovereign entity effectively has tied the future cash outflow into the domestic currency.

Compared to the currency swap market, the long-dated forward agreements are less flexible, since swap transactions can change the interest rate basis and at the same time be applied to almost any cash flow pattern. However, the long-dated forward agreement provides an efficient mechanism to lock in long-term future cash flows in most international cross currencies, and the transaction volume continues to blossom.

CONCLUSION

The OTC market offers institutional clients a wide variety of interest rate and currency hedging services which provide these institutions with complete hedges. As opposed to the exchange-traded hedging contracts, there are no basis risk and no unknown cash flow implications. Also, the complexity of exchange trading rules are avoided, since dealings are done on a bilateral basis with a known financial intermediary. The OTC market is less flexible than the exchange-traded contracts with regard to selling off an established hedging position which is rarely possible in the OTC market. However, the lack of trading flexibility appears to be outweighted by the wide range of financial services offered, many of which cannot be obtained by accessing the exchanges.

A major part of the OTC services offered are long-dated, with maturities exceeding those of the futures exchanges.

Under this scenario, the international financial institutions function as direct hedgers on the financial futures exchanges. In turn they offer their institutional clients risk-free, tailor-made hedging services without the uncertainties that accompany hedging positions on the futures and options exchanges.

CHAPTER **13**

Concluding Remarks

The development of the international financial markets over the past decades has led to increasingly volatile interest and foreign exchange rates, which impose an increased financial exposure on institutions holding international commitments.

In response, the first financial futures contracts were introduced in the United States in the mid-1970s to provide a hedging mechanism to the financially exposed institutions. The financial futures markets have gone through a geographical expansion both through the establishment of independent futures exchanges in other currency jurisdictions and through cooperation with existing futures exchanges. Financial futures contracts provide an efficient means of locking in the future interest or foreign exchange rate. However, hedging over the financial futures market exposes the hedger to a basis risk because the price of the futures contract is not necessarily fully correlated with the price movement of the financial commitment being hedged. Financial futures contracts carry a standard denomination and fixed maturities, and consequently they can be difficult to adapt fully to the specific asset and liability characteristics to be hedged. Hedging over the financial futures market locks in the future rate and hence covers the downside risk, but at the same time it limits the upside potential for gains.

The exchange markets for option contracts were established in the early 1980s. The special feature of the option is that it covers the downside risk of an unfavorable price movement, and at the same time leaving open the upside potential for a gain from a favorable price development. As in the financial futures markets, the option contracts have a standard denomination and fixed contract maturities. Exchange-traded options contracts can be written and bought, providing participants with added flexibility to arrange suitable hedging positions. The maximum term of the exchange-traded option contract is nine months. Its limited life places some restrictions on the hedging opportunities.

The increased activity on the financial futures and options exchanges inspired the international banks to offer new financial hedging services, whose maturities often exceed those of the exchange-traded contracts, directly to the client over-the-counter. The size, term, and exercise price of these financial agreements are tailor-made to meet the specific financial needs of the customer. Such financial agreements provide the buyers with complete hedges, with no basis risk for the holders of the agreements.

The major portion of these over-the-counter hedging products is based on counter hedges in the financial futures and option exchanges. The financial institutions offering the hedging services act as intermediaries between the institutional clients and the financial contract exchanges. The institutions thereby eliminate the administrative burden attached to direct dealings on the exchanges, assuming and managing the basis risk inherent in the financial futures positions and providing a risk-free hedge to the end user.

This evolutionary process in the development of financial hedging services illustrates the interdependence of the financial markets. They supplement each other to the extent that one could hardly stand alone without the other. It also shows that the development of financial services is an interactive process.

A general observation is that, despite certain attempts to ease the interaction between the different futures and options exchanges, there is no overall consensus on denomination and market practice. The denomination of futures and options con-

tracts were initially introduced on the exchanges in similar denominations or in denominations representing multiples of each
other. For example, the initial currency option contracts of the
Montreal Exchange made up one-fifth the size of the corresponding financial futures contracts traded on the Chicago Mercantile Exchange. The currency option contracts of the Philadelphia Stock Exchange make up one-half the size of the corresponding CME futures contracts. With the introduction of new
currency option denominations on the Montreal Exchange and
the European Options Exchange, the comparability to the original option contracts has been disrupted. On the other hand,
the introduction of the new option denominations envisages a
better compatibility with the standard quotation on the interbank forward foreign exchange markets.

As time goes by, however, the increased interdependence
is likely to force increased standardization between the different
market segments.

Several exchanges are already directly interlinked. Among
these is the Singapore International Monetary Exchange
(SIMEX) which is directly linked to the International Monetary
Market in Chicago. The Montreal Exchange, The Vancouver
Stock Exchange, the European Options Exchange, and the Sydney Stock Exchange are linked through the same clearing system, the International Options Clearing Corporations based in
Amsterdam. The Chicago Board of Trade and the London International Financial Futures Exchange have agreed to link the
trading of their futures contracts by introducing interchangeable
contracts on, for example, the U.S. Treasury bond future. The
direct linkage through the same clearing entity and the compatibility of contract characteristics enable the exchanges to provide
close to 24 hours of trading in the major contracts offered. The
refinement of the electronic linkages between the exchanges,
also allows for the possibility of placing stop orders on option
deals that can be transferred automatically from exchange to
exchange as opening hours change during the day. National
traders are thus able to take advantage of market developments
even outside their normal work hours.

The possibility of establishing other similar interlinkages
between U.S.-based, European, and Far Eastern exchanges con-

tinues to be investigated. Such development, however, has been delayed by the fact that the various exchanges use different contract standards, are backed by different clearing organizations with different contract delivery systems and cost structures, and are under the supervision of different national regulatory bodies. However, despite these obstacles, the internationalization process is likely to continue, albeit it might take time.

New currency option contracts have been introduced, completing the supply of currency options on the major exchanges. Also, new option contracts against the ECU and cross currency option contracts add new dimensions to exchange-traded option contracts.

An increasing number of interest rate and index-linked option contracts have been introduced, a development likely to continue and probably to be supplemented by the introduction of corresponding interest rate options in the other major international currencies and index options linked to various national stock exchanges. As this continued development of exchange-traded futures and options contracts takes place, we will continue to see a flourishing development of related hedging services offered over-the-counter by the international financial institutions.

The future development of the markets for financial hedging services is likely to be as rapid as that witnessed over the past couple of years. Although the conceptual framework of this book still maintains its validity, several of the descriptive parts could be outdated a few years down the road. Nevertheless, it hopefully represents an "appetizer" for the continued study of the developments on the international financial markets.

Footnotes

Notes to Chapter 2

[1]See, for example, David K. Eiteman and Arthur I. Stonehill, *Multinational Business Finance* (Addison-Wesley Publishing Co , 1979), Chapter 3.

[2]Charles R. Nelson, *Applied Time Series Analysis for Managerial Forecasting* (Holden-Day, 1973).
   C. Chatfield, *The Analysis of Time Series, Theory and Practice* (Chapman and Hall, 1975).
   C.W.J. Granger and Paul Newbold, *Forecasting Economic Time Series* (Academic Press, 1977).
   George E.P. Box and Gwillyn M. Jenkins, *Time Series Analysis, Forecasting and Control*, Revised Edition (Holden-Day, 1976).

Notes to Chapter 4

[1]The delivery date of the futures contracts differs from exchange to exchange and also varies for different types of contracts as shown by the following examples:

Type of Futures Contract (Exchange)	Delivery Date
Three-month Eurodollar time deposit (IMM)	2nd London business day before the 3rd Wednesday of the delivery month.
Three-month Eurodollar time deposit (LIFFE)	2nd Wednesday of delivery month.

Type of Futures Contract (Exchange)	*Delivery Date*
Three-month certificate of deposit (IMM)	15th through last business day of delivery month.
Three-month U.S. Treasury bill (IMM)	lst day when 13-week T bills are issued in the delivery month (or one-year T bills have 13 weeks to maturity).
U.S. Treasury Bonds (CBOT/LIFFE)	Any business day in the delivery month.

[2]Calculation of par value multipliers:

A.

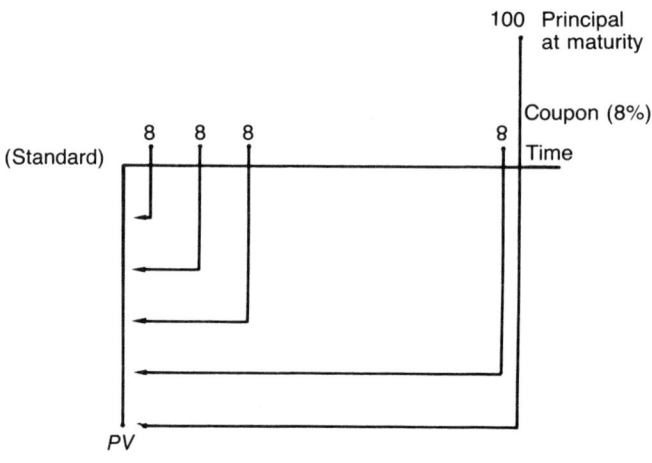

$$PV = \frac{8}{1.08} + \frac{8}{1.08^2} + \quad\cdots\quad \frac{8}{1.08^{15}} + \frac{100}{1.08^{15}}$$

$$= 8 \times \frac{(1 - \frac{1}{1.08})^{15}}{(0.08)} + \frac{100}{1.08^{15}} = 8 \times 8.5595 + \frac{100}{3.1722}$$

$$= 68.48 + 31.52 = 100 = \text{Principal}$$

B. 7% coupon / 15 years to maturity:

$$PV = 7 \times 8.5595 + \frac{100}{3.1722} = 59.92 + 31.52 = 91.44$$

The par value multiplier is .9144.

C. 7% coupon / 20 years to maturity:

$$PV = 7 \times 9.8181 + \frac{100}{1.08^{20}} = \mathbf{68.7267} + 21.4548 = 90.18$$

The par value multiplier is .9018.

D. 9% coupon / 15 years to maturity:

$$PV = 9 \times 8.5595 + \frac{100}{3.1722} = 77.04 + 31.52 = 108.56$$

The par value multiplier is 1.0856.

[3]For an excellent discussion of the interest rate parity theory, for example, refer to Jan H. Giddy, "An Integrated Theory of Exchange Rate Equilibrium," in *International Financial Management, Theory and Application*, ed. by Donald R. Lessard (Warren, Gorham & Lamont, 1980).

[4]For example, the Standard & Poors (S&P) 500 index is made up of 500 stocks representing industry, public utilities, transportation, and financial companies in relation to their proportions in the stock market. The shares represent around 80% of the value traded on the New York Stock Exchange.

The index is calculated by multiplying the number of stocks outstanding for each of the 500 institutions multiplied by their market prices. The total market value of these shares is then compared to the market value of the stocks outstanding in 1941-43. The index value for the base period is set at 10. Hence the S&P 500 index (x) is calculated as follows:

$$x = \frac{MV_P}{MV_{41\text{-}43}} \times 10$$

MV_P = Total market value of the 500 stocks at present.
$MV_{41\text{-}43}$ = Total market value of the 500 stocks during the base period 1941-43.

[5]To illustrate the diversity of stock indexes, see the following listing from the *Wall Street Journal* (Europe) of of February 12, 1985.

	1985		Change	1984
N.Y.S.E. Composite	104.50	— 0.89	—0.84%	89.28
Industrial	120.40	— 1.06	—0.87%	103.70
Utility	53.28	— 0.25	—0.47%	45.20
Transp.	100.66	— 1.64	1.60%	85.09
Financial	109.45	— 1.16	—1.05%	89.50
Am. Ex. Mkt Val Index	229.53	— 1.52	—0.66%	205.02
Nasdaq OTC Composite	287.43	— 0.92	—0.32%	250.57
Industrial	311.39	— 1.04	—0.33%	282.94
Insurance	319.66	— 1.08	—0.34%	244.71
Banks	251.26	— 0.88	—0.35%	205.23
Nasdaq Natl Mkt Comp	122.64	— 0.52	—0.41%	...
Industrial	117.71	— 0.52	—0.44%	...
Standard & Poor's 500	180.51	— 1.68	—0.92%	154.95
400 Industrial	201.85	— 1.95	—0.96%	174.18
Value Line Index	198.97	— 1.00	—0.50%	178.77
Wilshire 5000 Equity	1,865.081	—14.442	—0.77%	1,611.709

Note the difference in the index value, which is influenced by the choice of base period, the index value of the base period, and the development in share prices of the underlying stock portfolio. The change figures refer to the absolute changes (– or +) in the index value and the corresponding percentage change from the previous trading day.

[6]For a general description of the commodity futures markets, see, for example, William F. Sharpe, *Investments*, 2nd ed. (Prentice-Hall, 1981).

[7]The following ten exchanges are among those with the highest turnover of commodity futures contracts in the early/mid-1980s:

The Chicago Mercantile Exchange (CME)
The Chicago Board of Trade (CBOT)
The Commodity Exchange Inc. (COMEX)
The Coffee, Sugar & Cocoa Exchange (CS&C)
The New York Mercantile Exchange (NYMEX)
The Mid America Commodity Exchange (MIDAM)
The New York Cotton Exchange (NYCE)
The Kansas City Board of Trade (KCBOT)
The Minneapolis Grain Exchange (MGE)
The New Orleans Commodity Exchange (NOCE)

Notes to Chapter 5

[1]For a discussion of this, see: Mark J. Powers, *Inside the Financial Futures Markets*, 2nd ed. (John Wiley & Sons Inc., 1984).

[2]For a 15-year 8% coupon with $100 nominal value, to yield 11.00% p.a., it should be sold at a discount price of $78.43 ($78^{14}/_{32}$). (The calculations here assume that coupon is paid annually.)

$$8 \ \frac{1 - \dfrac{1}{1.11^{15}}}{0.11} \ + \ \frac{100}{1.11^{15}} \ = \ 57.527 \ + \ 20.900 \ = \ 78.43$$

When investing US $ 10,000,000, one achieves a nominal value of $100/78.427 \times 10,000,000$ equals $12,750,710.85, or rather by investing $9,960,230 one achieves a nominal value of $12,700,000. Applying the present value formula, the following present value calculations are worked out.

$$PV = \text{Coupon} \ \frac{[1-(1+i)^n]}{i} \ + \ \frac{\text{Principal}}{(1+i)^n} \quad \text{Coupon} = 8\% \text{ p.a., Principal} = 100$$

	$n = 15$	$n = 14$	(Change)
$i = 12.0\%$	$54.487 + 18.270 = 72.76$	$53.025 + 20.462 = 73.49$	(2.71)
$i = 11.5\%$	$55.974 + 19.538 = 75.51$		
$i = 11.0\%$	—	$55.855 + 23.199 = 79.05$	(2.85)
$i = 10.5\%$	$59.151 + 22.365 = 81.52$	$57.361 + 24.713 = 82.07$	(3.02)

Example 1: Actual return is calculated as follows:

Amount invested ($10,000,000)	$9,960,230
Current market price at year-end	
(12,700,000 × .7349)	$9,333,230
Loss from reduction in market price	$ (627,000)
Interest payment	$ 800,000
	$ 173,000

[3] *Example 2:* Actual return is calculated as follows:

Current market price at year-end	
(12,700,000 × .8207)	$10,422,890
Amount invested ($10,000,000)	$ 9,960,230
Capital gain from increase in market	$ 462,660
Interest payment	$ 800,000
	$1,262,660

[4] Principal	= $20,000,000
Semiannual coupon	= $800,000 (8% p.a.)
Maturity	= 15 years

$$PV = 800,000 \times \frac{1 - \frac{1}{1.05375^{30}}}{0.05375} + \frac{20,000,000}{1.05375^{30}} \quad i = 10.75\% \text{ p.a.}$$

$$= 11,789,267.94 + 4,158,171.21 = \$15,947,439.15$$

This implies sale at a discount price of

$$15,947,439.15 / 20,000,000 \times 100 = 79.74\%.$$

$$[5]PV = 800,000 \times \frac{1 - \frac{1}{1.055^{30}}}{0.055} + \frac{20,000,000}{1.055^{30}} \quad i = 11.00\% \text{ p.a.}$$

$$= 11,626,996.13 + 4,012,880.31 = \$15,639,876.44$$

This implies sale at a discount price of

$$15,639,876.44 / 20.000,000 \times 100 = 78.2\%$$

and a loss on the issue of

$$(\$15,947,439.15 - \$15,639,876.44) = \$307,562.71$$

[6]Of all the eligible bonds to be delivered under the U.S. Treasury bond contract, it is generally true to assume that sellers will deliver the bond cheapest for them. In general it is the security with the lowest value, calculated by taking the current cash market price and dividing it by the appropriate conversion factor.

[7]For more information on regression analysis, see Ronald J. Wannacott and Thomas H. Wannacott, *Econometrics* (John Wiley & Sons, Inc., 1970).

[8]Applying the present value formula $PV = $ Coupon:

$$\text{Coupon} = \frac{1 - \frac{1}{(1 + i)^n}}{i} + \frac{\text{Principal}}{(1 + i)^n}$$

The following calculations are performed assuming that the present interest rate for both the Eurobonds and the Treasury bonds is 12% p.a.

Eurobond

Nominal amount = 20,000,000
Coupon = 7% (annual payment)
Maturity = 20 years.

$i =$ 12% $PV =$ 12,530,556.38

$i =$ 12.01% $PV =$ 12,520,306.28, change $= - $ 10,250.10

$i =$ 11.99% $PV =$ 12,540,820.30, change $= + $ 10,263.92

Treasury Bond

Nominal amount = 20,000,000   Coupon = 8% (annual payment)

Maturity = 20 years.

$i =$ 12% $PV =$ 14,024,445.10

$i =$ 12.01% $PV =$ 14,013.12, change $= - $ 11,185.98

$i =$ 11.99% $PV =$ 14,035,645.89, change $= + $ 11,200.79

[9]See London International Financial Futures Exchange: "US Treasury Bond Futures," LIFFE Ltd., 1984.

[10]Remember here that the spot exchange rate quotation for all currencies is indicated as number of currency units per U.S. dollars with the exception of commonwealth currencies like the pound sterling, which is quoted as US $/£ Stg.

The futures contract prices, however, are always quoted in U.S. dollars. That is, a cash futures price of $0.0952 for a French franc contract implies a spot exchange rate of 10.5042 Fr. Frc./US $, and the cross rate is calculated as 1.0750 $\times$ 10.5042 (Fr. Frc./US $ \times$ $/£ Stg.) = 11.2920 Fr. Frc./£ Stg.

[11]The price variance of a stock portfolio is mathematically presented as follows:

$$\text{Var}(P) = \frac{1}{N^2} \sum_{i=1}^{N} \sum_{j=1}^{N} \text{Cov}(P_i, P_j)$$

Var (P) = Price variation of stock portfolio P.
Cov (P_i, P_j) = Price covariance of stock category i and j.

$$= \frac{1}{n - 1} \sum_{k=1}^{n} (P_{i,k} - \bar{P}_{i,k})(P_{j,k} - \bar{P}_{j,k})$$

i	=	$1, 2, ..., N$
j	=	$1, 2, ..., N$
i, j	=	Denotes specific categories of stock.
N	=	Total number of stock categories.
k	=	$1, 2, ... , n$
n	=	Total number of events in the statistical sample.
P_i	=	Average stock price of category i.
P_j	=	Average stock price of category j.

Then

Lim Var (P)	=	0 given a finite price fluctuation level for N approaching infinity.

When the number of stock categories in the portfolio increases, the price variation of the portfolio goes toward zero.

Notes to Chapter 6

[1]See a standard finance textbook like J. Fred Weston. Eugene F. Brigham. Poul Halpern. *Essentials of Canadian Managerial Finance* (Holt, Rinehart and Winston of Canada, Ltd., 1979).

[2]For a further discussion on the valuation of call options on stocks, refer to William F. Sharpe. *Investments*, 2nd ed. (Prentice-Hall, 1981).

[3]For a discussion of the Black-Scholes option evaluation equation, refer to Thomas E. Copeland and J. Fred Weston, *Financial Theory and Corporate Policy* (Addison-Wesley Publishing Co., 1979); or to the original source, F. Black and M. Scholes, "The Pricing of Options and Corporate Liabilities," *Journal of Political Economy* (May/June 1973), p. 637–659.

Example: Say the following data reflect the present market environment:

$P =$	US$ 120
$E =$	US$ 120.5
$T =$	.50 (six months being half a year)
$r_t =$	10% (reflecting the going interest rate on U.S. Treasury bills)
$s^2 =$	33.5

The price variance is calculated on the basis of the past year's end-of-month quotes on the stock price.

Month (*t*)	Market Price (*P*)	(P_t / P_{t-1})
1	119.75	—
2	119.95	0.00167
3	121.00	0.00872
4	120.85	− 0.00124
5	119.65	− 0.00979
6	118.95	− 0.00587
7	118.00	− 0.00802
8	117.45	0.00467
9	118.05	0.05096
10	118.35	0.00254
11	119.15	0.00674
12	119.50	0.00293
13	120.00	0.00418

Mean =	0.00401
Variances =	0.00232
Standard deviation (*s*) =	0.01589
Annual standard deviation =	$0.01589 \times \sqrt{12}$ = 0.05504

x_1 =   [ln 120/120.5) + (.05504 ^{2}/2) .50)] / (.05504 $\sqrt{.50}$)

   =   (− .00416 + .10076) / .03892

   =   2.48

x_2 =   (ln (120/120.5) + [.10 − (.05504 ^{2}/2) .50] / (.05504 $\sqrt{.50}$)

      (− .00416 + .09924) / .03892

   =   2.44

w =   120 × N (2.48) − $e^{-.10 \times .5}$ × 120.5 × N (2.44)

   =   120 × .9934 − .9512 × 120.5 × .9927

   =   19.21 − 113.78 = $ 5.43

[4]Refer to Lawrence G. McMillan, *Options as a Strategic Investment,* 2nd ed. (New York Institute of Finance, 1986).

Notes to Chapter 8

[1]*See Jack D. Schwager, A Complete Guide to the Futures Markets* (John Wiley & Sons, Inc, 1984).

[2]Refer to Lawrence G. McMillan, *Options as a Strategic Investment,* 2nd ed. (New York Institute of Finance, 1986).

Notes to Chapter 9

¹We have ignored the funding cost of the up-front premium from May to September. Assuming a per-annum rate of 10%, the four months' interest cost amounts to $500, which is relatively small compared to the premium itself.

²In this discussion the initial margin payment required to write an option has not been included in the profit and loss analysis. However, it is very important for option writers to fully understand the margin requirements of the exchange before engaging in any trading activities.

Notes to Chapter 10

¹In this calculation, however, we make an assumption that the dollar deposit interest amount in six months' time can be converted into Swiss francs at the spot foreign exchange rate prevalent at the date of the transaction initiation. To be precise, what should be done is to buy spot an amount of dollars that, including the six-month deposit interest amount, is equal to the required $1,000,000. Appling this principle the transaction:

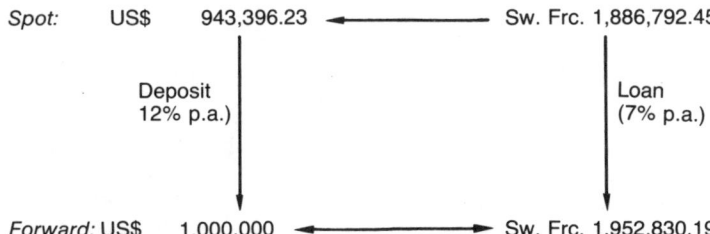

Hence the true outright rate is Sw. Frc./US$ 1.9528 and the swap is 0.0472 as opposed to 0.0500. However, the difference is considered too small to be material for general purposes.

²It is important to use the correct foreign exchange rate denomination when applying the general rules. In this example we trade U.S. dollars, so that the the "price" (foreign exchange rate) of the "goods" (US $) are denominated as Sw. Frc./US $.

Note to Chapter 11

¹These and other relationships are discussed further in an excellent unpublished paper by Jan H. Giddy, "Foreign Exchange Options," Columbia University and Claremont Economics Institute (September 1982).

Note to Chapter 12

¹For a very good overview of the counterparty technique behind swap transactions, David Pritchard, "Swap Financing Techniques," *Euromoney* (May 1984).

Index